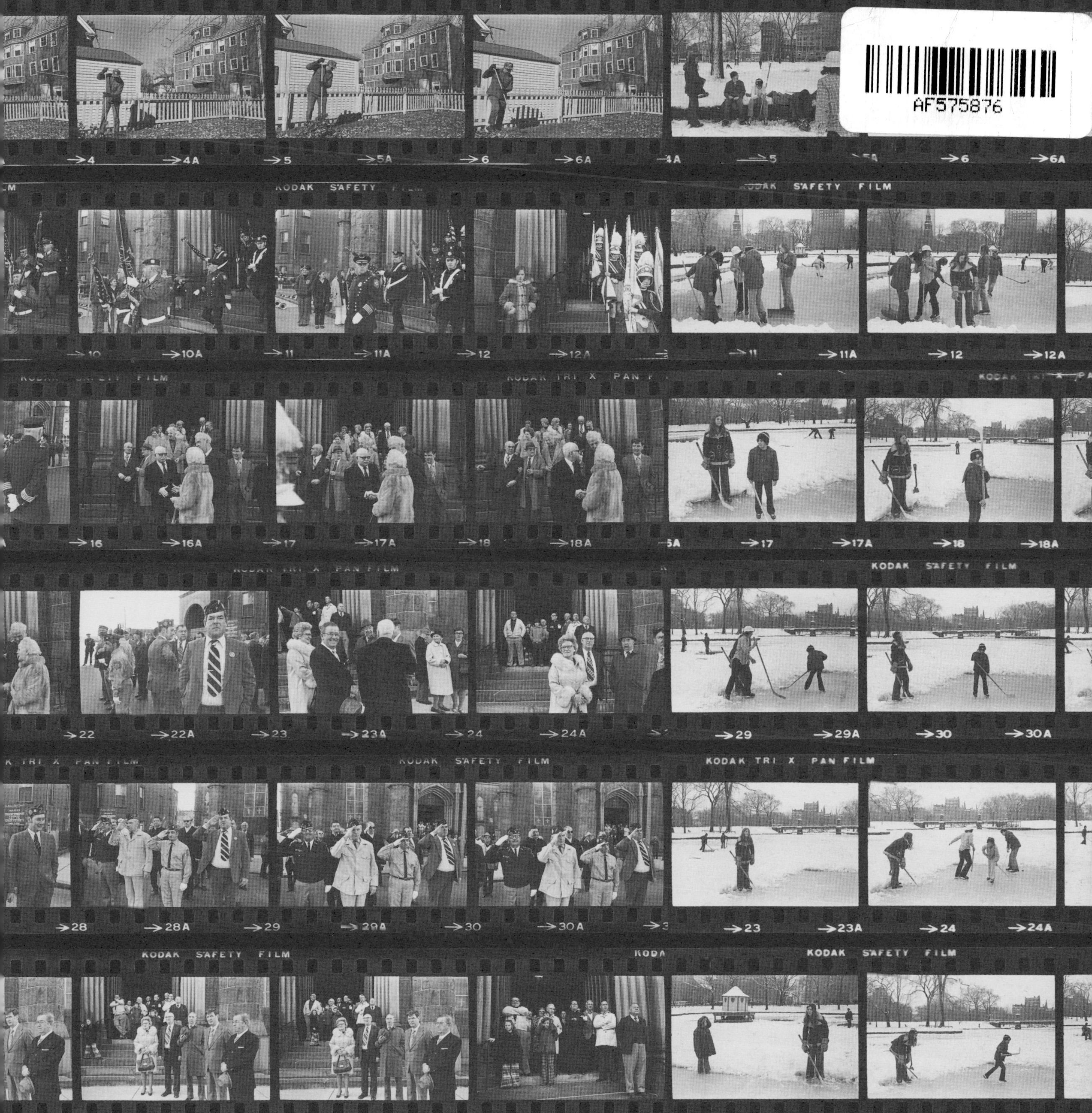
AF575876
KODAK SAFETY FILM
KODAK TRI X PAN FILM

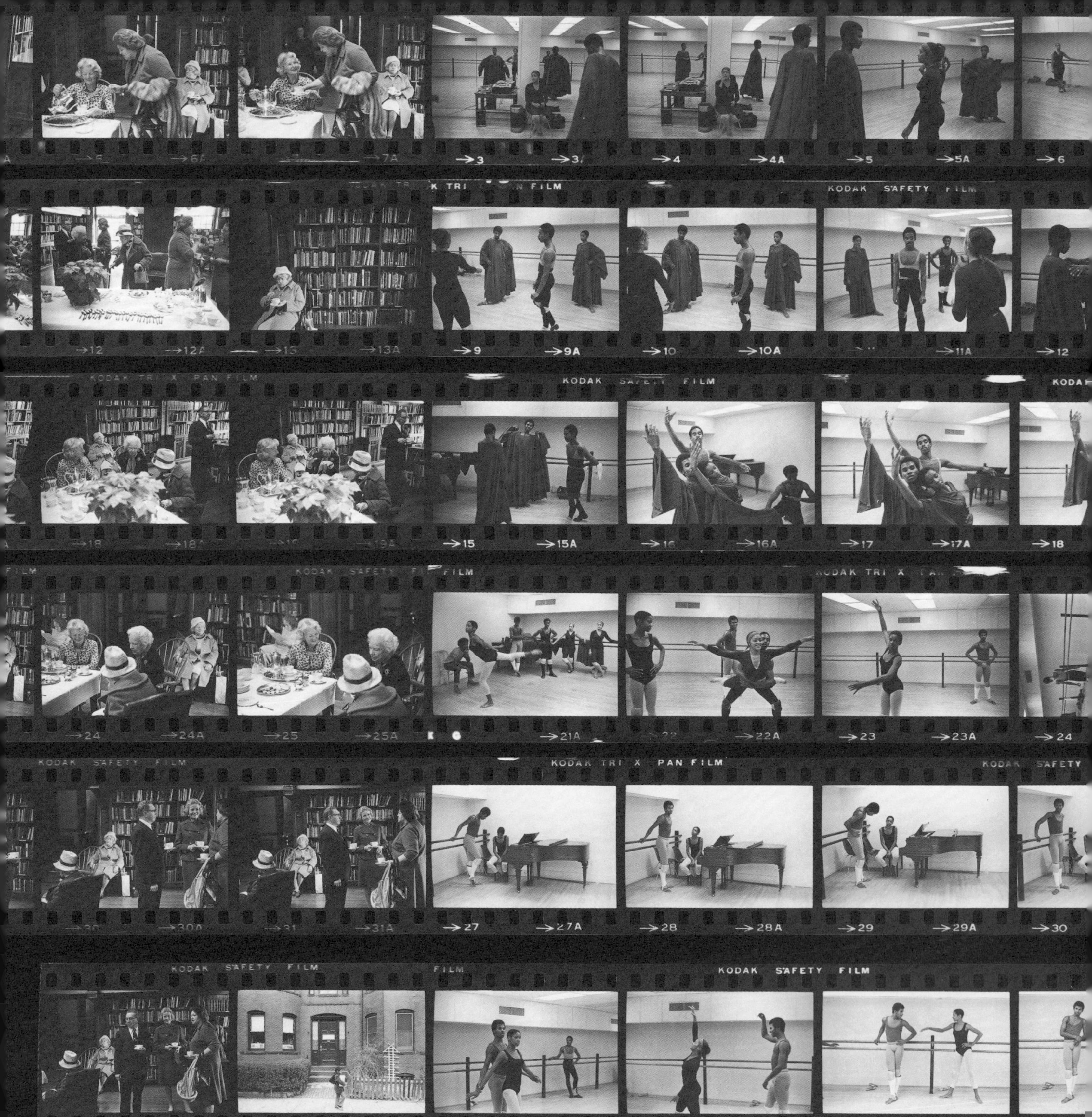
→6 →6A →7A →3 →3A →4 →4A →5 →5A →6
KODAK SAFETY FILM
→12 →12A →13A →9 →9A →10 →10A →11A →12
KODAK TRI X PAN FILM
KODAK SAFETY FILM
→18 →18A →19A →15 →15A →16 →16A →17 →17A →18
KODAK SAFETY FILM
KODAK TRI X PAN FILM
→24 →24A →25 →25A →21A →22A →23 →23A →24
KODAK SAFETY FILM
KODAK TRI X PAN FILM
→30A →31 →31A →27 →27A →28 →28A →29 →29A →30
KODAK SAFETY FILM

Constantine Manos

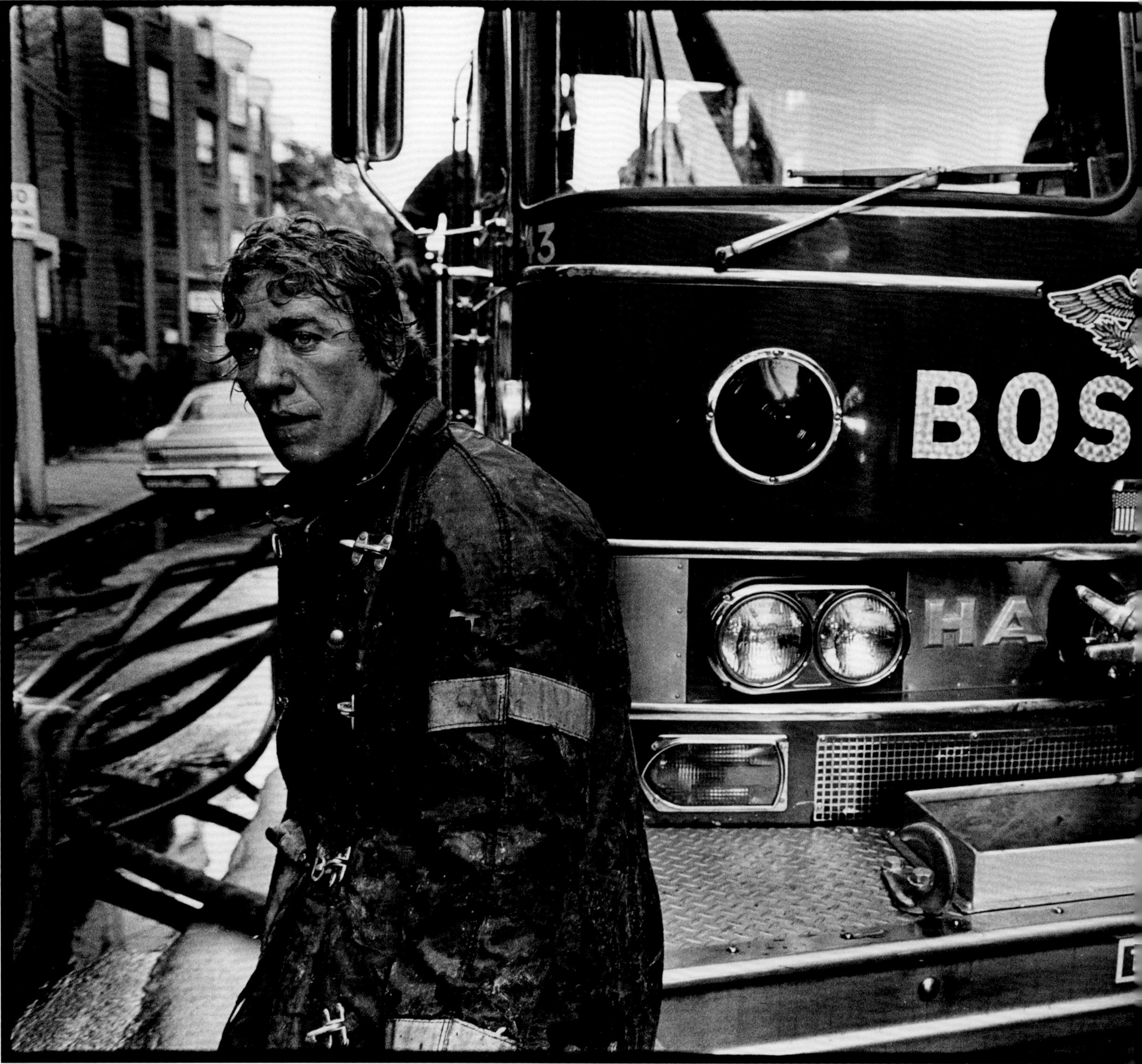
BOS
HA

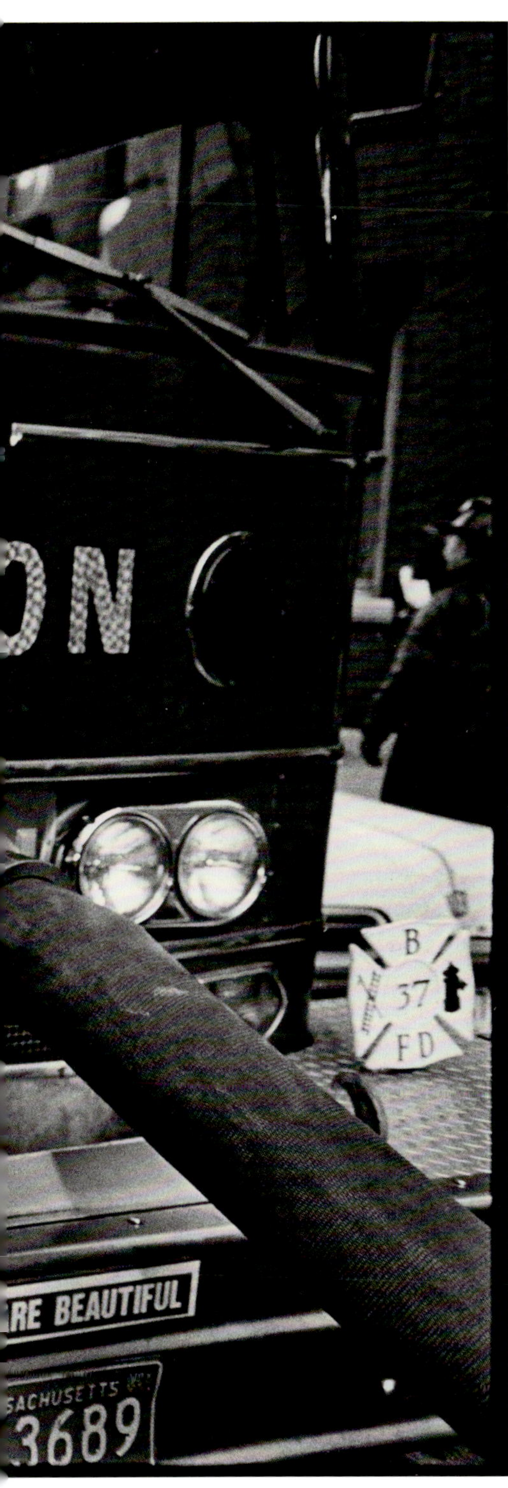

Constantine Manos
Bostonians

Edited by Lauren Graves,
with text by Constantine Manos,
Joseph Nevins, and Lauren Graves

Oral histories from Barney Frank,
Clara Wainwright, Jeri Robinson,
Pedro Santiago, Rosanne Solomon,
George and Carolyn Moran, Jim Stewart,
Cedric Turner, Naftali Brawer,
and Roger Chesebrough

Boston Athenaeum

Contents

Director's Foreword

This exhibition and publication celebrate how Boston remembers —and reimagines—itself. In 1975, the popular exhibition *Where's Boston?* opened to the public in Boston's Back Bay neighborhood. The exhibition, coinciding with America's bicentennial, celebrated Boston as a living city, shaped by the people who inhabit it. On the exterior of the red, white, and blue exhibition pavilion was a series of 154 black-and-white photographs by Constantine Manos titled *Bostonians*. Arranged in two rows and measuring 4 by 6 feet each, these images formed a public portrait gallery of Boston's residents. Capturing candid portraits of people from almost every neighborhood, the photographs celebrated the city's diversity, complexity, and distinctive character.

Today, as we commemorate the 250th anniversary of American independence, we revisit Manos's series *Bostonians*. The images reproduced in the following pages carry a visual intensity and emotional warmth that captivated audiences half a century ago. Looking at the images today inevitably leads us to ask what has—and hasn't—changed in the past 50 years.

The Boston Athenaeum has long been a steward of Boston's topographic and cultural history in books, prints, and photographs from the 18th century to today. Continuing in that tradition, we are proud to mount this exhibition and to republish *Bostonians* in an edition that reframes Manos's photographs with new contextual essays and interviews. This endeavor has been made possible by the Athenaeum's recent acquisition of a substantial group of vintage prints from the *Bostonians* series. Together with works on loan from the Manos estate, these photographs not only capture Boston in a moment of profound transition, but signal our institution's commitment to preserving and sharing a visual record of the richness and contradictions of Boston's civic life.

We are deeply grateful to the late Constantine Manos and to his estate for its generous support of the exhibition and publication. It is our honor to share this work with a new generation of viewers and to examine it with voices from those who lived, shaped, and witnessed the city then and now. We extend special thanks to the individuals pictured in the photographs, especially those with whom we've connected and who shared their oral histories, as well as to the artists, activists, and politicians of the era who contributed their reflections. Their voices give the photographs new resonance, allowing Boston's past to speak more fully to its present.

Manos honed his vision in real time, capturing fleeting moments with a clarity that still feels immediate and profound. It is a testament to Manos's keen eye that so many of these photographs remain fresh, urgent, and alive today. Revisiting the series 50 years after it was originally made still reveals much about Boston as a city. We hope this exhibition and publication will reintroduce audiences to Manos's vision and invite fresh reflection on Boston's past, present, and future.

Leah Rosovsky
Stanford Calderwood Director
Boston Athenaeum

Preface

Constantine Manos

To photograph the people of a great city is at once an awesome undertaking and a pleasant one. My visual quest after the people of Boston began and ended appropriately in the heart of the city, the Boston Common. It started with an American Indian rally on a warm spring day in late March and ended with the first heavy snowfall in late December.

The Boston Common is a good place to start, for here one finds Bostonians of every description, either relaxing or passing through on their way to business or shopping. It is a place of free concerts and political rallies, of sports and dog walking. And the Common is the center of town. A small circle drawn around it easily encompasses the adjacent neighborhoods of Beacon Hill, the Back Bay, the North End, and the South End. A somewhat wider circle takes in quiet residential streets in East Boston, Charlestown, Mattapan, Roxbury, Jamaica Plain, Dorchester, and South Boston. And the adjoining towns of Cambridge, Brookline, and Somerville cannot be excluded from the overall spirit that is Boston. On important civic occasions, all these neighborhoods and towns turn to the heart of the city, be it the Boston Common or Government Center.

Government Center not only draws the citizenry for such mundane matters as water bills and taxes, it is also the place where the people ultimately bring their causes. And Boston has traditionally been a city of causes, where citizens take to the streets to demonstrate their beliefs. One can disagree with one side or the other, but one must admire the fact that Bostonians do not take things lying down. If there is a complaint, banners are unfurled, and the people speak out.

At the end of the day the tired marchers roll up the placards and return to the quiet of South Boston or Roxbury or Dorchester. The businessmen and shoppers go home to suburbia, and the inner city reverts to its permanent tenants—mostly young newcomers and elderly long-time residents.

The young and old, how well they co-exist in Boston. The youth come from all over America to pursue their dreams within the framework of lifestyles that might raise eyebrows back home. And even the oldest Bostonians, after their first tentative encounters, generally find this influx of informal youth not only harmless but interesting and sometimes charming. One sees little old ladies earnestly taking in an impromptu rock concert or scrutinizing the wares of a young street vendor. And if the costumes and lifestyles of the young are highly individualistic, so too are those of the old—each stamped with that unbending character that is pure Boston.

Looking down upon this public side of the city are the variegated and often noble facades of its institutions, public and private and social and scholarly and sometimes a combination of all these. Boston is a city of institutions in every sense of the word, elevating to that status even its burlesque theaters, its sports arenas, and certain individuals. Its universities, libraries, hospitals, museums, social clubs, and churches give it a sense of permanence and history one associates more with Europe than with the newer cities of America. With its abundance of new architecture amidst the old, Boston is perhaps the best city in America in which to observe the end of the Old World and the beginning of the New.

Only minutes away from this imposing inner core of institutions and fine old townhouses are the neighborhoods. Boston has probably the most varied collection of distinct neighborhoods in the country, neighborhoods that have survived the urban explosion because of people who care. Each neighborhood is so unique in its architecture, inhabitants, and traditions that it could be thought of as an institution in itself.

For the photographs, neighborhoods and institutions and public events are only abstractions until the camera captures the individual people who breathe life into them. Going out into the city with a small camera and making hundreds of pictures of people doing hundreds of things is a dizzying odyssey. It's like gathering the bits of an infinite mosaic: even in thousands of photographs, it's impossible to fit all the bits together. They are fragments, suggestions of the myriad human moments in the daily life of a great city.

The possibilities are many, for the city had much to offer not only the camera but its citizens: a Summerthing senior-citizens event at Jamaica Pond . . . a Special Mass at the Cathedral on Washington Street . . . Waltz Evening at the Copley . . . the annual Latin-English high school football game . . . the Columbus Day parades in East Boston . . . block parties in the South End . . . unloading the day's catch at the Boston Fish Pier . . . a Saturday afternoon Red Sox game at Fenway Park . . . the Fourth of July ceremonies at the Old State House . . . a religious procession in the Italian North End . . . Kite Day at Franklin Park.

And there are the lovely moments one stumbles across: the lovers sitting on an old tombstone in the Granary Burying Ground . . . the old lady hoeing her plot in the Victory Gardens in the Fenway . . . the bride leaving the church at Roxbury Crossing . . . the fiddler on the Common beneath the American flag . . . the comedian greeting the stripper backstage at the Pilgrim Theatre.

Out of these events and chance encounters come these photographs of the people of Boston. One wishes that all the citizens of Boston could see the thousands of images the camera has seen in the course of this odyssey—could see each other at work and play in their neighborhoods, could see that everyone wants simply to live a good and happy life.

The photographs that follow are presented to all Bostonians with the hope that we can know and love each other and our city better.

Situating the Hub
Boston in the Mid-1970s

Joseph Nevins

Boston's identity, like that of any place, is multiple. The city's complexity cannot be captured by a single descriptor. This was as true in the mid-1970s—and is reflected in Constantine Manos's images of the time—as it is today. Still, inequality, and efforts to maintain and enhance it, has always been central to Boston's identity—as have efforts to contest that inequality with the goal of bringing about a more just city and a more equitable world.

Taken in 1974 and published in the photobook *Bostonians* in 1975, Manos's photographs show a city of significant diversity, not least in terms of age, class, race, and religion. They also bear witness, beautifully, to everyday activities—from individuals working, playing, or socializing to those contemplating, celebrating, or worshipping. There is little overt evidence of dissent and social struggle, though Manos gestures toward those activities in the book's text.

In the preface, the photographer writes, "One must admire the fact that Bostonians do not take things lying down. If there is a complaint, banners are unfurled and the people speak out."[1] To those unfamiliar with the contexts out of which specific

Figure 1. J. Berndt for *The Boston Phoenix*, STOP flyer, Symphony Road, March 1, 1977. Courtesy of Northeastern University Library Archives and Special Collections.

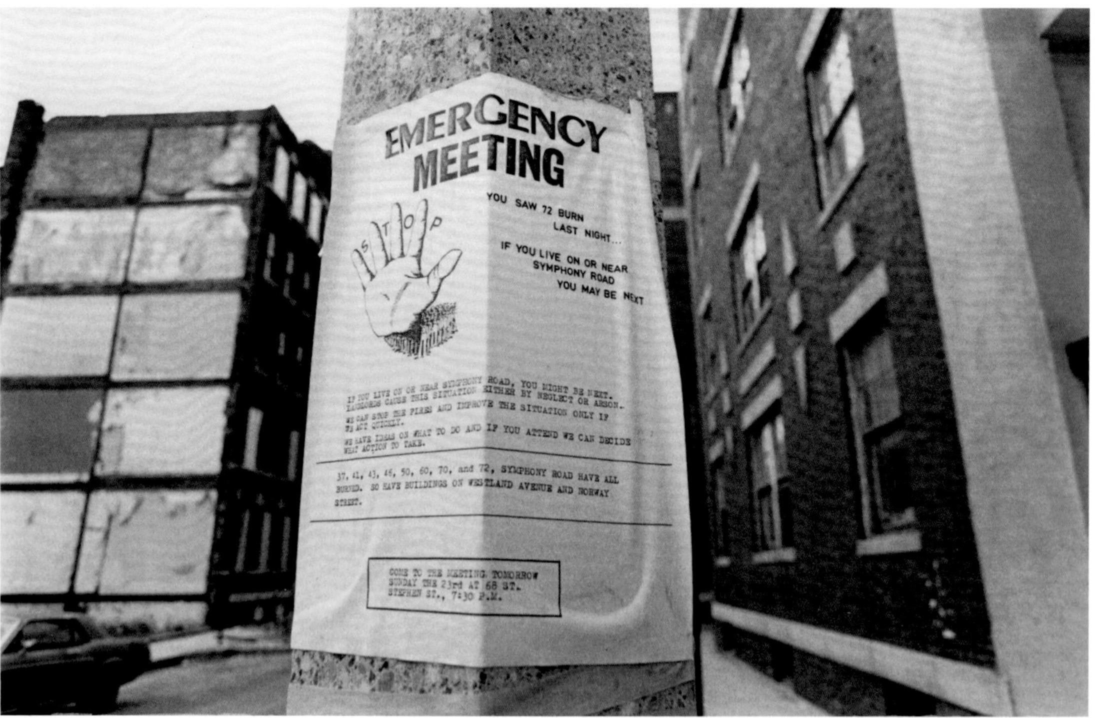

photographs emerge, however, most of the images suggest something different—a Boston area devoid of active protest, conflict, and upheaval. While Greater Boston was many things in the mid-1970s, quiescent it was not.

Banners Unfurled in Manos's Boston

Take the photograph originally published on page 47 of the 1975 photobook (page 83 of this volume), for instance. According to the caption at the end of the book, it shows a fireman resting after fighting a blaze on Symphony Road in the Fenway neighborhood. Today, few people know that arson was a frequent occurrence in Boston at the time, particularly in the Symphony Road area—composed of an ethno-racially diverse population made up of the elderly, working-class families, the poor, and students, as well as gay and lesbian residents. The first fire struck at 40 Symphony Road in January 1974. Over the next three to four years, 23 major fires occurred in a one-block area, displacing hundreds and killing five, including a four-year-old girl. Convinced that the fires represented a pattern of arson perpetrated by outside actors against a vulnerable area suffering from disinvestment, residents came together to form STOP, the Symphony Tenants Organizing Project, to fight back (figure 1).[2]

One indication of such grassroots organizing in *Bostonians* is the photograph originally published on page 33 (page 71 of this volume). The image might appear to show a patriotic celebration, but the caption, alluding to the struggle over the court-mandated desegregation of the Boston Public Schools, tells us otherwise: "Busing demonstration at Federal Building, Government Center."

The only other photograph that clearly reflects unrest is on page 83 of the original volume (page 118 of this volume), but in this case, it's the caption that suggests something more innocuous: "Commencement Day procession at Harvard University, Cambridge." Unlike the anti-busing image, the content of the commencement photograph is obviously political, as it shows graduating women with armbands championing gender equality. Female graduates, Harvard's student newspaper explained, were concerned about "equal admissions, better job opportunities for women, equal pay, better facilities and equal access to prizes

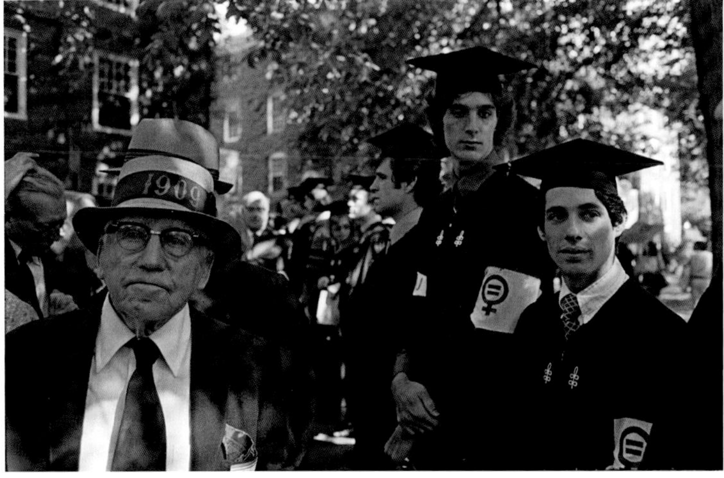

Figure 2. Constantine Manos, *Harvard commencement*, 1974. Courtesy of the Boston Athenaeum.

and facilities."[3] Some male graduates, seen in one of Manos's photographs not included in *Bostonians*, shared these concerns (figure 2).

Some of the female graduates also carried signs that referred to a strike. They were likely manifestations of support for workers in the university's Printing Office and the Typing and Copy Center. Members of the Graphic Arts International Union, they struck for better wages beginning in late April 1974. (The strike was not resolved until late July of that year.)[4]

Such dissent was hardly unknown at Harvard or at other Boston-area institutions of higher education at the time. (The horrific US wars in Vietnam and, later, Cambodia and Laos, were by far the biggest issues on campus.)[5] Four years earlier, about 20 Cambridge residents and student supporters stormed the graduation stage in Harvard Yard to protest the university's predatory housing policies in the Riverside neighborhood, a long-time home of the city's Black community (figure 3).[6]

Sexism, inadequate wages for workers, and real estate practices that threatened to displace low-income residents—as well as efforts to end such injustices—speak to the overlapping forms of inequality that characterized Harvard in the 1970s. More importantly, they reflected the larger Boston area at a time when, demographically speaking, the city was changing dramatically.

The "New Boston"

Boston proper was a shrinking city. Its population had dropped by about 25 percent of what it had been in 1950, when it peaked at just over 800,000 residents. Boston experienced its greatest decline in the decade that followed, losing more than 100,000 people, a decrease greater than that experienced by any other major US city at the time, as many wealthy residents and members of the largely white middle class left the city for the suburbs.[7]

At the same time, elements of the city's government were marked by severe dysfunction. In the case of the Symphony Road fires, for instance, a state task-force investigation revealed ties between real estate and insurance profiteering and official corruption, leading to the indictment and conviction of 32

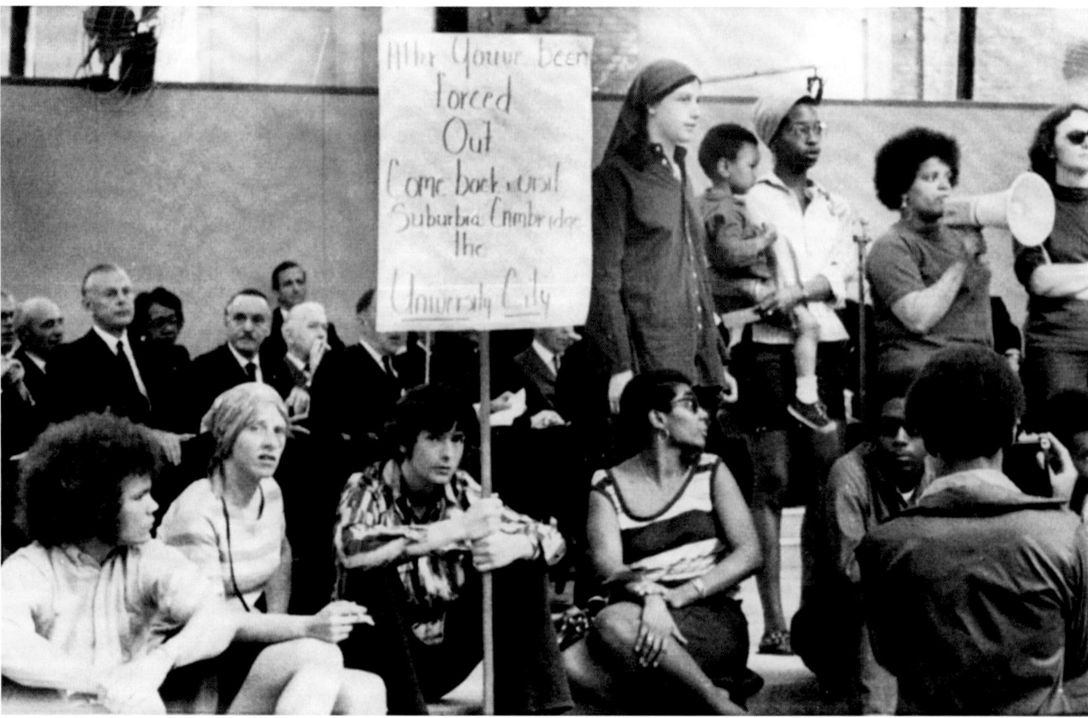

Figure 3. Associated Press, Harvard commencement interrupted, June 11, 1970. Courtesy of the Cambridge Photo Morgue Collection.

Figure 4. Faye Photo Service, Scollay Square, 1933. Courtesy of the Arts Department, Boston Public Library.

Figure 5. The construction of Government Center and the New Boston's City Hall in what was Scollay Square, circa 1968. Courtesy of Boston City Archives.

individuals. In addition to real estate agents and insurance adjusters, the convicted included a City of Boston housing inspector and two police officials, one of whom was the head of the city's arson squad.[8] Robert diGrazia, at the time the Boston Police Department's reform-minded commissioner—he arrived from San Francisco in 1972 with the charge of cleaning up the department—would probably not have been shocked by such official malfeasance. He was convinced that the city's police force was the most corrupt in the United States. According to diGrazia, District One, which was responsible for policing the downtown area, was Boston's most crooked; he estimated that about half of its cops were on the take.[9]

Meanwhile, Boston's ethno-racial composition had changed substantially and was continuing to do so. In 1930, only 2.6 percent of the city's residents were people of color; by the mid-1970s, about a quarter of its population was non-white, largely due to growth in the city's Black population.[10] The Black population more than doubled between 1960 and 1970, as people of African descent migrated from the southern United States and the Caribbean, particularly the West Indies.[11] This diversity was not reflected in Boston's halls of power, however. All nine members of the City Council were white from 1974 to 1976, for example, and only one was a woman.

The mid-1970s was also a time of political and economic transition, one that unfolded over decades, from the "Old Boston," a city ruled by cronyism and corruption and characterized by marked economic decline, to something very different. This "New Boston," the birth of which is often associated with the electoral defeat, in 1949, of long-time mayor James Michael Curley—the "Rascal King" to his detractors—was, for its champions, one that would be focused on high tech, the knowledge economy, and financial capital, with power concentrated politically and economically in the downtown area. It was to be a city led, shaped, and saved by leading lights of the business community and trained experts.[12]

Transforming Boston from the old to the new involved a great deal of destruction and displacement, in addition to a lot of construction. Among the changes that the New Boston's leadership

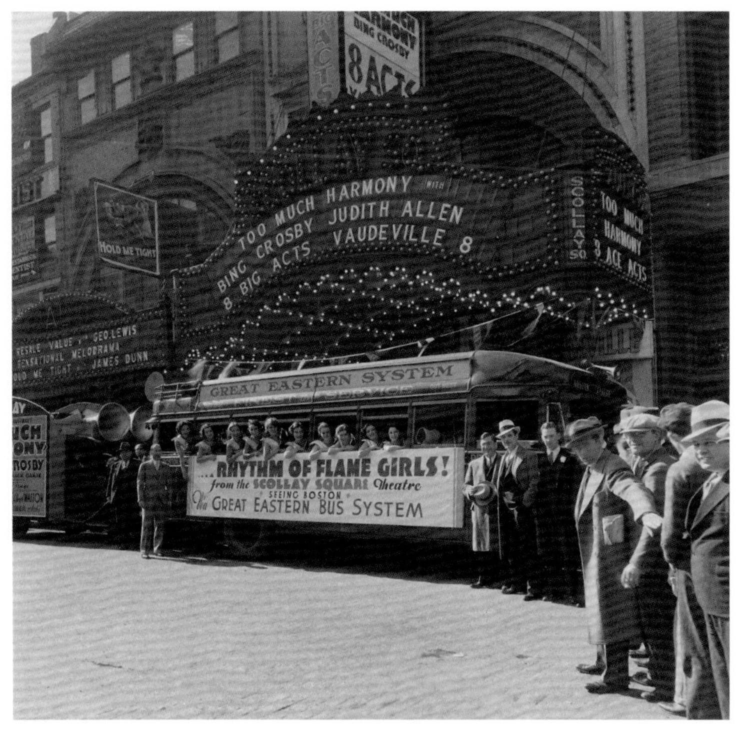

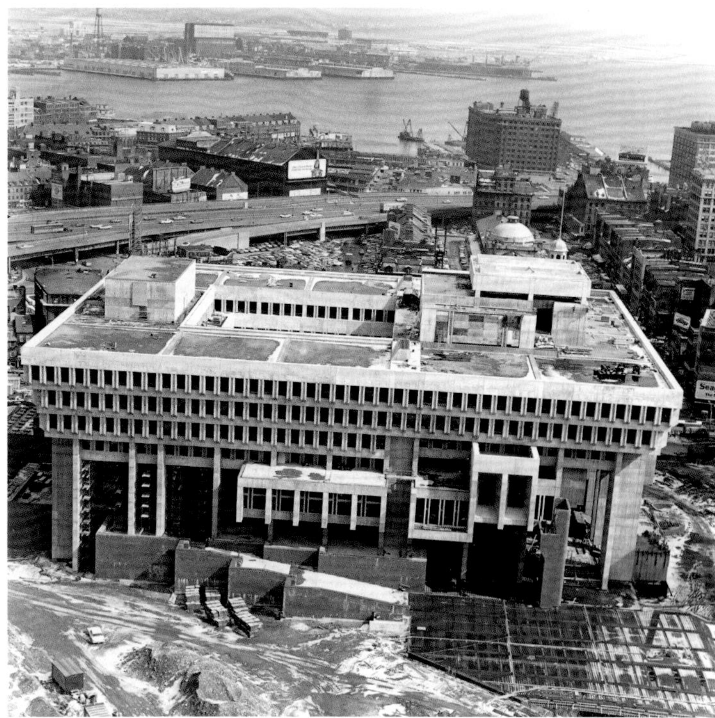

helped to bring about in the heart of the city was the demolition, in 1962, of Scollay Square. Boston's entertainment hub, it was home to movie theaters, burlesque shows, vaudeville acts, bars, and a diverse set of other businesses. A new city hall and Government Center (figures 4 and 5) were built in its place, and in the mid-1970s, Faneuil Hall Marketplace was developed.

As manifested in Scollay Square's transformation, "urban renewal"—the tearing down and redevelopment of areas characterized by local elites as "blighted"—was central to this project of salvation.[13] Unfolding most intensely in the 1950s and 1960s, urban renewal beyond the downtown area saw the razing of streets and neighborhoods that had always been largely composed of working-class people and often had significant immigrant or non-white populations. The first to go was a multi-ethnic and multi-racial part of the South End called the New York streets.[14] Parts of Chinatown were also devastated. Most infamously, urban renewal saw the razing of the city's West End almost in its entirety—displacing 12,000 residents, mostly working-class people of Italian and, to a lesser extent, Eastern European (largely Jewish) descent—and the building of luxury apartments in much of the cleared area (figure 6). Highway construction and expansion often overlapped with these efforts. In the case of East Boston, airport expansion demolished large swaths of the heavily working-class neighborhood.

These undertakings engendered a great deal of grassroots opposition and anger, providing fertile ground for neighborhood-based and citywide activism in the 1970s. So, too, did the long history of civil rights organizing in Boston's Black communities. The explosion of anti-war activism and the rise of the New Left, as well as the emergence of movements in support of women's rights and gay rights, helped fuel what took place outside the gates of college campuses. Student activists often worked with off-campus groups. And many left-wing activists and large numbers of students, especially following their graduations, lived and worked in working-class areas. In this regard, there was a great deal of cross-fertilization between "town and gown" and between political radicals and those who identified with more mainstream politics. At the same time, there was considerable

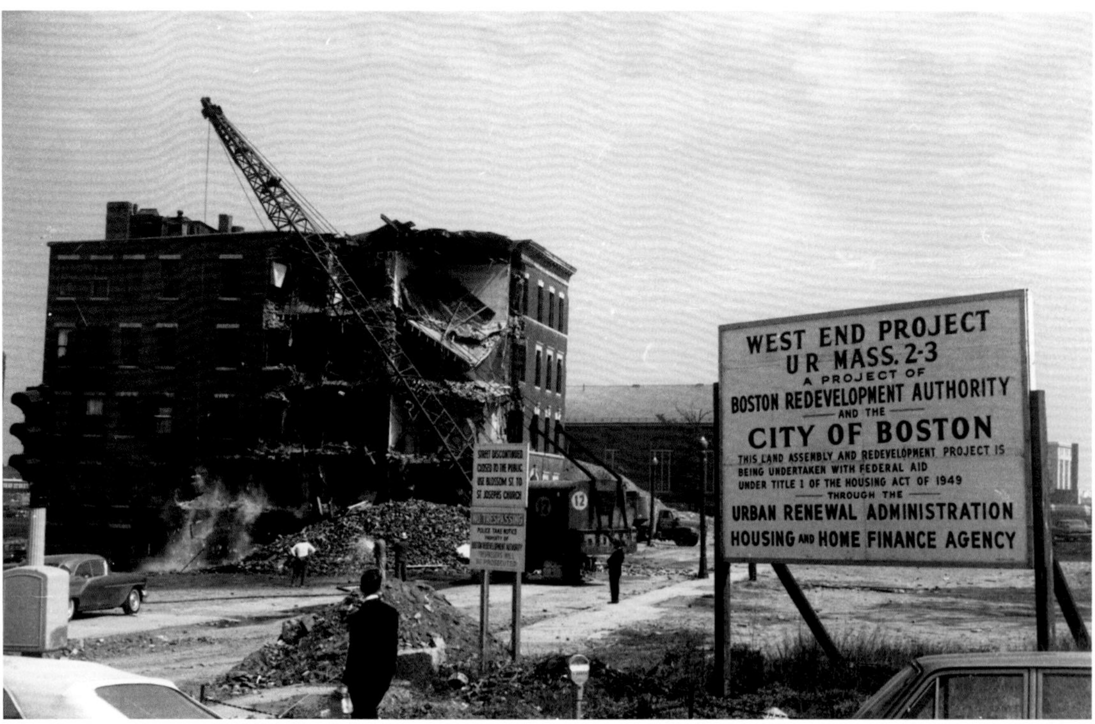

Figure 6. Charles Frani, The razing of the West End, 1963. Courtesy of the West End Museum.

interracial organizing, particularly in the fight against the massive highway project (which was ultimately defeated) known as the Inner Belt.[15]

A Story of (at Least) Two Cities

Even so, with the exception of a few neighborhoods (for example, the South End, Mission Hill, the Fenway), Boston was a highly segregated city, a fact reflected in Manos's photographs.[16] Racial boundaries, especially those related to where people lived, were difficult to cross, particularly for Black Bostonians. As the number of Black residents grew, the newcomers found limited residential options; they were confined largely to parts of Dorchester, Jamaica Plain, Roxbury, and Mattapan through a combination of redlining and discriminatory lending and illegal real estate practices such as "steering."[17]

In this regard, the image on page 108 of white residents of Mattapan is quite striking. Captioned by Manos as "Girls with baby carriages at neighborhood grocery, Mattapan," the photograph reflects a neighborhood that was, demographically speaking, radically different from the one of today. In the 1960s, Mattapan, a neighborhood made up of largely Jewish and Irish Catholic residents, was almost exclusively white. In the late 1960s and early 1970s, with "white flight" to the suburbs already happening, real estate interests engaged in blockbusting practices (not exclusive to Mattapan) to encourage homeowners to sell by stoking fears of Black residents moving into the neighborhood. This had the effect of rapidly and radically changing Mattapan. By the late 1970s, the neighborhood was predominantly Black.[18] (Today, it remains the Boston neighborhood with the highest percentage of Black residents.)

Such change illustrates the power of racial segregation in Boston in the mid-1970s. Combined with the antipathy toward what many saw as a state apparatus dominated by unaccountable elites, it also helps explain the highly charged efforts at the time to prevent the desegregation of the Boston Public Schools.

What critics called "forced busing" (more broadly known simply as "busing") was a federal court-ordered program initiated in September 1974. It grew out of longstanding concerns among

Boston's Black community, its allies, and civil rights activists, about a school system characterized by dozens of racially imbalanced schools and, relatedly, a skewed allocation of resources (not least in terms of funding). In the face of the Boston School Committee's refusal to accede to the orders of the Commonwealth of Massachusetts to remedy the segregation, the federal courts stepped in, with Judge W. Arthur Garrity mandating, among other things, a program that bused students between largely white and Black schools to achieve integration.[19] While a great majority of white people in Boston opposed the desegregation program, they did so for numerous, often overlapping, reasons. In addition to racism, opposition was fueled by economic class divides, urban-suburban tensions, and loyalties to turf and neighborhood schools.[20] Opposition was often militant, and sometimes violent. That said, it is important to remember that desegregation unfolded peacefully at most schools,[21] a fact that gets overshadowed by the incidents of racialized violence that marked the process, while obscuring larger, underlying dynamics that fueled the conflict surrounding busing.

The late Boston journalist Alan Lupo spoke to these dynamics in a 1989 interview for *Eyes on the Prize II*, the famed civil rights documentary. A reporter asked him to reflect on the first day of school desegregation in September 1974. "Despite a couple of centuries of racism and bigotry, and class warfare," Lupo responded, the process began "with a minimum of violence." He added, "The real story of Boston is a story of two cities."

One story, Lupo explained, was that of "the traditional, alleged liberal abolitionist Boston, the progressive Boston." The other Boston "is a very hidebound, distrustful, turf-conscious, class-conscious, parochial city full of people who did not make much progress over the years. . . . They were poor folk and they were running hard-scrabble operations. And they were scared folk and they had had plenty of things done to them."[22]

One way to think about the fight against busing was that it was part of a struggle against an anti-democratic status quo. Of course, it was a lot more than that: for many, it was an often ugly struggle to maintain segregation through the perverse process by which many students were assigned to schools (and the underlying residential boundaries that were drawn for those schools) to maintain educational apartheid. Nonetheless, it was also a fight to uphold the the importance of neighborhoods and the ability of the city's children to attend schools in proximity to where they grew up.

Constantine Manos's Boston 50 Years Later

Efforts to desegregate the city's public schools, and what transpired in the 1970s more broadly, greatly changed Boston, for better and for worse. In many ways, today's Boston is a far more inclusive and welcoming place than it was when Manos took his photographs. It is now a majority-minority city. Meanwhile, the mayor, Michelle Wu, is a Chicago transplant and the daughter of Southeast Asian immigrants, and more than half of the 13 members of the Boston City Council are women and people of color. Boston is also far less turf-conscious than it was, with neighborhoods dramatically more open to people of diverse backgrounds than was the case not too long ago.

That said, segregation in neighborhoods and schools persist, and Boston is now one of the most unequal cities in the United States.[23] Indeed, in 2021, Boston had the largest gap between the richest 20 percent and the poorest 20 percent (by a factor of more than 35) of any US city.[24] Such pronounced inequality is also manifest in the larger metropolitan area, and yawning racial disparities remain. A 2015 study found that the median net worth of Black (non-immigrant) households in the Boston Metropolitan Statistical Area was $8; the corresponding figure for whites was $247,500.[25] In 2017, 61 municipalities (of 147 in total) that make up Greater Boston were at least 90 percent white.[26]

In various ways, school desegregation contributed to the inequality that today scars the Boston area. Busing helped to fuel "white flight" from the public-school system—half of the district's white students left the school system between 1973 and 1978—and, in many cases, emigration to the suburbs.[27] And in focusing exclusively on racial difference and not on economic inequality as well, school desegregation helped both obscure and enshrine Boston's pronounced class distinctions and how they related to educational inequities. In addition, by limiting the plan to address racially imbalanced schools to Boston proper, it reinscribed the boundaries (and thus the socioeconomic gaps) between city and suburbs (especially affluent ones), limiting more profound remedies.[28] When coupled with the type of capital-fueled development schemes associated with the New Boston—the Seaport District, one of Boston's wealthiest and whitest areas, is the most recent example[29]—some of the downsides of the slow death of Old Boston become evident.

In a 2014 essay, Michael Patrick MacDonald pondered the results of busing. He quoted the 1985 edition of Jonathan Kozol's *Death at an Early Age*. A champion of racial and educational justice, Kozol called school desegregation a "Pyrrhic victory," asserting that it did little to improve access to quality education. "Poor whites, poor blacks and poor Hispanics now become illiterate together," he wrote. MacDonald added to this class-based analysis by observing that Boston is also a place where "poor and working-class people of all complexions can no longer afford to live," a city "whose turf we fought over, died on, and ultimately lost to speculators and developers."[30]

Constantine Manos's 1974 photographs remind us that Boston proper was once a city where poor and working-class people of all complexions could and did live—as well as work, play, worship, celebrate, and struggle—and did so with the expectation that those who followed them would also be able to do so. Fifty years later, these images remain powerful not only as documents of their time, but as prompts for reflection. They remind us of what has been lost and what has been gained, while offering a lens through which to recognize enduring inequality and the urgent need to confront its evolving forms and sources in today's Boston.

Notes

1. Constantine Manos, *Bostonians* (CambridgeSeven Associates, 1975).

2. See Steven Syre and Andrew Gully, "Fear—and Arson?—in the Symphony Road Neighborhood," *The Boston Phoenix*, March 8, 1977, 6–7, 33–34, 38; Jim Vrabel, *A People's History of the New Boston* (University of Massachusetts Press, 2014); and Sonia Weinhaus (producer), *Burning Greed: Arson, Profit, and Murder in the Fenway* (documentary), (Live Lobster Group, 2016).

3. Emily Fisher, "Radcliffe Seniors Plan Picket at Commencement Exercises," *The Harvard Crimson*, May 31, 1974, https://www.thecrimson.com/article/1974/5/31/radcliffe-seniors-plan-picket-at-commencement/.

4. Adithya V. Madduri and Saketh Sundar, "'Can't Survive on 5.5': The Months-Long Printer Strike in 1974," *The Harvard Crimson*, May 31, 2024, https://www.thecrimson.com/article/2024/5/31/harvard-printers-strike/.

5. See, for example, Michael Ansara, *The Hard Work of Hope: A Memoir* (Cornell University Press, 2025).

6. "Residents Occupy Stage in Graduation Protest," *The Harvard Crimson*, June 11, 1970, https://www.thecrimson.com/article/1970/6/11/residents-occupy-stage-in-graduation-protest/. See also "Riverside Rezoned," *Harvard Magazine*, January-February 2004, https://www.harvardmagazine.com/2004/01/riverside-rezoned-html; and Henry N. Lear and Bear Wall-Feng, "Treeland: The High-rises Harvard Never Built," *The Harvard Crimson*, October 6, 2022, https://www.thecrimson.com/article/2022/10/6/Treeland-riverside-harvard-1970/.

7. Vrabel, *A People's History of the New Boston*.

8. Howard Husock and Michael Matza, "The Arson Probe: How STOP Got Bellotti Going," *The Boston Phoenix*, October 25, 1977, 6–7, 30; Weinhaus, *Burning Greed*.

9. Jan Brogan, *The Combat Zone: Murder, Race, and Boston's Struggle for Justice* (University of Massachusetts Press, 2021).

10. Jeffrey Brown, "Profile of Boston, 1920–1980: Economic and Demographic Characteristics" (Boston Redevelopment Authority, Research Department, October 1982), https://archive.org/details/profileofboston00brow/page/n1/mode/2up.

11. See Zebulon Vance Miletsky, *Before Busing: A History of Boston's Long Black Freedom Struggle* (University of North Carolina Press, 2022); James C. O'Connell, *Boston and the Making of a Global City* (University of Massachusetts Press, 2025).

12. An important expression of this leadership was the "Vault." Formally known as the Boston Coordinating Committee, the self-appointed group was composed of the heads of the city's major corporate and financial entities—from Ropes & Gray (a law firm) and Filene's department store to the Gillette Company (manufacturer of safety razors and other personal-care products) and the First National Bank of Boston.

Beginning in 1959, Vault members met regularly at the Boston Safe Deposit and Trust Company with the goal of gaining control over the city's finances—they exercised a lot of leverage because some of its members were major lenders to the City of Boston—and "saving" the city from economic ruin. Regarding the Vault, see J. Anthony Lukas, *Common Ground: A Turbulent Decade in the Lives of Three American Families* (Knopf, 1985); Mel King, *Chain of Change: Struggles for Black Community Development* (South End Press, 1981).

13. For a nuanced take on urban renewal and how it unfolded through the career of one of its central figures in Boston, see Lizabeth Cohen, *Saving America's Cities: Ed Logue and the Struggle to Renew Urban America in the Suburban Age* (Farrar, Straus & Giroux, 2019).

14. For an account of life in the New York streets area, see King, *Chain of Change*.

15. Ansara, *The Hard Work of Hope*; Karilyn Crockett, *People Before Highways: Boston Activists, Urban Planners, and a New Movement for City Making* (University of Massachusetts Press, 2018); Amy Hoffman, *An Army of Ex-lovers: My Life at the Gay Community News* (University of Massachusetts Press, 2007); Michael Liu, *Forever Struggle: Activism, Identity, and Survival in Boston's Chinatown, 1880–2018* (University of Massachusetts Press, 2020); Miletsky, *Before Busing*; Dorothy Nelkin, *Jetport: The Boston Airport Controversy* (Transaction Publishers, 1974); Joseph Nevins, Suren Moodliar, and Eleni Macrakis, *A People's Guide to Greater Boston* (University of California Press, 2020); and Vrabel, *A People's History of the New Boston*.

16. Regarding the long history of residential segregation along ethnic and racial lines, see John R. Logan and Weiwei Zhang, "White Ethnic Residential Segregation in Historical Perspective: US Cities in 1880," *Social Science Research* 41, no. 5, 2012, 1292–1306; and Catherine Elton, "How Has Boston Gotten Away with Being Segregated for So Long?," *Boston Magazine*, December 8, 2020, https://www.bostonmagazine.com/news/2020/12/08/boston-segregation/.

17. Steering is when prospective homebuyers are directed away from particular residential areas on the basis of race, religion, gender, or some other legally protected category.

18. Elton, "How Has Boston Gotten Away with Being Segregated for So Long?" The reasons for the departure of most of Boston's Jewish residents for areas outside the city proper is a complex matter; see Gerald Gamm, *Urban Exodus: Why the Jews Left Boston and the Catholics Stayed* (Harvard University Press, 1999).

19. See Ronald P. Formisano, *Boston Against Busing: Race, Class, and Ethnicity in the 1960s and 1970s* (University of North Carolina Press, 2004); Bruce Gellerman, "How the Boston Busing Decision Still Affects City Schools 40 Years Later," *WBUR.org*, December 19, 2014, https://www.wbur.org/news/2014/06/20

/boston-busing-ruling-anniversary; and Lukas, *Common Ground*.

20. There was, of course, a minority of white Bostonians who supported the desegregation plan; and there were white Bostonians who were supportive of the broad goals of desegregation but opposed the specific remedies mandated by Judge Garrity. See, for example, Adam Reilly, "50 Years After Busing, Its Legacy Remains Ambiguous and Contested in Boston," *WGBH.org*, June 27, 2024, https://www.wgbh.org/news/politics/2024–06–21/fifty-years-after-busing-its-legacy-remains-ambiguous-and-contested-in-boston. See also Gellerman, "How the Boston Busing Decision Still Affects City Schools 40 Years Later."

21. Lewis Finfer, "A Difficult Anniversary: 50 years Ago, the Busing Crisis Exploded in Our City," *Dorchester Reporter*, September 11, 2024, https://www.dotnews.com/2024/difficult-anniversary-50-years-ago-busing-crisis-exploded-our-city.

22. "Eyes on the Prize II; Interview with Alan Lupo," March 16, 1989, Film and Media Archive, Washington University in St. Louis, American Archive of Public Broadcasting (WGBH and the Library of Congress), Boston, MA, and Washington, DC, http://americanarchive.org/catalog/cpb-aacip-fd426486e1c.

23. Regarding schools, see Max Larkin, "The Complicated History of School Choice in Boston," *WBUR.org*, *The Emancipator*, June 19, 2024, https://theemancipator.org/2024/06/19/topics/education/wbur-the-complicated-history-of-school-choice-in-boston/.

24. Katharine Swindells, "Income in US cities is most unevenly distributed in a decade," *City Monitor*, December 22, 2022, https://www.citymonitor.ai/analysis/us-income-inequality-cities-revealed/.

25. Ana Patricia Muñoz, Marlene Kim, Mariko Chang, Regine O. Jackson, Darrick Hamilton, and William A. Darity Jr., "The Color of Wealth in Boston," Federal Reserve Bank of Boston, March 25, 2015.

26. Elton, "How Has Boston Gotten Away with Being Segregated for So Long?"

27. Larkin, "The Complicated History of School Choice in Boston."

28. See Michelle Adams, *The Containment: Detroit, the Supreme Court, and the Battle for Racial Justice in the North* (Farrar, Straus & Giroux, 2024).

29. See Nevins, Moodliar, and Macrakis, *A People's Guide to Greater Boston*.

30. Michael Patrick MacDonald, "Whitey Bulger, Boston Busing and Southie's Lost Generation," *WGBH News*, September 2, 2014, https://www.michaelpatrickmacdonald.com/articles-backend/2016/9/2/whitey-bulger-boston-busing-and-southies-lost-generation.

Where's Boston? *Constantine Manos's* Bostonians

Lauren Graves

In April 1974, Constantine Manos began his nine-month project photographing the streets of Boston. Camera in hand, Manos traveled to nearly every corner of the city, creating a dynamic visual record of urban life. Describing the endeavor as a "dizzying odyssey," he focused his lens on Boston's medley of old and new architecture, residents of all ages, and the city's richly layered cultural traditions.[1] The result is a composite portrait of the city and its people, one that is both celebratory and attuned to the tensions and transformations shaping Boston in the mid-1970s. Commissioned for *Where's Boston?*, part of the city's bicentennial celebrations, Manos's portfolio emerges from a city in transition. The photographs reflect the broader historical moment—an era marked by desegregation battles, shifting demographics, and political uncertainty. Many images document everyday life and subtly probe questions of access and belonging in Boston's public spaces. Manos's photographs, singularly and serially, celebrate Boston's diversity, complexity, and idiosyncrasies.

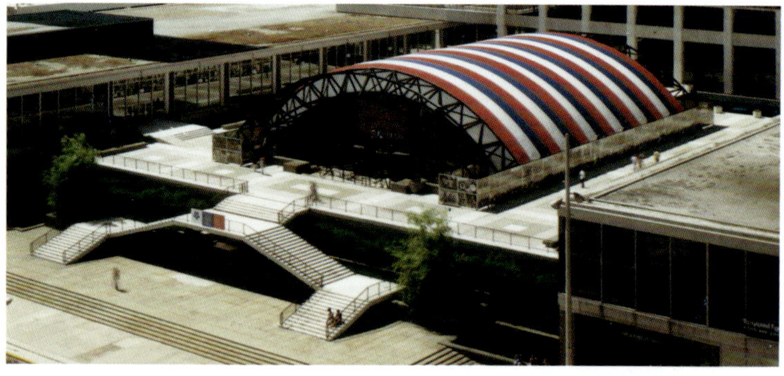

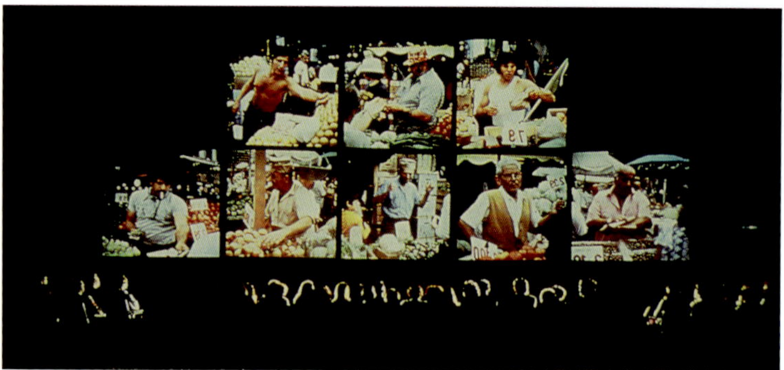

Figure 1. *Where's Boston?* Pavilion, 1975. Copyright Steve Rosenthal, courtesy of CambridgeSeven.

Figure 2. *Where's Boston?* Slideshow, 1975. Copyright Steve Rosenthal, courtesy of CambridgeSeven.

A City on Display: *Where's Boston?* and Boston 200

Bostonians was originally commissioned for the exhibition *Where's Boston?*, which opened in 1975 in Boston's Back Bay (figure 1). Sponsored by the City of Boston and the Prudential Company, and designed and produced by the architectural firm CambridgeSeven Associates, *Where's Boston?* was part of Boston 200, a large-scale, citywide celebration marking the nation's Bicentennial.[2] Boston 200 featured numerous public events and installations, including exhibitions exploring Boston in the 18th, 19th, and 20th centuries; citywide walking tours; games; and a reenactment of the Battle of Bunker Hill.[3] As its title suggests, *Where's Boston?* focused on the Boston of the 20th century and celebrated the "living city." Located in front of the Prudential Center, the symbol of the "New Boston," the exhibition complemented the historic pavilions and oriented visitors to the contemporary city as told by and through Bostonians.[4] While it functioned as a tourist destination, *Where's Boston?* sought to convey the idea that Boston's true value, what made it worth visiting and worth calling home, lay in its people. For tourists and residents alike, *Where's Boston?* aimed to foster a sense of civic awareness and pride, offering a view of the city that was not merely geographic or architectural, but deeply human. Promoted by Boston 200 as the principal gateway to the city during the bicentennial year, the pavilion framed the modern city not only in terms of urban renewal or economic development, but in terms of lived experience. The creators of *Where's Boston?* succinctly explained their thesis—to emphasize the ways in which Boston had always relied on the "resourceful ingenuity and steadfast endurance" of its people. Or, "Put more directly: Since Bostonians are convinced that Boston is worth keeping, they do what is necessary to keep her."[5]

Upon entering the pavilion, visitors were greeted by a "word wall," a mural based on the "special language, verbal associations and special names that contribute to Boston's diverse and unique flavor."[6] Further into the lobby was an exhibition of "Boston artifacts," objects that were designed, conceived, or made meaningful by Bostonians. These included a Celtics jersey, the prototype of the Polaroid camera, and track shoes worn in the Boston Marathon.[7] Deeper into the pavilion was the main attraction of

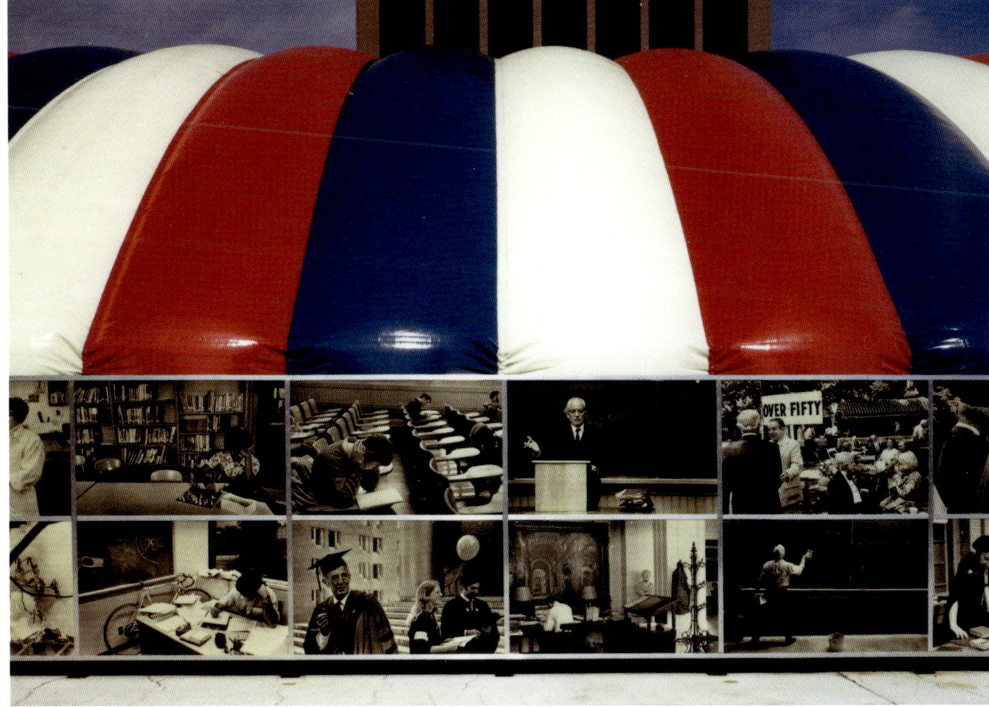

Figure 3. *Where's Boston?* Pavilion, 1975. Copyright Steve Rosenthal, courtesy of CambridgeSeven.

the exhibition—a large-scale multimedia installation of an eight-screen slideshow documentary composed of more than 3,000 slides and using 40 projectors, interwoven with hundreds of oral histories collected from a broad range of Bostonians playing over a quadraphonic sound system that immersed viewers (figure 2).[8] These included voices as varied as State Representative Barney Frank, poet David McCord, Richard Parker (the "Oldest Fenway Gardener"), and the proverbial "man on the street."[9] A press release for the exhibit described the show:

> Over 2,500 views of 20th-century Boston to portray the city's charms, traditions, and excitement. Would-be explorers can familiarize themselves with Boston's people, neighborhoods, and institutions at the Prudential Pavilion, then organize their own tours around favorite subjects. *Where's Boston?* is an orientation tour of each ethnic area of the city, which weaves the tapestry that is called Boston. *Where's Boston?* is about the people who live in each neighborhood, their festivals, their traditions, and their ways of life.[10]

Constantine Manos was a principal photographer for the slideshow, and his photographs also had a significant physical presence, functioning as part of the architecture of the pavilion (figure 3). One hundred and fifty-four of Manos's 35mm slides were blown up to 4 × 6 feet, creating a two-level frieze on the pavilion's exterior.[11] The series served as a public-art gallery, a large-scale portrait album of Boston and its people. The same year, CambridgeSeven Associates published a photobook, *Bostonians*, as a companion to the exhibition. This more intimate volume presented a selection of Manos's photographs, allowing viewers to engage with the images beyond the fleeting encounter at the pavilion. Together, the frieze, slideshow, and book emphasized the centrality of photography in shaping public memory and urban identity during the bicentennial celebrations.

Manos and Magnum

Manos, a native of Columbia, South Carolina, born to Greek-immigrant parents, began his photographic training at age 13 and continued to develop his eye in college at the University of South Carolina, working as a photojournalist for his university's paper. In the early 1950s, Manos began his first series, photographing African American sharecropper communities in Daufuskie Island, South Carolina. At this same time, Manos published a series of anti-segregation articles in his university's paper, a striking indication of his early political engagement and ethical commitment. In 1953, at the age of 19, he had his first encounter with Boston, when he was hired as the official photographer for the Boston Symphony Orchestra. The photographs from this work are dynamic and emotive and resulted in the publication of his first photobook, *Portrait of a Symphony* (1960). In the 1960s, Manos traveled to rural parts of Greece and commenced work on his seminal book *A Greek Portfolio* (1972). A few years later, he began work on *Bostonians* and, by the 1980s, Manos was a pioneer in the field of color photography. Throughout his decades-long career, Manos remained dedicated to photographing the American experience, picturing the country's costumes, rituals, and diverse communities. In their range of subject matter, from an orchestra to Mardi Gras celebrations to a gay pride parade, his photographs hold an "impossibly intense intimacy."[12]

In 1963, Manos was invited to join the photography collective Magnum Photos, a membership he retained until his death in early 2025. Magnum Photos was founded in 1947 by Henri Cartier-Bresson, Robert Capa, George Rodger, and David Seymour. Established in the wake of World War II, Magnum aimed to give photographers full control over their work—ownership of their negatives, independence in assignments, and the freedom to pursue stories that mattered to them, rather than being directed by the editorial agendas of newspapers or magazines.[13] Its founding principles centered on integrity, curiosity, and the belief that photography could serve as both witness and agent in understanding the world. Roughly a decade into his Magnum membership, Manos returned to the streets of Boston to create *Bostonians*, a project that reflects the ethos of the collective. Like his Magnum peers, Manos worked independently, driven by observation rather than direction, attuned to the particularities of place and moment. By the time he began *Bostonians*, Manos had been living in Boston for more than a decade, residing in the South End, a racially and culturally diverse neighborhood that mirrored the very communities he would come to photograph. To make *Bostonians*, Manos used a Leica camera, the same camera used by Cartier-Bresson. Manos, like many photographers, celebrated the Leica for its sharp lens and ability to capture the world in a manner most similar to the human eye.[14] Rather than distorting scenes through a wide-angle lens or homing in on singular details, the Leica distills action into sharp, translatable focus. In *Bostonians*, as in much of his earlier and later work, Manos combines formal rigor with emotional resonance, offering not only a portrait of a city but a meditation on what it means to see people in their everyday lives.

Manos's *Bostonians*

The prints in *Bostonians* underscore Manos's curiosity and the clarity of vision that he brought to the project. The series reveals the lively streets and bustling buildings of Boston, always bubbling with activity. Manos goes well beyond downtown Boston and its newer skyline, and his photographs document almost all of Boston's neighborhoods and communities. There is an emphasis throughout his portfolio on humanity and how people activate space and give life to a city.[15] In the series, Manos documents a great diversity of ages, classes, ethnicities, religions, and races. Pictured are busy public spaces balanced with intimate interior shots. In selecting his interiors, Manos chooses spaces that are still considered "public" or "shared." While Manos's portfolio captures Boston's true diversity, many photographs uncover the segregated spaces of the city. Rarely do prints include both white and Black subjects, and when the photograph shows a diverse scene, groupings tend to be divided by race. In photographs that seem apolitical in nature—socializing at Franklin Park, lounging on the beach at Castle Island, or playing in the snow in the Public Garden—the photographs raise questions of access to the city's "shared" spaces.

The project itself was born out of a clear directive from Boston 200, the organizing body behind the bicentennial exhibition. As an internal memo explained, "Mr. Constantine Manos and his camera have been contracted by Boston 200 to produce the photographs which will be hung on the exterior walls of the Bicentennial Pavilion at the Prudential Center. These photographs will capture Bostonians in all their variety, and will document the City of Boston at work, at play, at rest, etc."[16] In making the series, Manos immersed himself in the city's life firsthand—attending parades, hockey games, factory lines, and community celebrations—prioritizing spontaneous encounters. The openness of this approach is reflected in Manos's own words:

> None of the pictures are posed or arranged; they are all true and candid moments. I find that photographing people in this manner is the most exciting and challenging kind of photography. Things are in constant flux, and one must always be alert for the right moment. Public events such as parades and street festivals provided much material, but many of the photographs are simply the result of wandering in the neighborhoods. I went into every neighborhood in the city of Boston and found them all to be rich in variety and in humanity. The people were great and helpful everywhere I went. My experiences in making these photographs make me believe that Bostonians are very proud of their city. [17]

In many prints, subjects are in the midst of action, suggesting that this series is only a partial document of the city and that life continues beyond the four corners of the prints. Throughout the portfolio, Manos experiments with what the camera reveals and conceals, framing his subjects with their backs to us, behind a barrier of glass, or with an accessory (glasses, a hat, a book) that hides the subjects' faces. Rather than simply transcribing the world around him, Manos uses the camera to play with reality, extracting uncanny relationships between subjects and their shared spaces. Building on his experimentation with what the camera reveals and conceals, Manos prefers to photograph people's reactions to action, events, and activities instead of the actual event itself, asking the viewer or reader to continue the narrative. This framing technique also provides a distance or boundary between the viewer and the photographic subject, allowing them to live in anonymity and limiting the viewer's, and his own, access to their personhood.

Manos's practice of wandering, observing, and patiently waiting for moments of authenticity manifests throughout *Bostonians* as a "dizzying odyssey," as Manos himself describes it, capturing "hundreds of pictures of people doing hundreds of things."[18] His photography resists tidy narratives or definitive statements. Instead, it offers fragments, "suggestions of the myriad human moments in the daily life of a great city."[19] These photographs accumulate into a rich, layered portrait that celebrates Boston's complexity, its contradictions, and the ordinary people who give it life.

Neighborhood life and everyday intersections

Manos's series is organized around the spatial experience of the city, moving through occupied sidewalks, weathered streets, public commons, and quiet interior spaces. This geographical structure allows for a nuanced exploration of Boston's multifaceted social fabric, its layers of public and private life. In this way, *Bostonians* is less a linear story and more an evocative portrait assembled from fragments that reveal the diversity and contradictions of the city. Manos's *Bostonians* immerses the viewer in the rhythms of everyday life within Boston's varied neighborhoods. These images celebrate the city's communities by capturing candid moments where personal lives intersect with public spaces, offering a rich, textured portrait of urban life. Manos's keen compositional choices, such as reflections, balanced frames, and repeated motifs, invite viewers to look beyond the obvious and consider the layered social dynamics at play. Here, the city is both intimate and expansive, shaped by its residents' daily interactions and subtle exchanges.

In one photograph, for example, a seemingly ordinary street scene in Mattapan transforms into a layered portrait of youth, community, and photographic observation (figure 4). Three girls stand confidently with baby carriages and a dog in front of a small grocery store, presenting a sense of balance and symmetry that echoes across Manos's work. The framing is precise: three young figures, two carriages, and a canine companion squarely in the

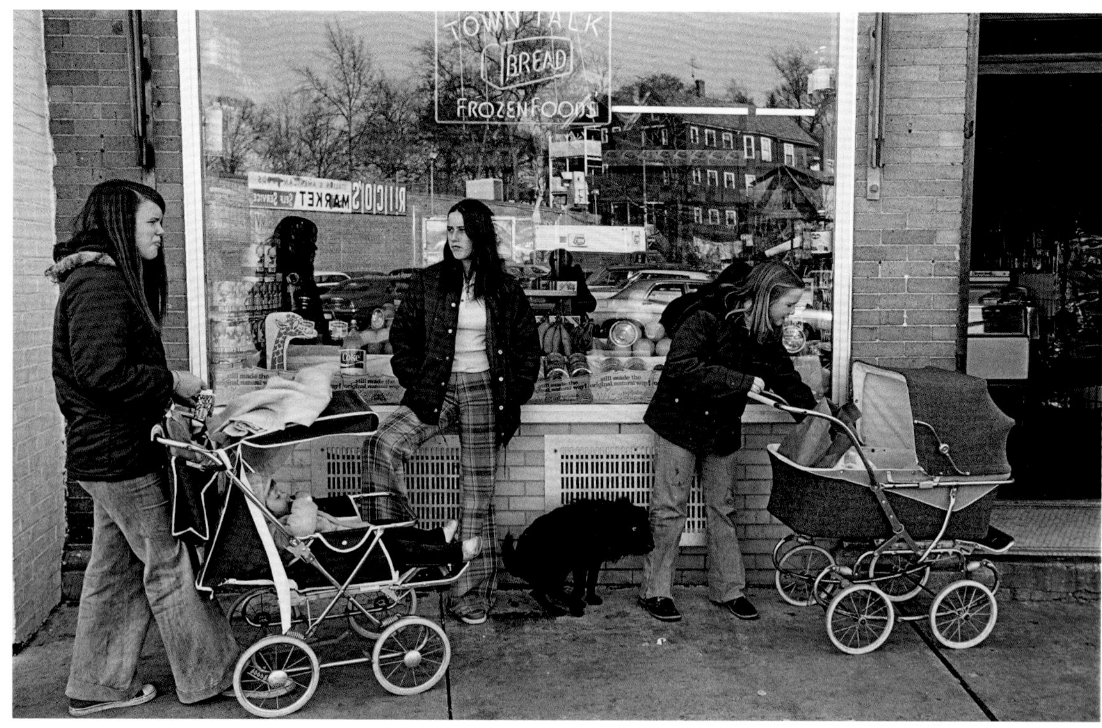

Figure 4. Constantine Manos, *Girls with baby carriages at neighborhood grocery, Mattapan*, 1974. Courtesy of the Boston Athenaeum.

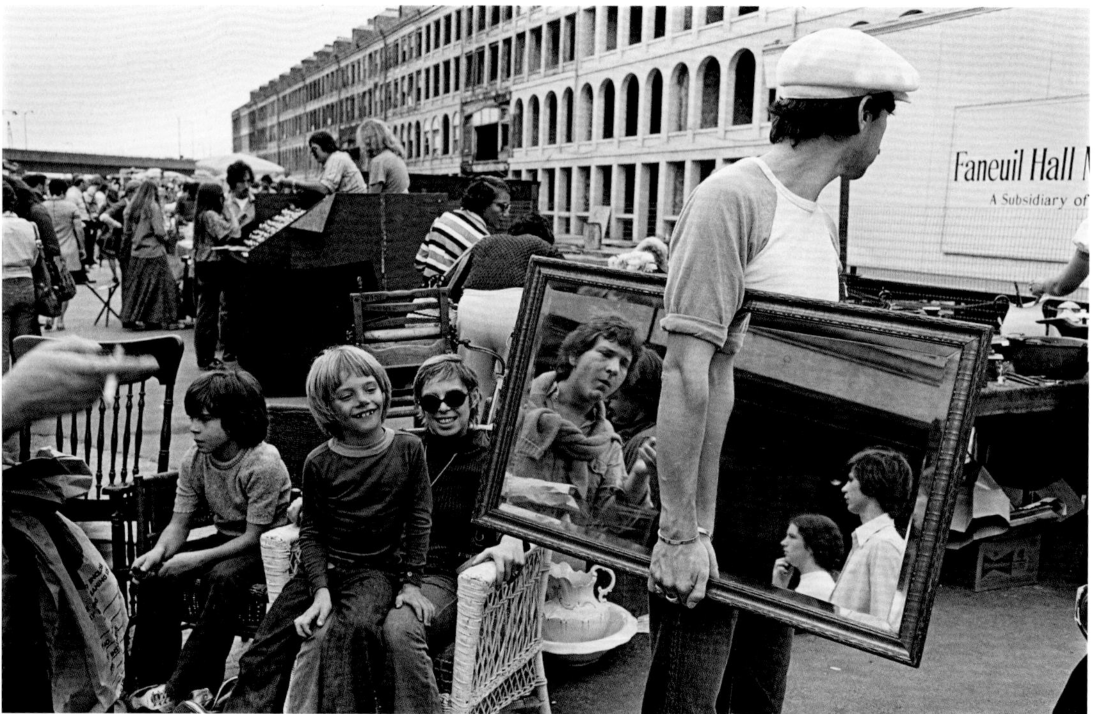

Figure 5. Constantine Manos, *Sunday morning flea market, Faneuil Hall*, 1974. Courtesy of the Boston Athenaeum.

center—mid-action—relieving itself on the sidewalk. This tiny disruption at the core of the image is quintessential Manos, puncturing compositional harmony with a touch of irreverent humor. The photograph invites us to consider roles and performances, even in casual moments: girls tending to siblings (perhaps) and standing on the threshold between childhood and adult responsibility. Manos's own presence is subtly revealed in the window's reflection, anchoring him within the narrative and reminding the viewer of his role as both participant and documentarian. Taken in Mattapan, a neighborhood in flux during the 1970s, the image captures an intersection of age, place, and gaze.[20] While the central focus appears to be the trio, Manos cleverly turns our attention to the act of seeing itself, complicating the relationship between photographer, subject, and viewer.

Manos also explored a flea market outside of Faneuil Hall, presenting a dynamic study of public space and human interaction (figure 5). The photograph is alive with movement and commerce, a microcosm of Boston's bustling urban life. Manos employs a pyramidal composition that balances activity across the frame, directing the viewer's eye not only to the central figures but equally toward the edges, where smaller, seemingly incidental moments unfold. At the heart of the image, a man holds a mirror, which reflects the crowd around him, creating layers of visual complexity and a "frame within a frame." This reflective surface echoes Manos's recurring exploration of visibility and concealment, challenging the viewer to question what is seen, what is hidden, and where attention is directed. A cigarette peeking through the frame's left edge points the viewer to the central action of the photograph, an ephemeral marker that grounds the scene in everyday reality. The photograph's formal structure exhibits Manos's characteristic blending of modernist principles—clarity, geometry, and balance—with idiosyncratic subject matter that retains emotional resonance. Through this image, Manos captures the city's layered social fabric, showing how public markets serve as vital crossroads for community life.

In Franklin Park, Boston's largest open green space, which borders the majority Black neighborhoods of Roxbury and

Dorchester, Manos captures a different expression of public life. By the late 1960s, Franklin Park had become neglected by the city, a hotbed for crime and vice and a dumping ground for industrial waste.[21] In response, community leaders such as Elma Lewis, founder of the Elma Lewis School of Fine Arts, established the Franklin Park Coalition (1971) to clean up the park. In the summer of 1966, Lewis began the Playhouse in the Park, a program that offered underprivileged children from surrounding neighborhoods training in drama, set design, and other skills.[22] In another effort to revitalize the park, in 1974, Lewis began Uptown in the Park, a series of soul concerts at White Stadium, a football stadium in the western section of the park.[23] In Manos's photograph, the park bustles with activity on a summer Sunday, revealing its role as a vital green space where Boston's diverse communities gather to relax, socialize, and celebrate (figure 6). At the center, a group of men listen intently to a saxophonist whose sound seems to resonate beyond the frame, creating a sensory bridge between image and viewer. To the right, a cluster of Girl Scouts chat, while scattered groups in the distance play, rest, fly kites, and gather, emphasizing the park's importance as a shared refuge.[24] The image strikes a balance between intimacy and expansiveness, capturing both individual encounters and collective energy. An outtake from the same day (ultimately left out of the final portfolio) reveals a wider demographic spread, showing more diverse groups of people across age and race engaged with the space (figure 7).[25] Manos's photograph captures the vitality of these efforts. The imagined sounds of music and laughter imbue the print with a kind of living presence, making the image resonate far beyond its static form. Through this photograph, Manos explores how green spaces become vital arenas for joy, connection, and the performance of cultural life.

Intimate interiors

In his photographs of interior spaces, Manos turns his lens toward Boston's cultural and educational institutions—spaces that both reflect and shape the city's identity and reveal moments of quiet and intellectual engagement. Manos experiments with framing to explore themes of access, concealment,

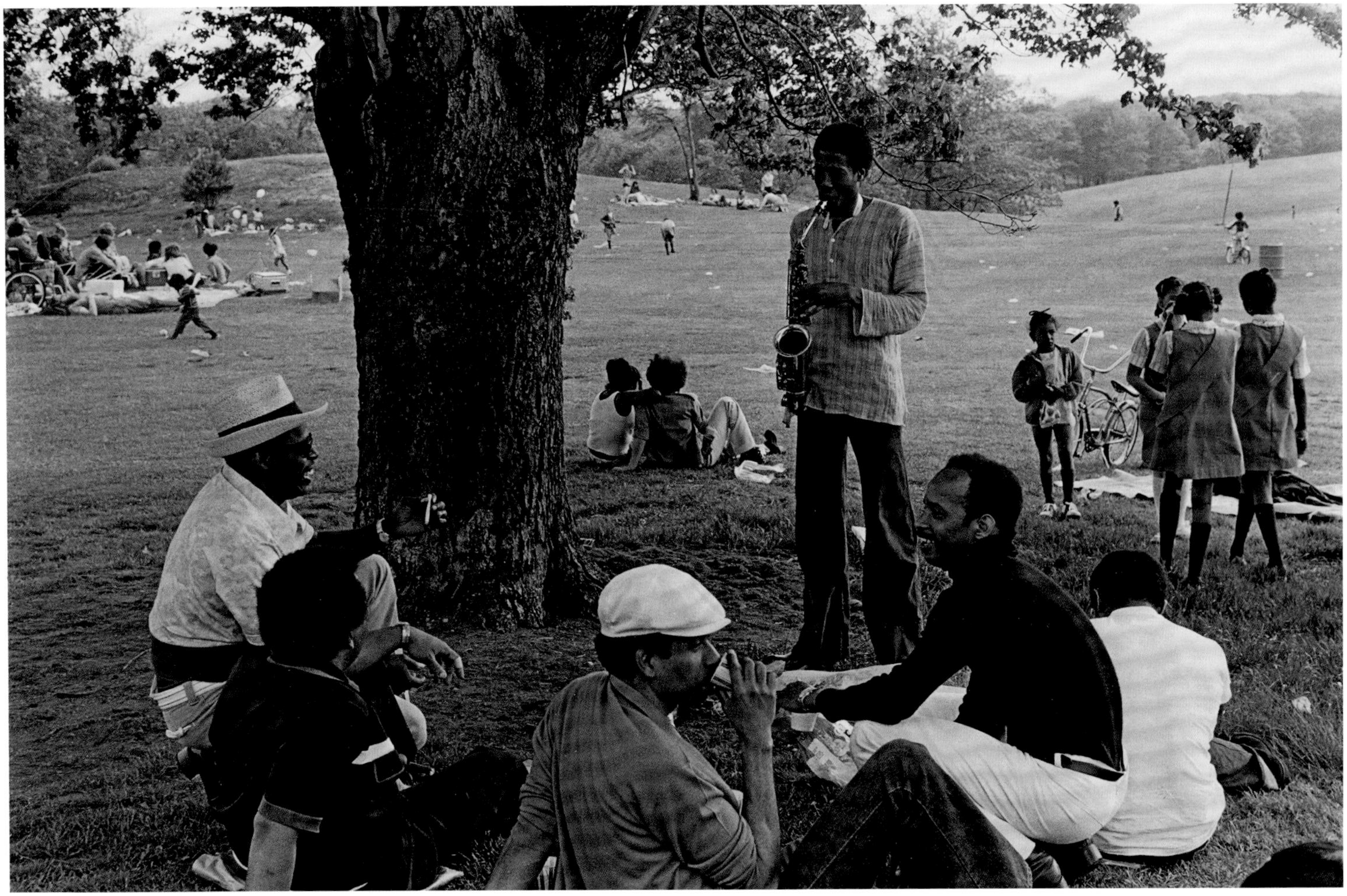

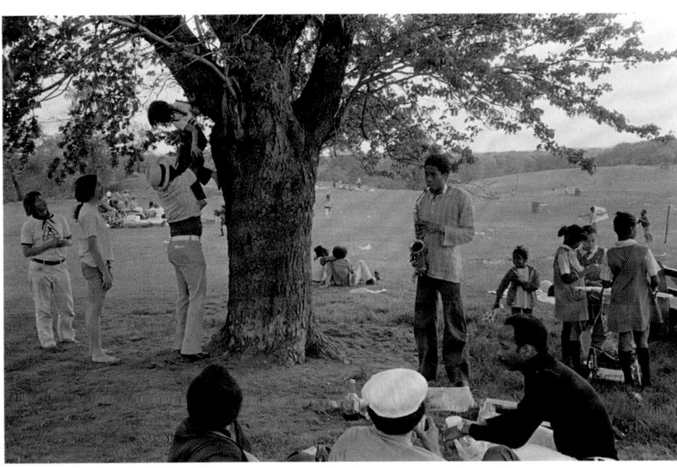

Figures 6 and 7. Constantine Manos, *Sunday Afternoon Gathering of Friends, Franklin Park, Boston, Massachusetts*, 1974. Courtesy of the Boston Athenaeum.

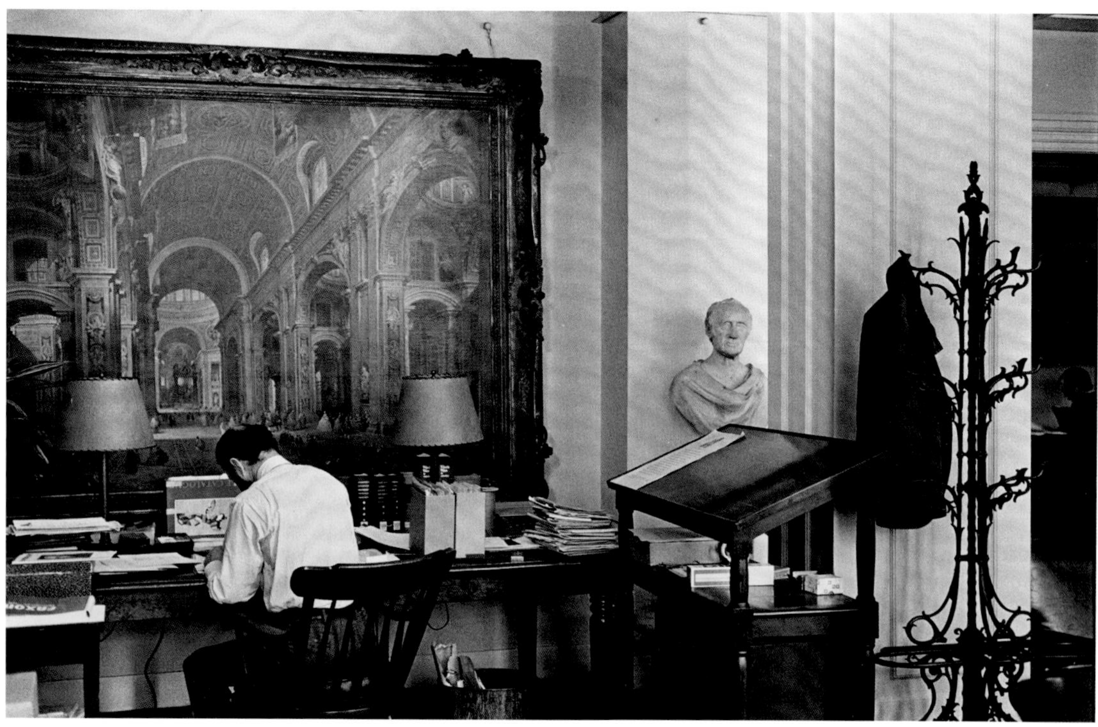

Figure 8. Constantine Manos, *Librarian at work, Boston Athenaeum*, 1974. Courtesy of the Boston Athenaeum.

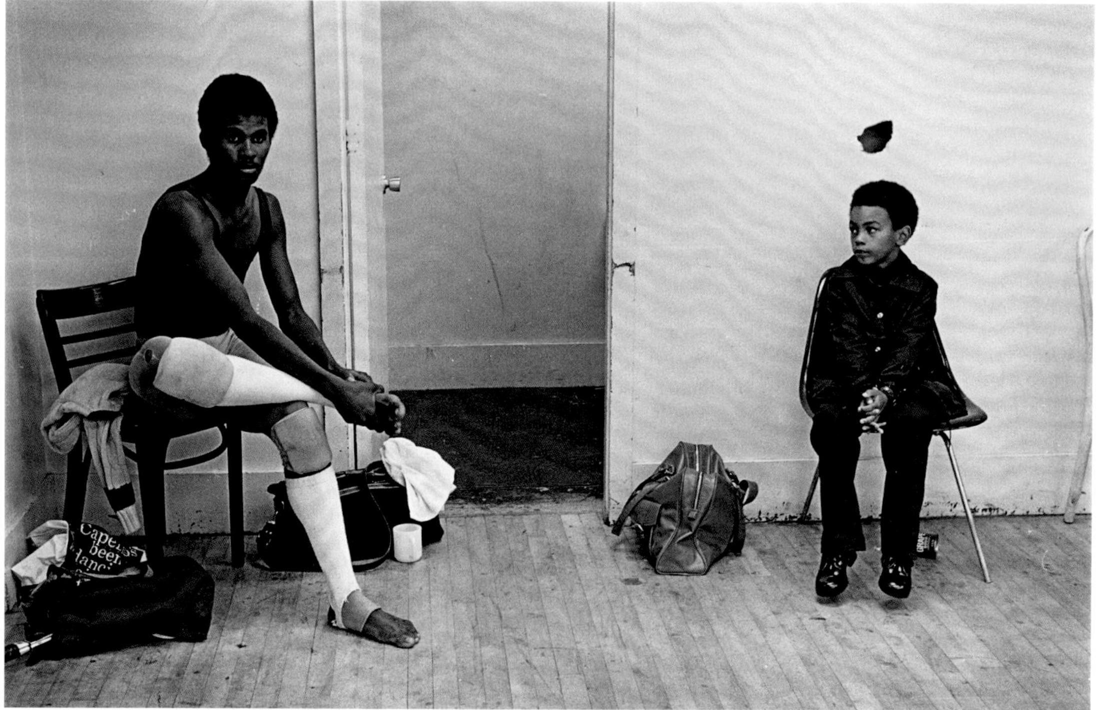

Figure 9. Constantine Manos, *Dancer and admirer at rehearsal, Elma Lewis School*, 1974. Courtesy of the Boston Athenaeum.

and intimacy, prompting reflections on who inhabits these spaces and how cultural knowledge is transmitted. The layered spatial dynamics of these interiors highlight the city's complex interplay between public visibility and private experience. In *Librarian at work*, Manos captures a quietly charged scene within the Boston Athenaeum (figure 8). The librarian, Richard McDonald, seated at his desk and engrossed in his work, is framed by the imposing backdrop of Giovanni Paolo Panini's *Interior of St. Peter's, Rome*, visible on the wall behind him. Notably, Manos composes the photograph with an intriguing play on presence and absence: the librarian's back is turned to the camera, creating a subtle barrier between subject and viewer, while the classical bust in the foreground faces forward, as if silently observing the unfolding scene. This trio of figures—the librarian, the bust, and the painting—forms an uncanny assembly, linking the living, the sculpted, and the painted worlds. The photograph subtly critiques the exclusivity of elite cultural spaces and shows the quiet, often unseen work that sustains them. Here, Manos uses spatial arrangement and perspective to evoke questions about access, authority, and the custodianship of knowledge in Boston's cultural spaces.

In one especially quiet image, *Dancer and admirer at rehearsal, Elma Lewis School*, a dancer sits at rest in a chair to the left, while a small child gazes up at him in quiet reverence from the right (figure 9). The room is spare, almost austere, punctuated by an open door at its center that subtly emphasizes the spatial and emotional distance between the two figures. Yet the intimacy is palpable: the dancer's grounded pose, one foot firmly planted, and the child's small frame, feet hovering just above the floor, suggest a moment suspended between admiration and aspiration. Their glances don't meet, but the space between them hums with unspoken dialogue. Manos frames this fleeting moment with care, using tonality and architectural elements to build a quiet tension. The Elma Lewis School, founded to support Black youth in Roxbury and Dorchester through arts education, provides an essential backdrop to this image's layered meaning. Through a subtle interplay of posture, glance, and space, Manos offers a meditation on mentorship and the possibilities of cultural transmission.

Figure 10. Constantine Manos, *Parade inaugurating Puerto Rican Festival, City Hall*, 1974. Courtesy of the Boston Athenaeum.

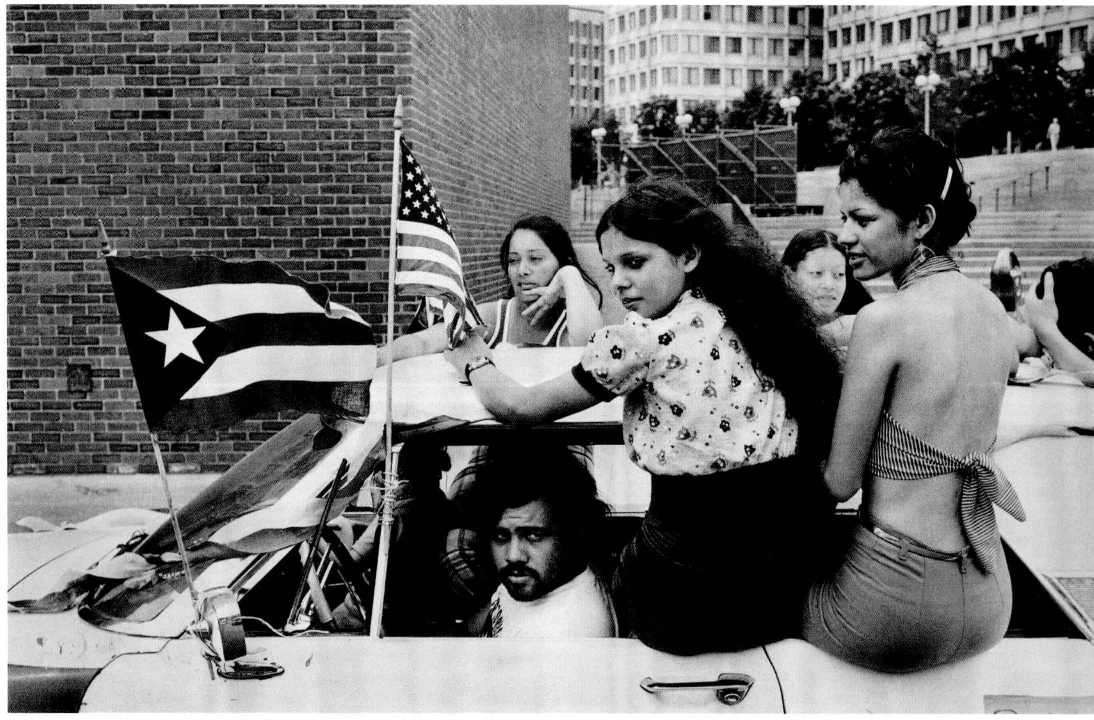

Figure 11. Constantine Manos, *Busing demonstration at federal building*, 1974. Courtesy of the Boston Athenaeum.

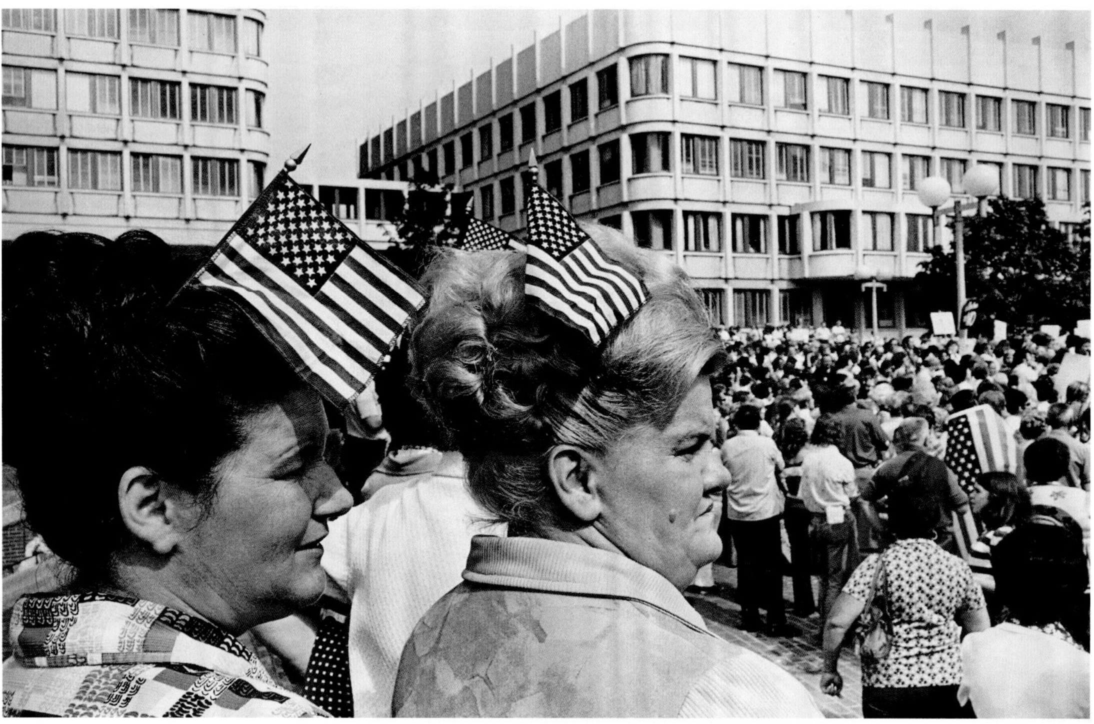

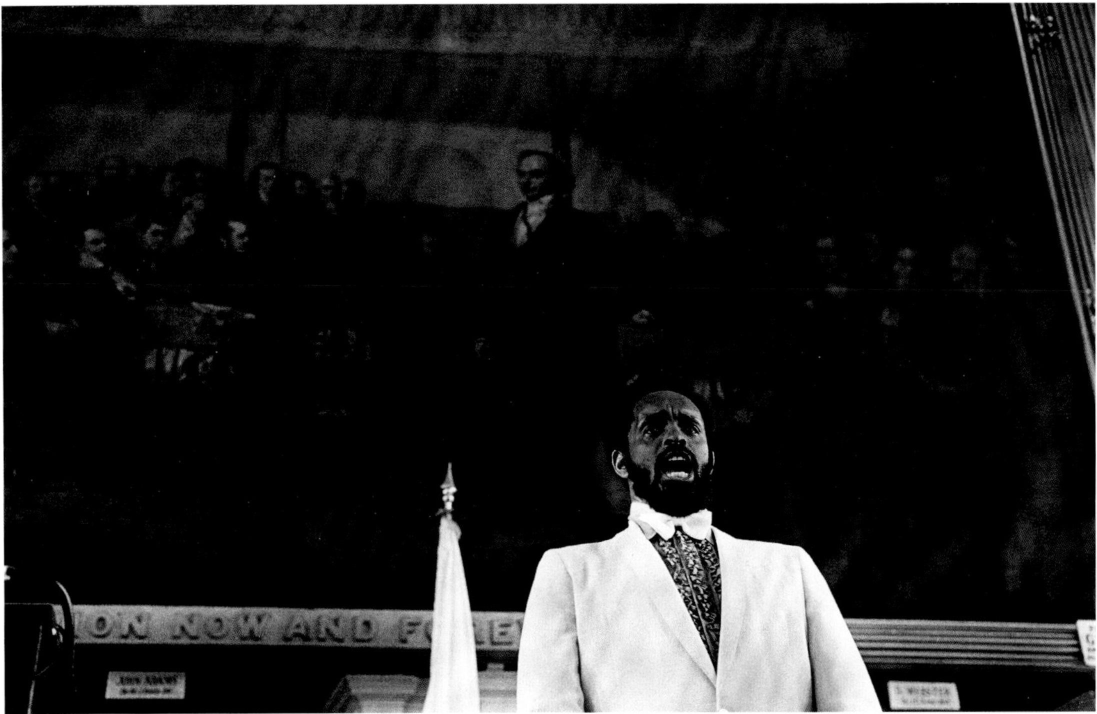

Figure 12. Constantine Manos, *Singing of National Anthem at July Fourth ceremonies, Faneuil Hall*, 1974. Courtesy of the Boston Athenaeum.

Political and patriotic tensions

Set against the backdrop of the American Bicentennial, Manos's portfolio captures Boston's political contradictions and social unrest. His photographs reveal a city negotiating its identity amid celebrations of nationalism and struggles for civil rights. A recurring motif throughout *Bostonians* is the American flag, an emblem that Manos returns to repeatedly, both in the photographs displayed on the *Where's Boston?* pavilion and in the original photobook publication. This symbolic presence recalls the work of Robert Frank and his seminal photobook *The Americans* (1958), which presents a critical view of postwar America. Within the book, Frank utilized the flag as a visual and thematic device to disrupt and punctuate the photographic sequence.[26] Like Frank, Manos uses the flag not simply as a patriotic icon but as a complex marker of identity, division, and belonging within the American urban landscape. The American flag is peppered throughout Manos's series, stuck in a woman's bouffant hairdo at an anti-busing protest, displayed at an American Legion Memorial Day service, and coupled with a Puerto Rican flag during the city's Puerto Rican festival (figures 10 and 11). The cover photograph of this edition of the *Bostonians*—featuring a demonstrator holding an American flag in front of City Hall—and the 1975 book's concluding image of a fiddler on Boston Common next to a billowing American flag (page 120), function as bookends to the narrative, framing the city's tensions and celebrations through visual metaphors.

Through scenes of protest and patriotic ceremony, Manos presents a layered narrative that questions who is included in public displays of belonging and who remains marginalized. In *Singing of National Anthem at July Fourth ceremonies, Faneuil Hall*, Manos centers singer Ernest Triplett mid-performance, just in front of a flagpole (figure 12). The singer stands before George Peter Alexander Healy's painting depicting Daniel Webster's famous Senate rebuttal to Senator Robert Hayne's claim that the North was trying to destroy the South through high tariffs and a vocal opposition to slavery. This symbolically charged backdrop visually anchors the ceremony in the historic struggle over federalism, liberty, and union, connecting the scene to broader narratives of American identity, justice, and democracy. The interplay

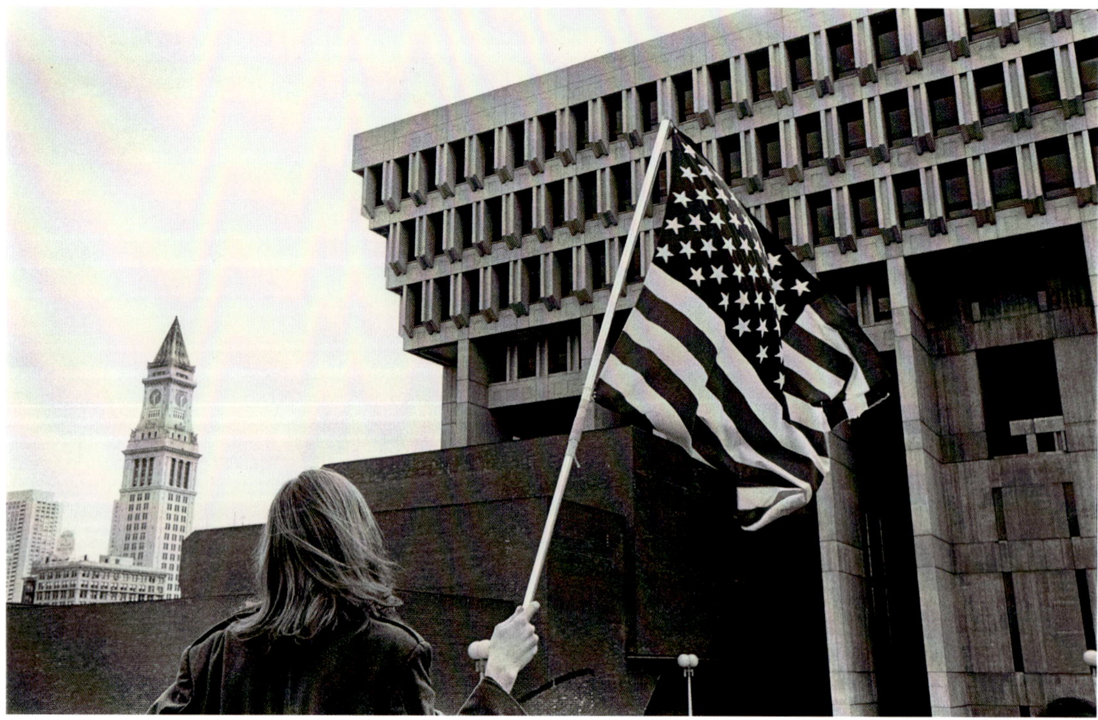

Figure 13. Constantine Manos, *Demonstrator in front of City Hall, Government Center*, 1974. Courtesy of the Boston Athenaeum.

between the singer's presence and the historic painting evokes a continuum between past and present struggles for inclusion and equality. The photograph invites reflection on the complex layers of patriotism—how an African American singer leads the national anthem celebrating freedom even as many in Boston and beyond continue to fight for civil rights.

Just outside where that photograph was made is another from the series, *Demonstrator in front of City Hall* (figure 13). This stark, evocative image captures a demonstrator clutching an American flag outside the imposing modernist facade of Boston's City Hall. The figure stands off-center in the frame, creating a tension between human scale and the monumental architecture in front of them. The flag, a potent symbol of national identity and contested belonging, is both a banner of patriotism and a provocative claim to rights in a city grappling with racial segregation and school desegregation conflicts. The flag's stark white stripes contrast sharply with the gray concrete surroundings, visually asserting the presence of dissent within a cold, bureaucratic environment. Manos's composition emphasizes lines and geometry—the rigid verticals of the flagpole, building edges, and the flag itself are juxtaposed with the more organic human form. By leaving the demonstrator's cause ambiguous, Manos invites the viewer to grapple with the nuances of the period's protests, whether for or against busing and civil rights, highlighting the fractured nature of civic identity and belonging in 1970s Boston.

Viewed together, these images embody the duality of Boston's bicentennial moment: celebration and struggle, unity and division. The anthem singer inside Faneuil Hall represents a hopeful, patriotic performance rooted in cultural affirmation and inclusion, while the lone demonstrator outside City Hall personifies the ongoing fight for justice. Manos's inclusion of these moments challenges the viewer to consider for whom America's promises ring true, especially as Boston navigated its own fraught history of race, class, and power during the 1970s. Through his nuanced framing, Manos invites us to reflect on the complexities of urban citizenship, reminding us that patriotism and protest are often intertwined expressions of belonging and resistance within the American city.

Conclusion

Constantine Manos's varied and intimate series reveals a city caught in a moment of profound growth and change. The dynamism and complexity of Boston in the mid-1970s resonate through these photographs, inviting viewers to forge connections across time with the anonymous city dwellers who animate each frame. Whether experienced as a complete portfolio or as singular prints, Manos's work celebrates Boston's communities, public spaces, and everyday rituals. Today, *Bostonians* offers not only a window into the past but also a mirror reflecting ongoing conversations about identity, inclusion, and urban life in Boston. The themes Manos explored—the tensions of patriotism and protest, the power of community spaces, and the diversity of experience—remain relevant as the city continues to evolve. *Bostonians* stands as both a historical document and a living dialogue, reminding us that the stories of a city are always in motion, shaped by the everyday moments and the countless individuals who call that city home.

Notes

1. Constantine Manos, *Bostonians* (CambridgeSeven Associates, 1975), preface.

2. CambridgeSeven was brought on to design the 20th-century pavilion and came up with the name *Where's Boston?*. This was led by CambridgeSeven co-founder Peter Chermayeff (conversation with the author, April 4, 2024). A budget breakdown in November 1974 estimated that the *Where's Boston?* pavilion would cost $460,000. Project # 188 Contemporary Boston Show, Envision, personal records of Fred Brink.

3. Boston 200 was led by Katherine Kane, Boston deputy mayor under Kevin White. The citywide celebration opened in the summer of 1975 and included three World's Fair-like pavilions. The 20th-century pavilion, *Where's Boston?*; the 19th-century pavilion, *The Grand Exposition of Progress and Invention*; and the 18th-century pavilion focused on the revolution. See Caryl Rivers, "Boston's Bicentennial Hallmark: Participatory Tourism, *The New York Times*, June 22, 1975.

4. Caryl Rivers, "Boston's Bicentennial Hallmark: Participatory Tourism, *The New York Times*, June 22, 1975.

5. Boston City Archives, Boston 200, collection 0279.001, box 18, folder 8, "Treatment: Prudential Pavilion Bicentennial show," May 3, 1974. A 1973 planning document described the pavilion as "the most important orientation point in the modern city. . . . It will be the location from which people will begin their exploration of the 20th-century city. Promoted by Boston 200 as a prime orientation point during the Bicentennial years, it will become the principal gateway to Boston." Boston City Archives, Boston 200, collection 0279.001, box 51, folder 4, "Boston, at Prudential Center," September 21, 1973. A later document spells out the thesis of the *Where's Boston?* endeavor: "Originally sited on a tiny peninsula, lacking abundant natural resources, and with an abundance of problematic weather, Boston has, and continues to compensate through the resourceful ingenuity and steadfast endurance of people attracted by the city's distinctly flavorful, slightly eccentric, occasionally exasperating, but generally civilized style of living. Put more directly: Since Bostonians are convinced that Boston is worth keeping, they do what is necessary to keep her." Boston City Archives, Boston 200, collection 0279.001, box 18, folder 8, "Treatment: Prudential Pavilion Bicentennial show," May 3, 1974.

6. Boston City Archives, Boston 200, "Boston 200 Pavilion," July 1974, record 0279.001 box 18, folder 4. The goal of the "word wall" was to catch the rich texture of Boston through its verbal expressions. Words/phrases included "Quahogs . . . Lace-Curtain Irish . . . The Common," *Where's Boston?* (CambridgeSeven Associates, 1975).

7. Boston City Archives, Boston 200, collection 0279.001, box 18, folder 8, "Boston collection."

8. The Boston-based company Envision began the early planning stages of this project, beginning in 1973. This planning and script treatment was managed and led by

Fred Brink. About a year into planning, CambridgeSeven brought in the multimedia artist Rusty Russell, previously known for his films *The New York Experience* and *The San Francisco Experience*. The *Where's Boston?* slideshow was a huge endeavor, employing two principal photographers, Constantine Manos and Kevin Burke, and later Lou Jones, as well as 13 additional photographers. The field recording and sound editing was done by Mary Jane Soule. The slideshow was around 45 minutes and ran on the hour every day from 10 a.m. until 10 p.m. The admission fee was $2 for adults, $1 for children. (Conversation with Peter Chermayeff and the author, April 4, 2024, and *Where's Boston?* [CambridgeSeven Associates, 1975].)

9. Project # 188 Contemporary Boston Show, Envision, personal records of Fred Brink.

10. Boston City Archives, Boston 200, collection 0279.001, box 51, folder 8, press release, n.d.

11. Boston City Archives, Boston 200, collection 0279.001, box 51, folder 9, press release, n.d.

12. Alison Nordström, "Who Are You Looking At?," *Art on Paper* 12, no. 4, March/April 2008, 74.

13. For more information about the founding of Magnum Photos, see Nadya Bair, *The Decisive Network: Magnum Photos and the Postwar Image Market* (University of California Press, 2020).

14. Constantine Manos, "From Black and White, to Color, and Back Again," Magnum Photos, Jun 17, 2019.

15. In an interview, Manos claimed to never make a photograph without a person in it. "I am a people photographer and have always been interested in people. I also have always looked for a *moment* in my pictures. I have been very serious about photographing people as individuals, as human beings. I don't think I have ever taken a photo without a person in it. (Constantine Manos, "From Black and White, to Color, and Back Again," Magnum Photos, June 17, 2019.)

16. Boston City Archives, Boston 200, collection 0279.001, box 51, folder 6, Internal memo to all Boston 200 staff, March 22, 1974.

17. Boston City Archives, Boston 200, collection 0279.001, box 51, folder 9, Constantine Manos, "Comments on the photographs," n.d.

18. Constantine Manos, *Bostonians* (CambridgeSeven Associates, 1975), 13.

19. Ibid.

20. For more information about the ethnic make-up of Mattapan, see Jim Vrable, *A People's History of the New Boston* (University of Massachusetts Press, 2014), 223.

21. Daniel McClure, "Brokering Culture: Elma Lewis, Cultural Politics, and Community Building in Postwar Boston, *Black Women, Gender & Families* 6, no. 2, 2012, 65.

22. Ibid, 62. Founded by Elma Ina Lewis in 1950, the Elma Lewis School of Fine Arts was established to meet the social, cultural, and artistic needs of Boston's African American community. Lewis believed in the importance of fostering the arts not

only in the local Roxbury-Dorchester community but also in the African American community of Boston at large, and her philosophy was to instill racial pride while teaching.

23. Tanya Hart, "Sly Stone: A soulful revolution," *Bay State Banner*, June 25, 2025.

24. As a number of figures are shown flying kites, it is possible that this photograph was taken during the Franklin Park Kite Festival, founded by Clara Wainwright in 1969 with the support of the Boston Parks Commissioner, another effort to revitalize the park.

25. Thanks to Robert Klein Gallery for sharing additional unpublished photographs from the series.

26. For more information on Robert Frank's *The Americans*, see Sarah Greenough, *Looking In: Robert Frank's The Americans*, expanded ed. (National Gallery of Art, 2009).

The Photographs

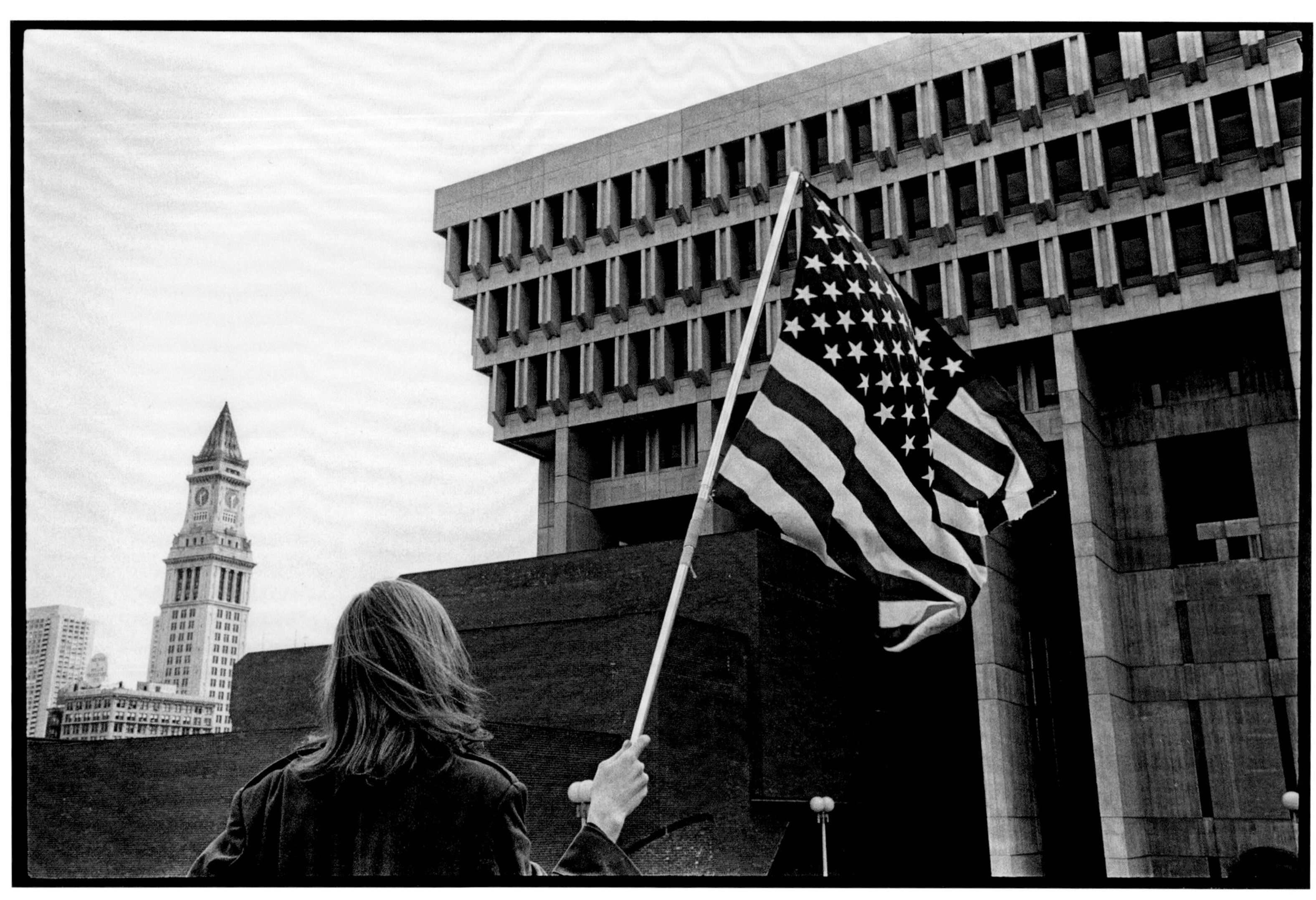

Demonstrator in front of City Hall,
Government Center

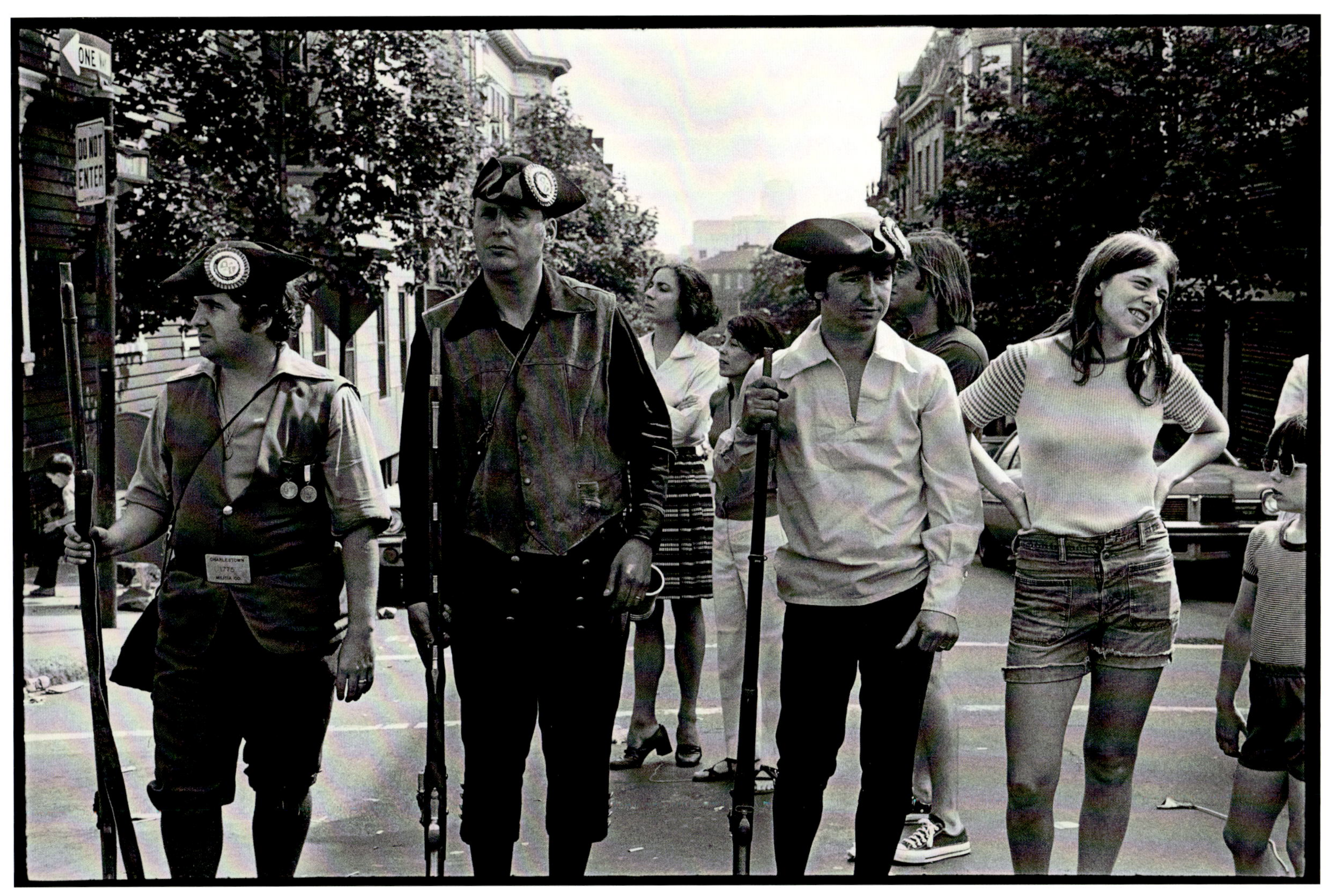

Participants and spectators at
Bunker Hill Day, Charlestown

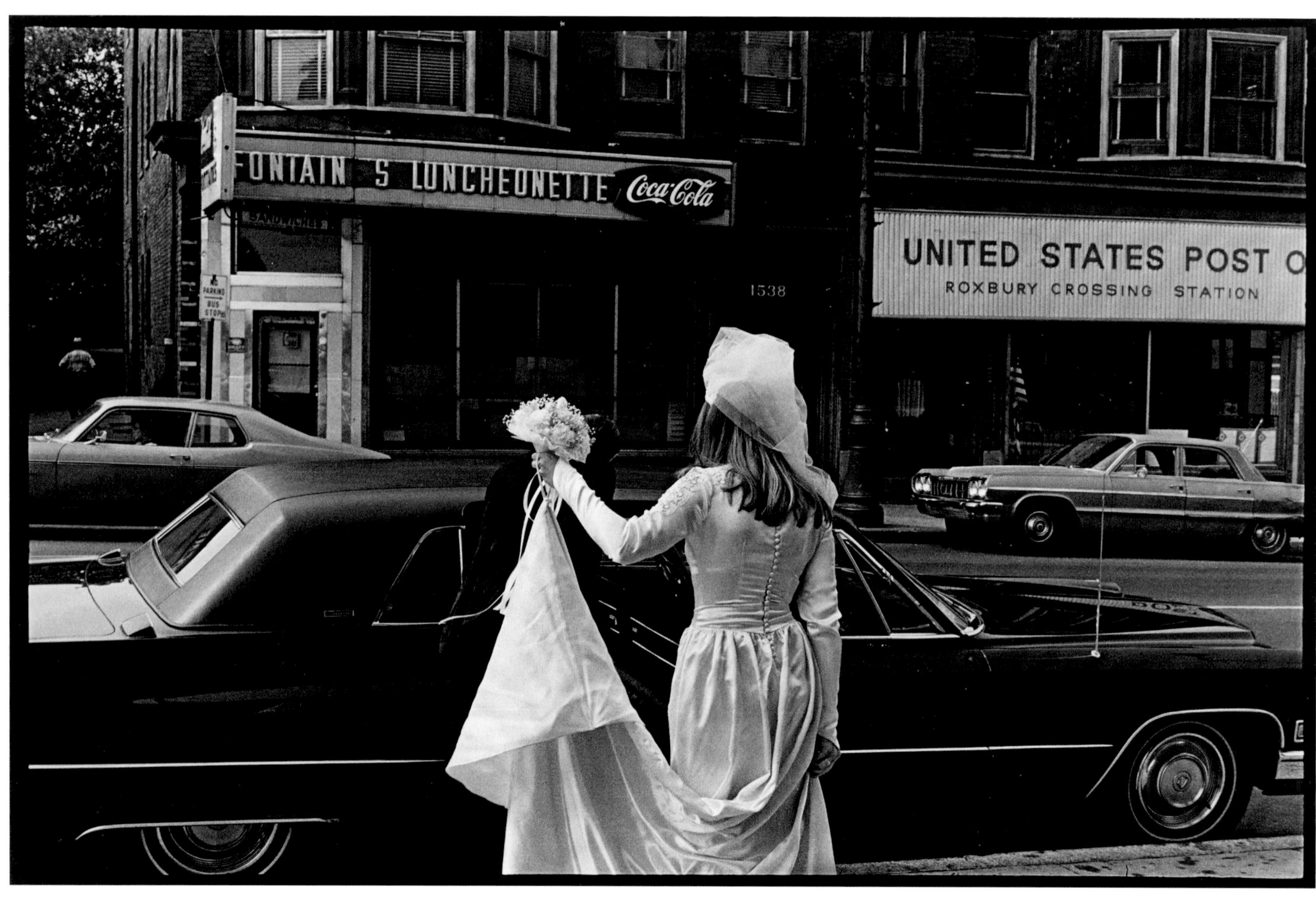

Bride leaving church,
Roxbury Crossing

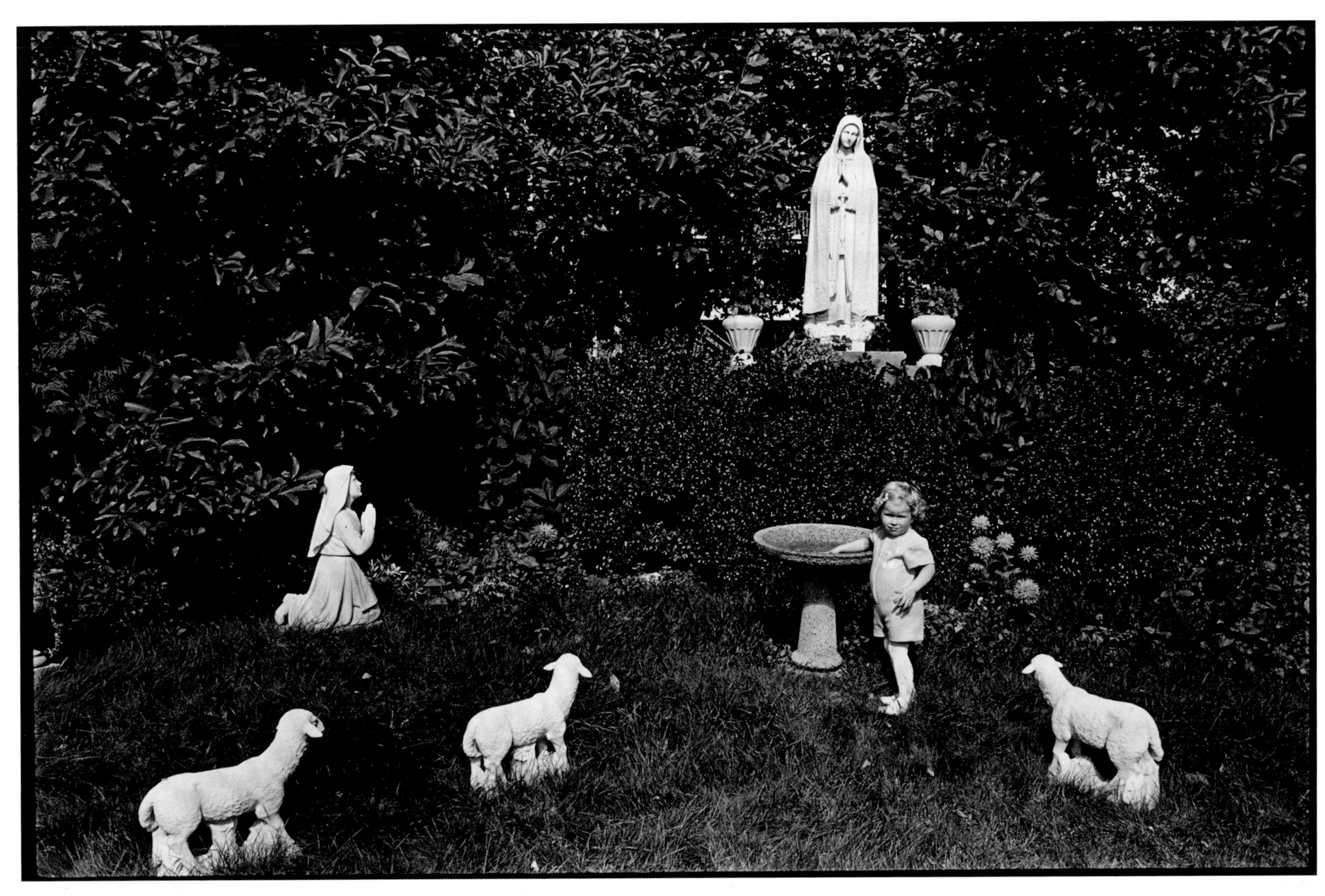

Child at shrine of St. Lazarus Church,
East Boston

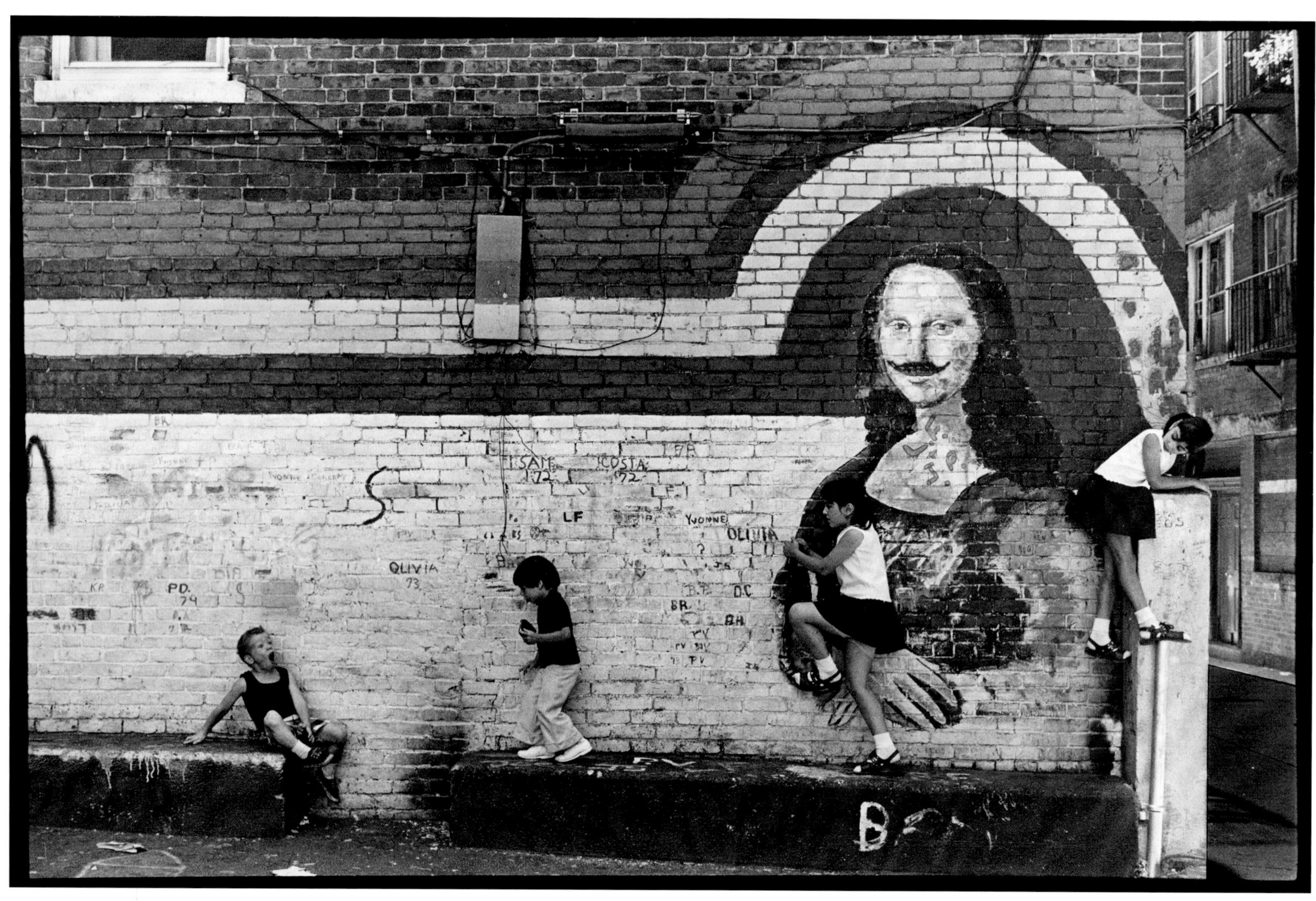

Children and Mona Lisa wall,
North End

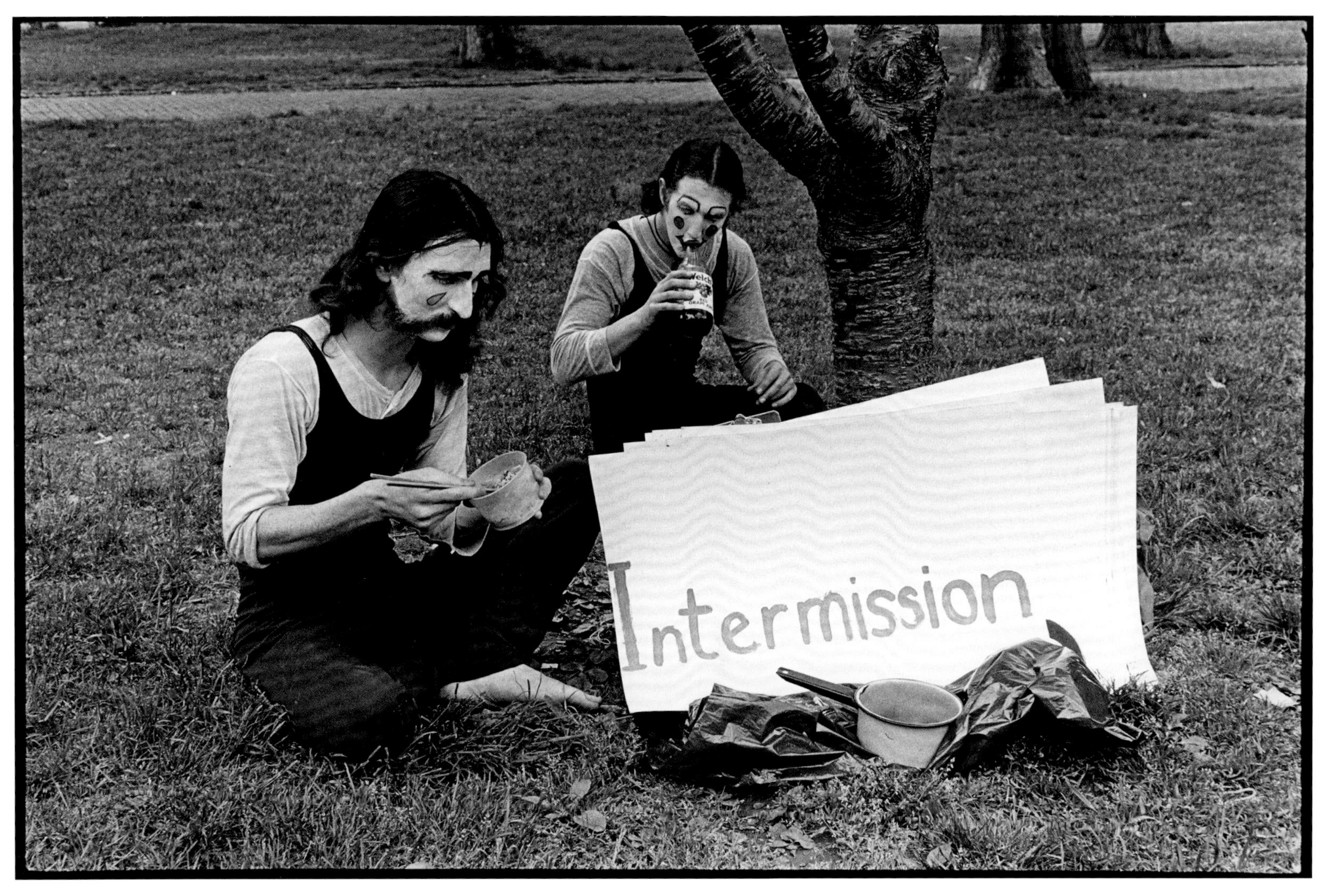

Wandering mime actors having lunch,
Boston Common

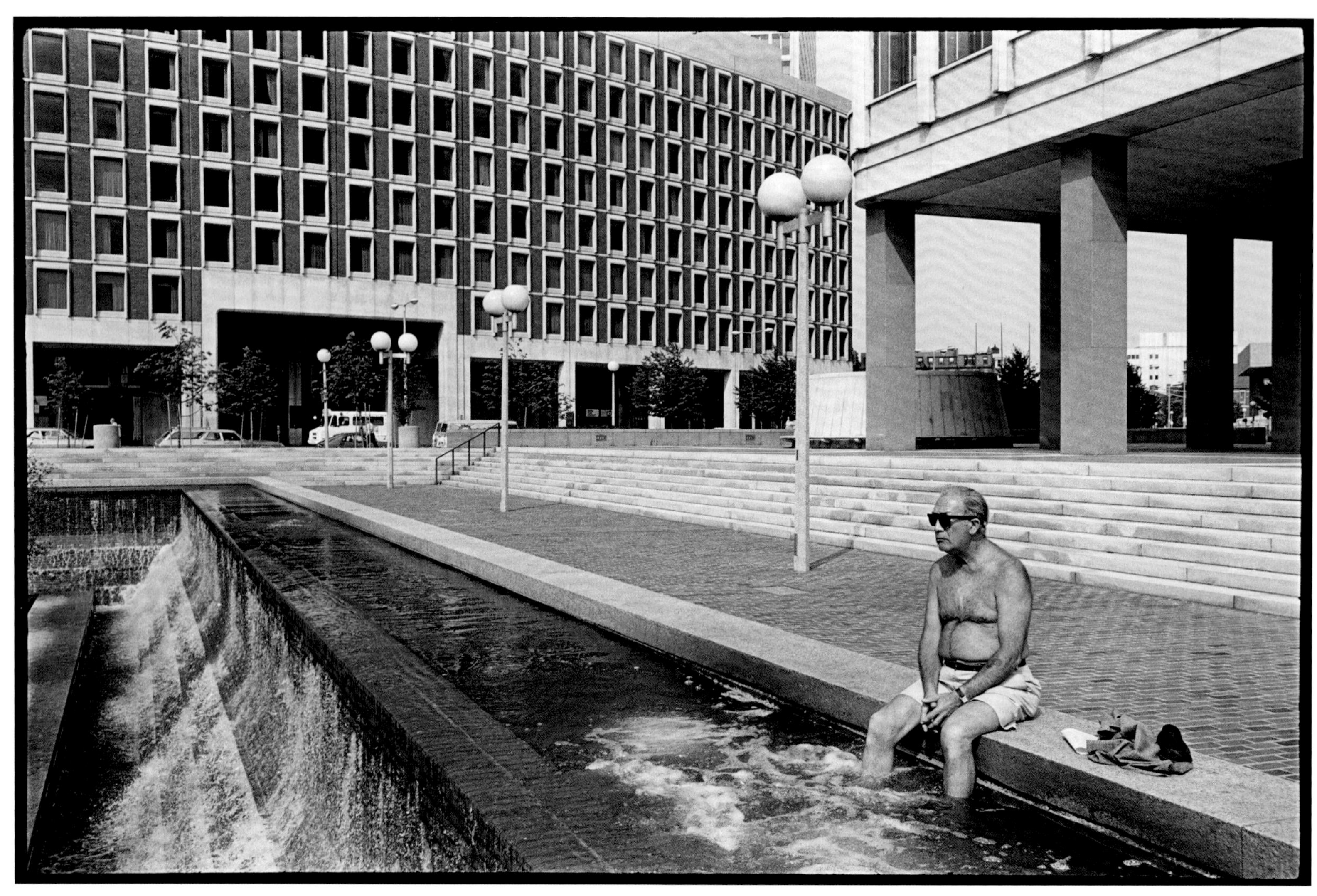

Man sunning himself on Fourth of July, Government Center

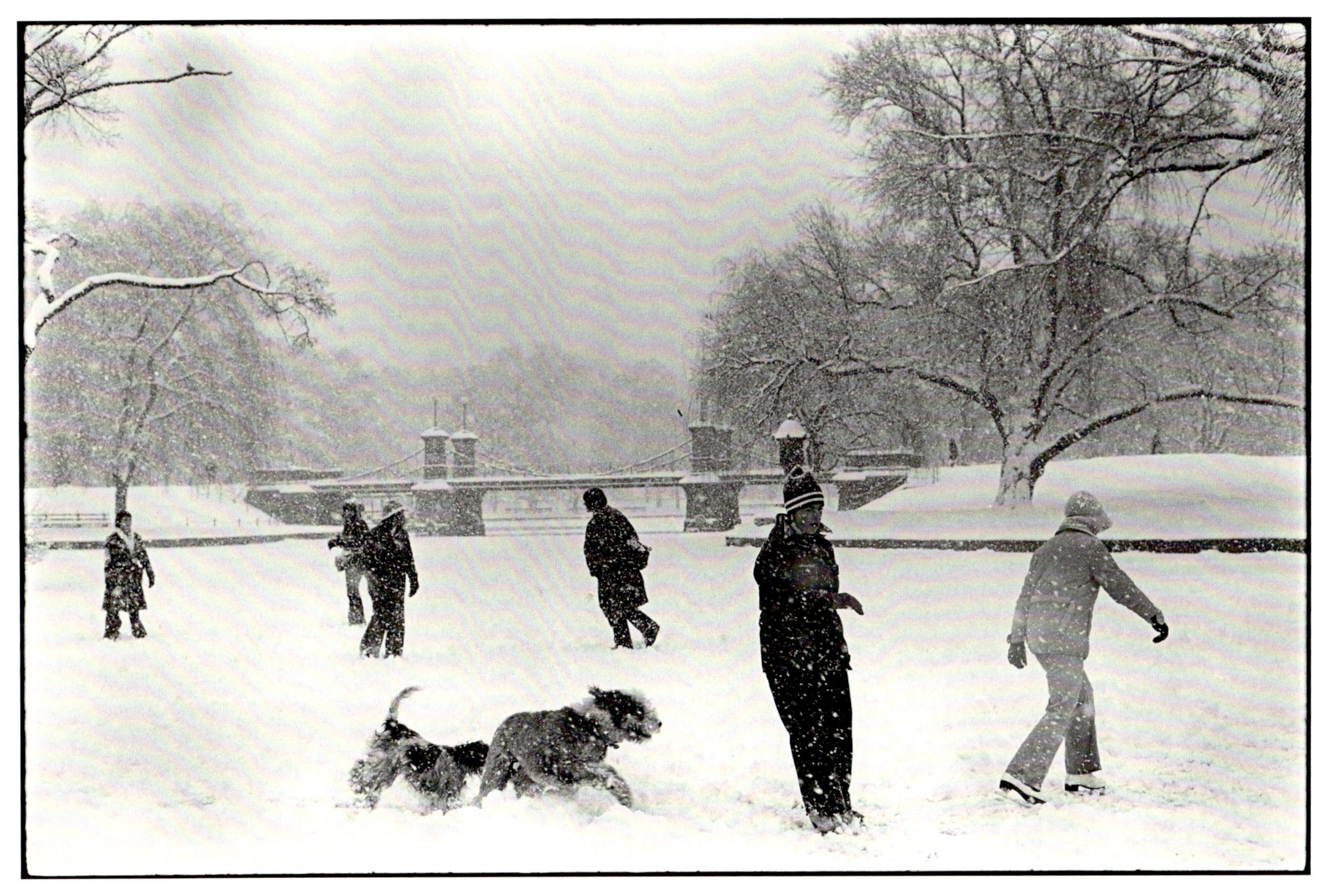

The first snow of Winter,
Public Garden

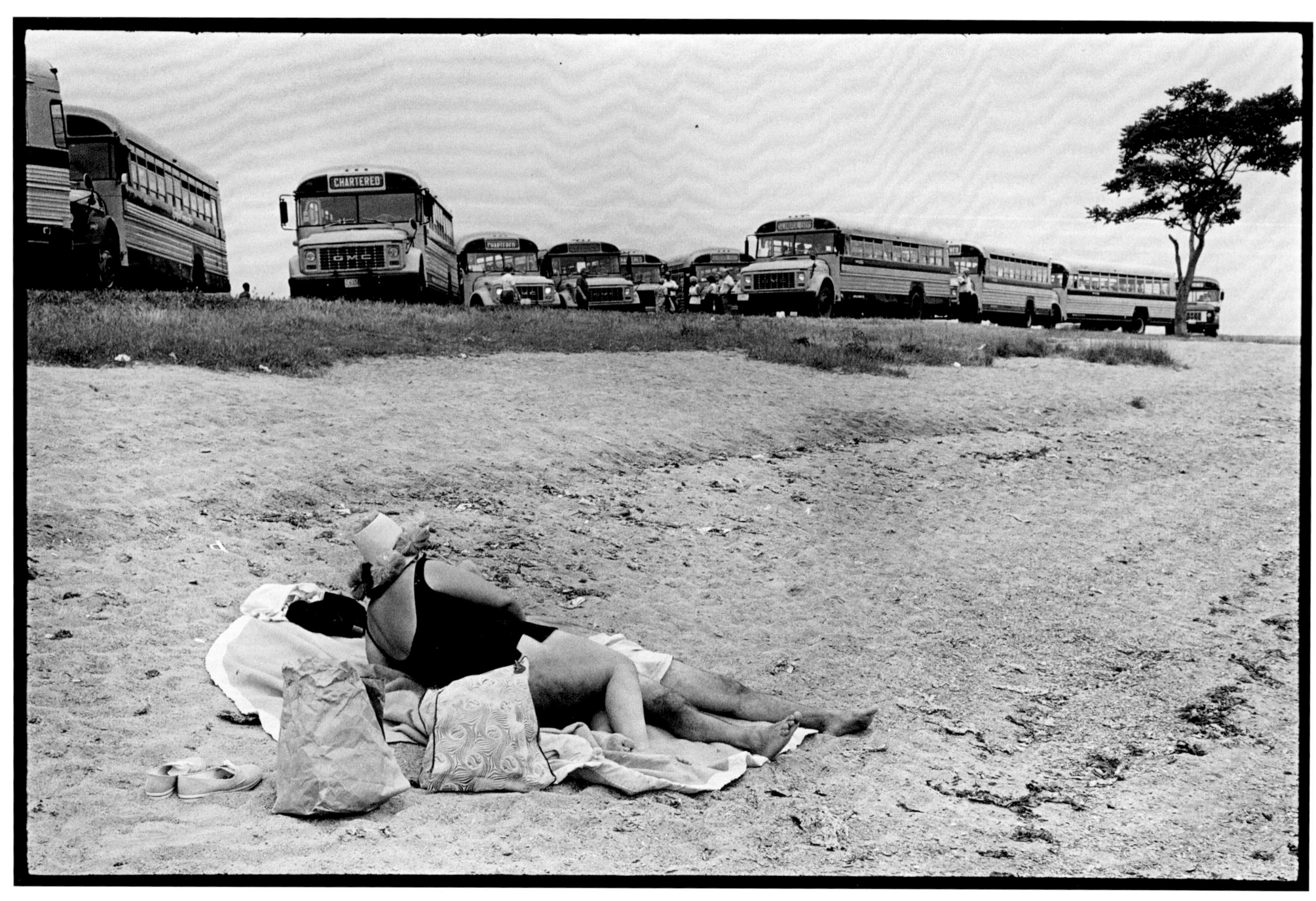

Couple and buses at an outing,
Castle Island

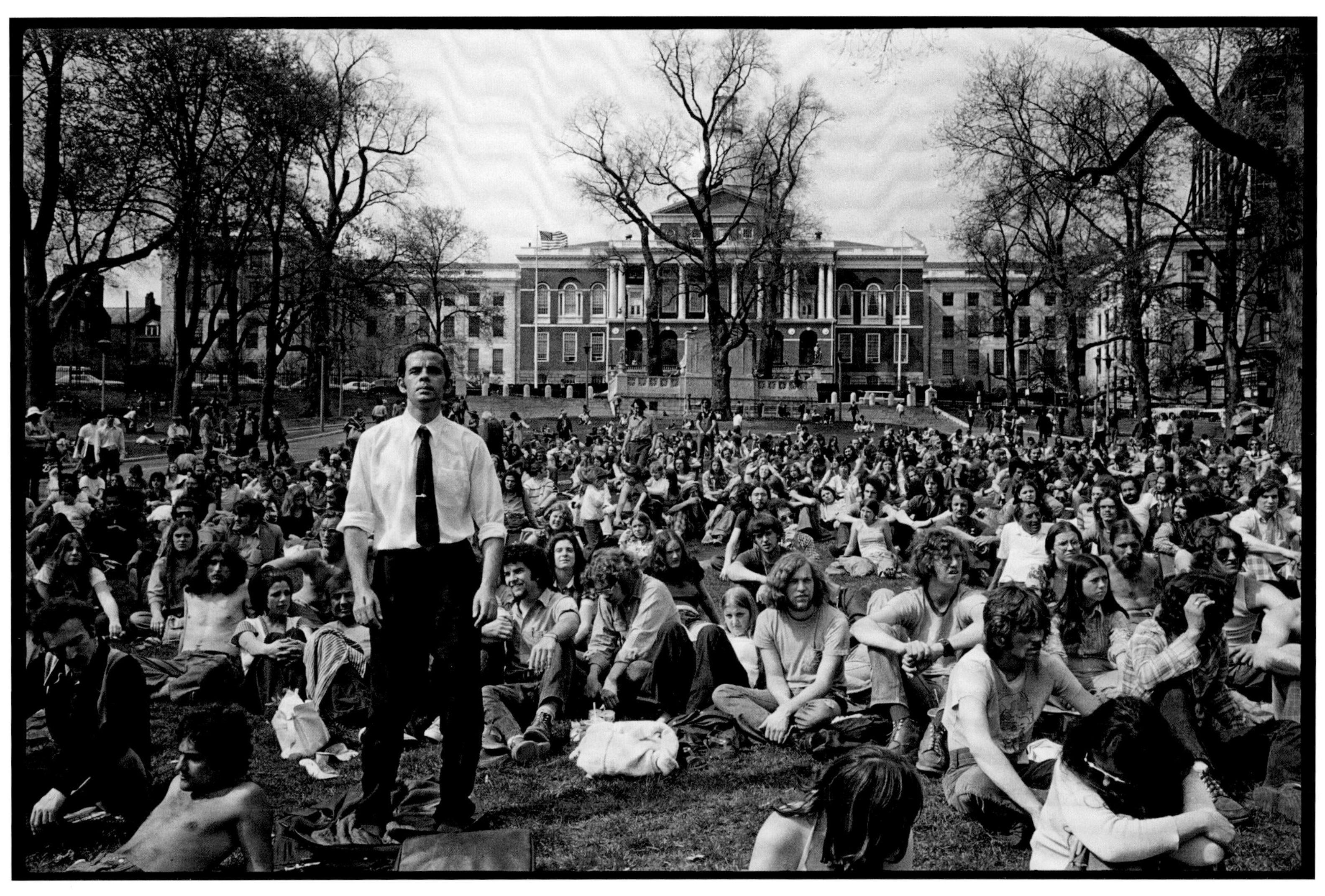

Concert in front of the State House, Boston Common

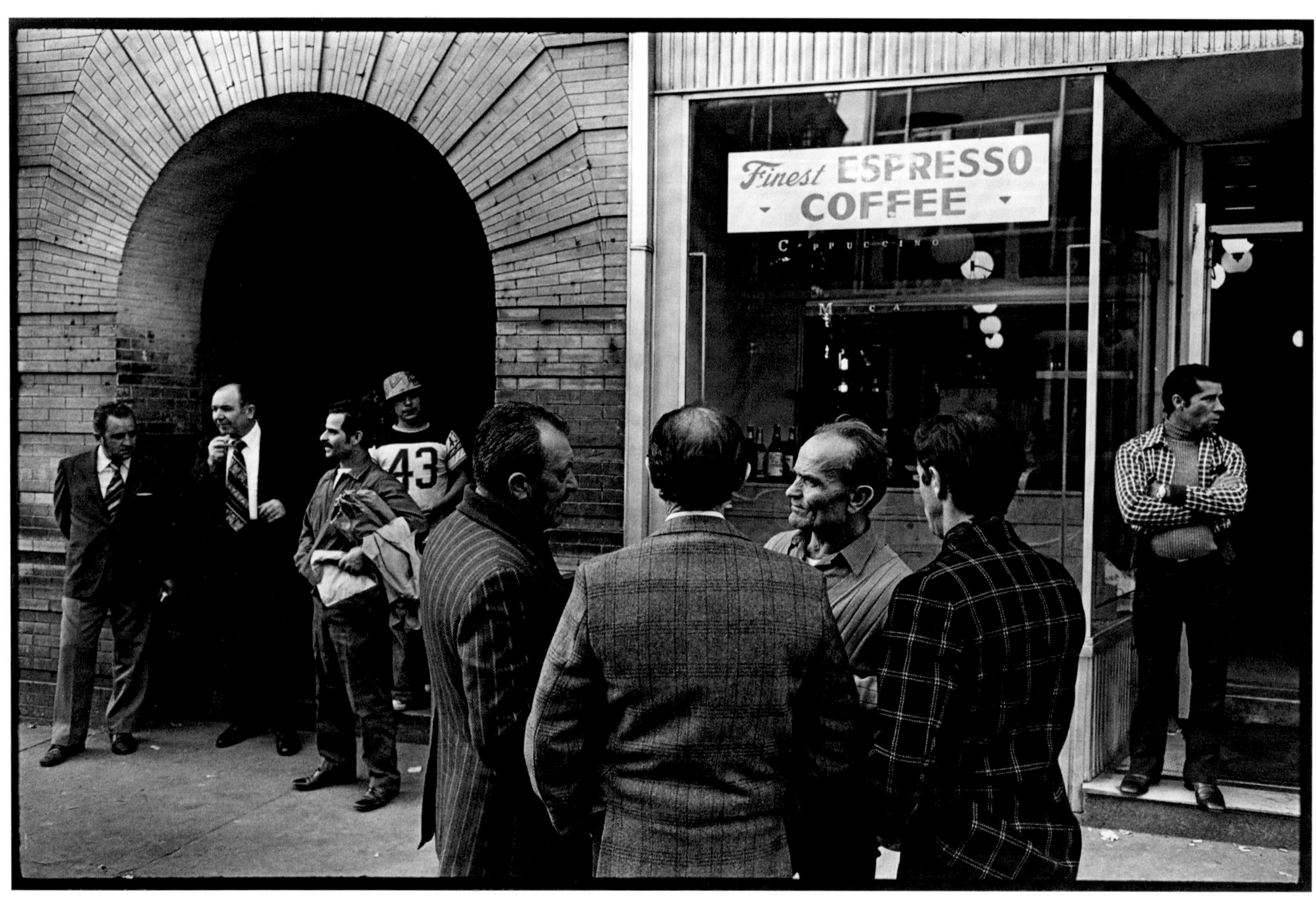

Sunday morning on Hanover Street,
North End

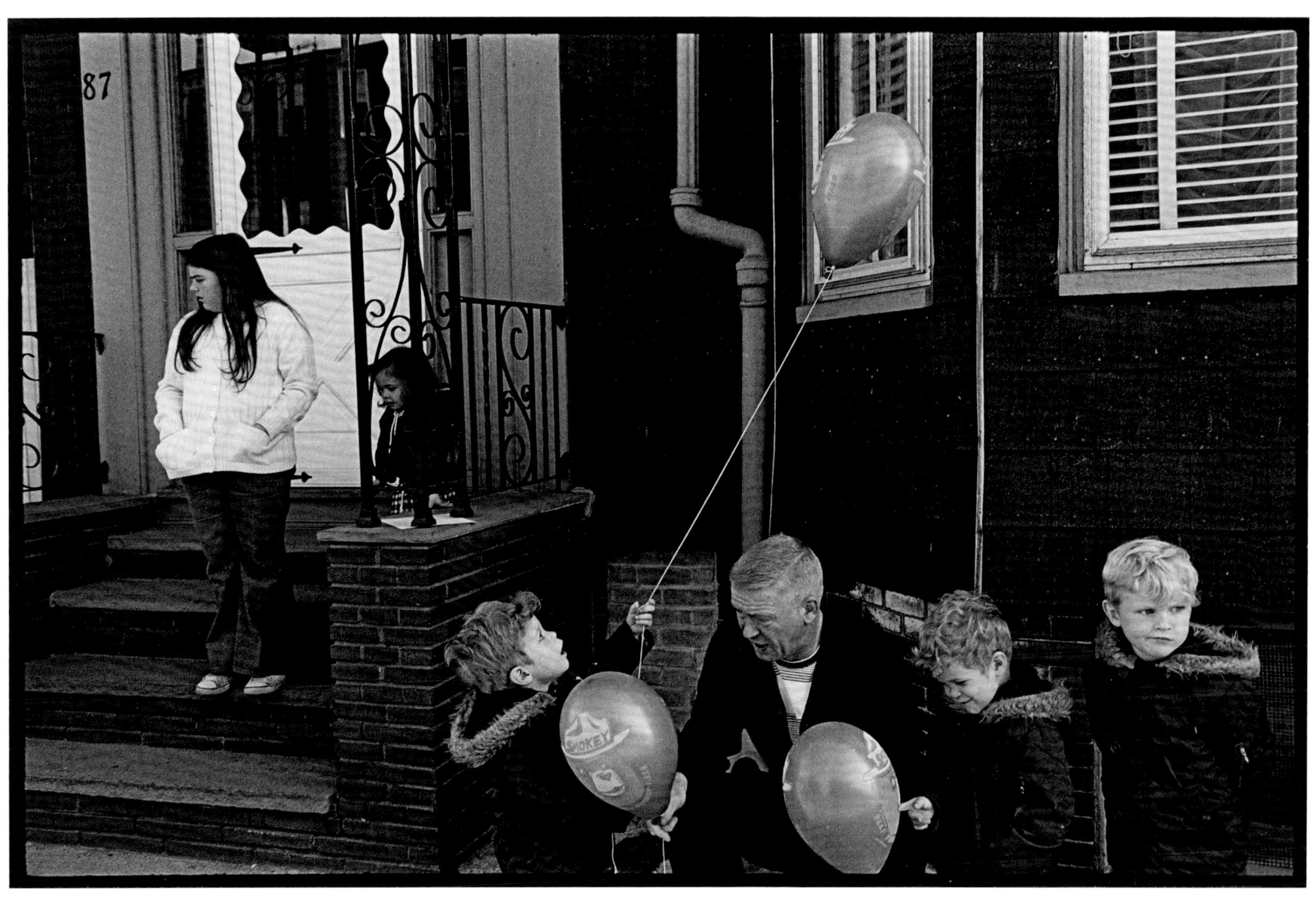

Waiting for the Columbus Day
Parade, East Boston

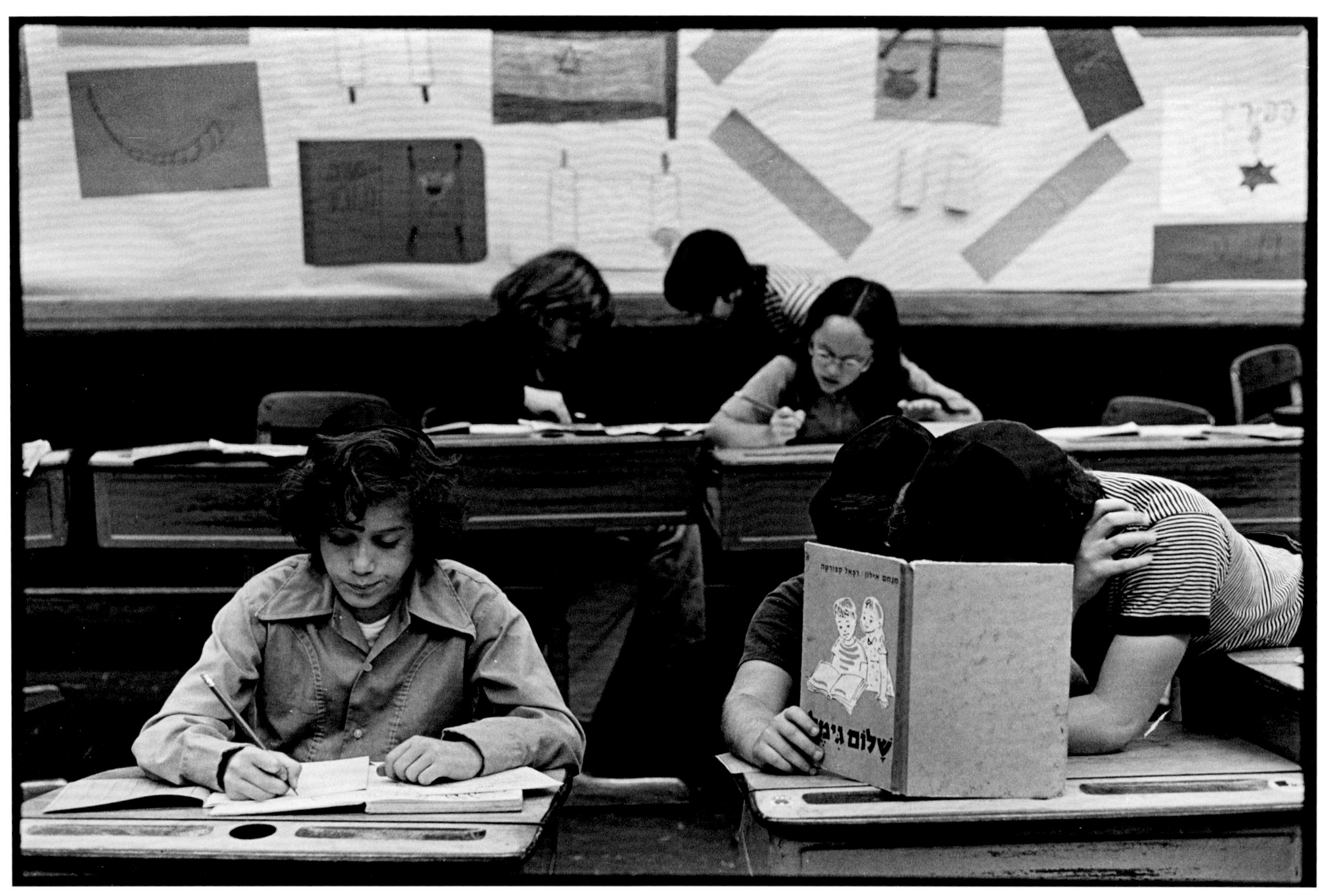

Hebrew class at Congregation
Kehillath Israel, Brookline

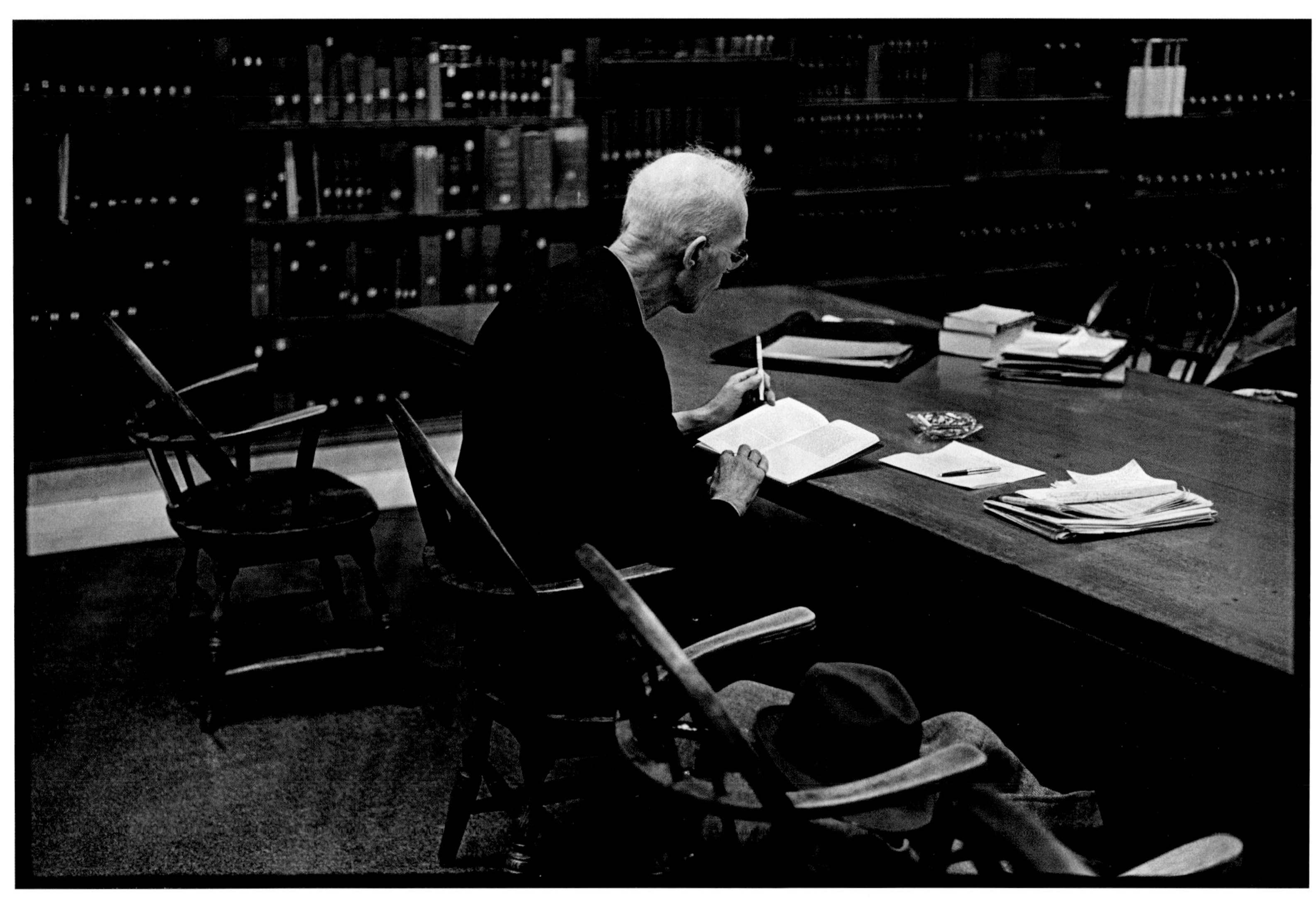

Reading room of Widener Library,
Harvard University

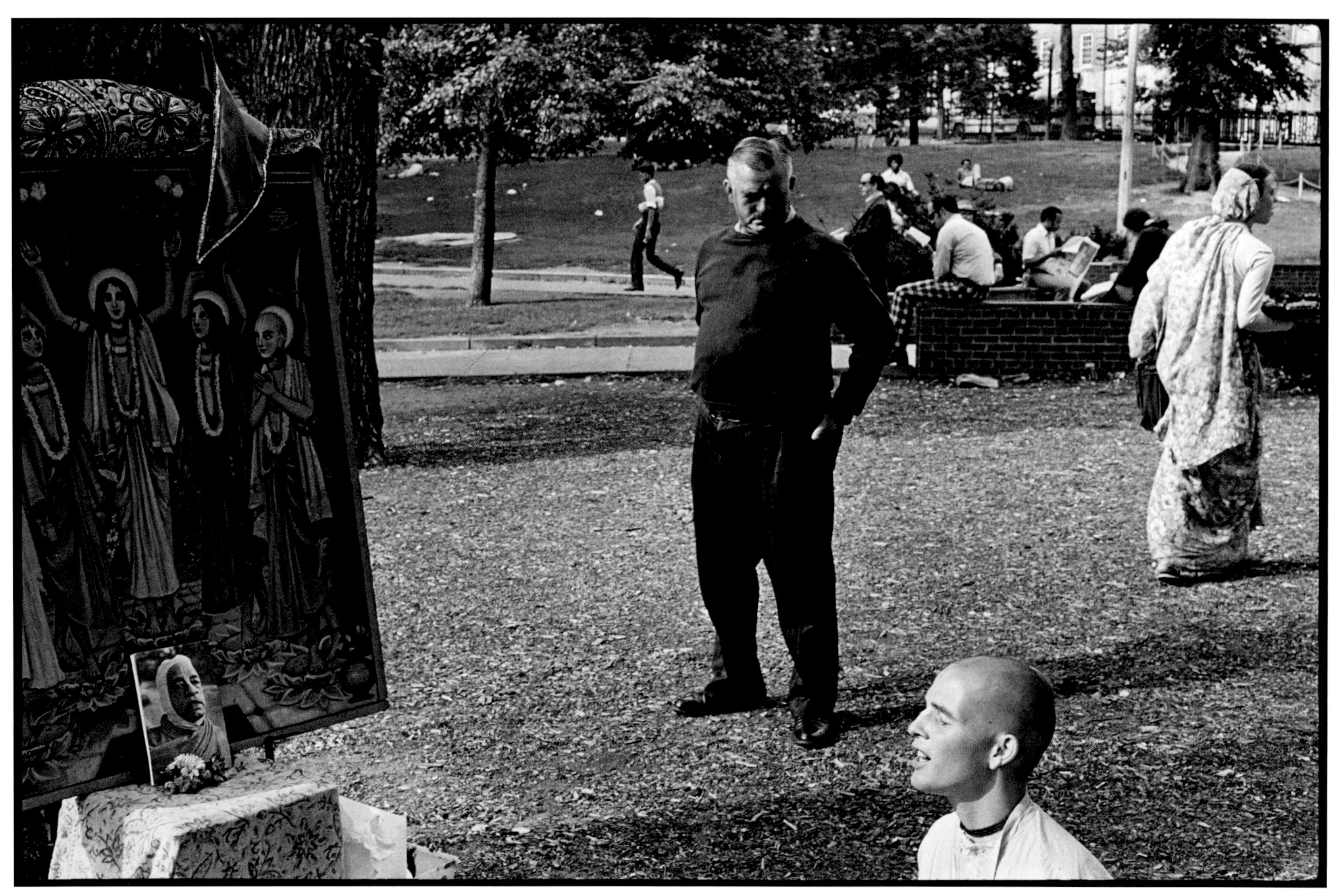

Hare Krishna disciple and spectator,
Boston Common

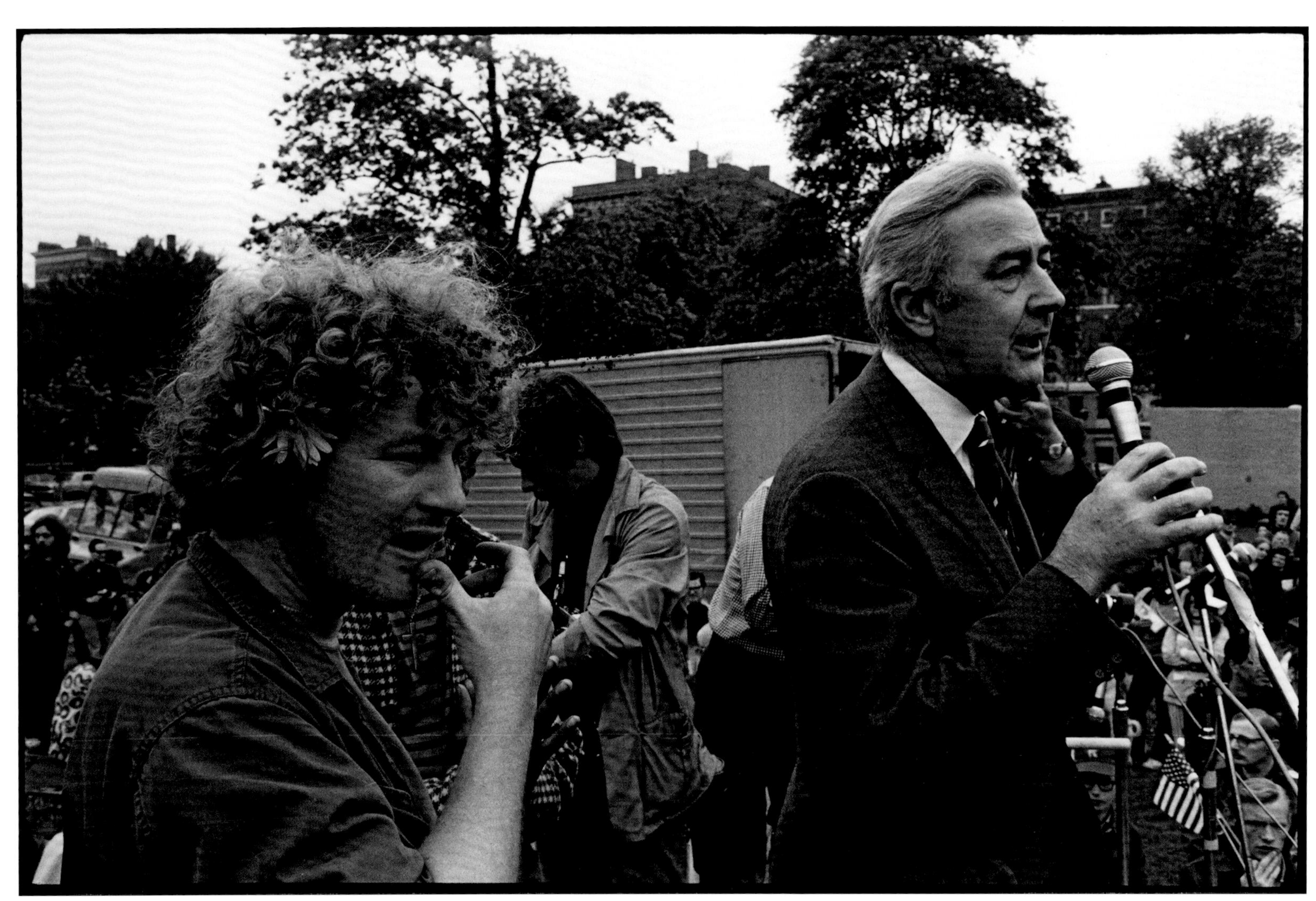

Political rally, Fenway

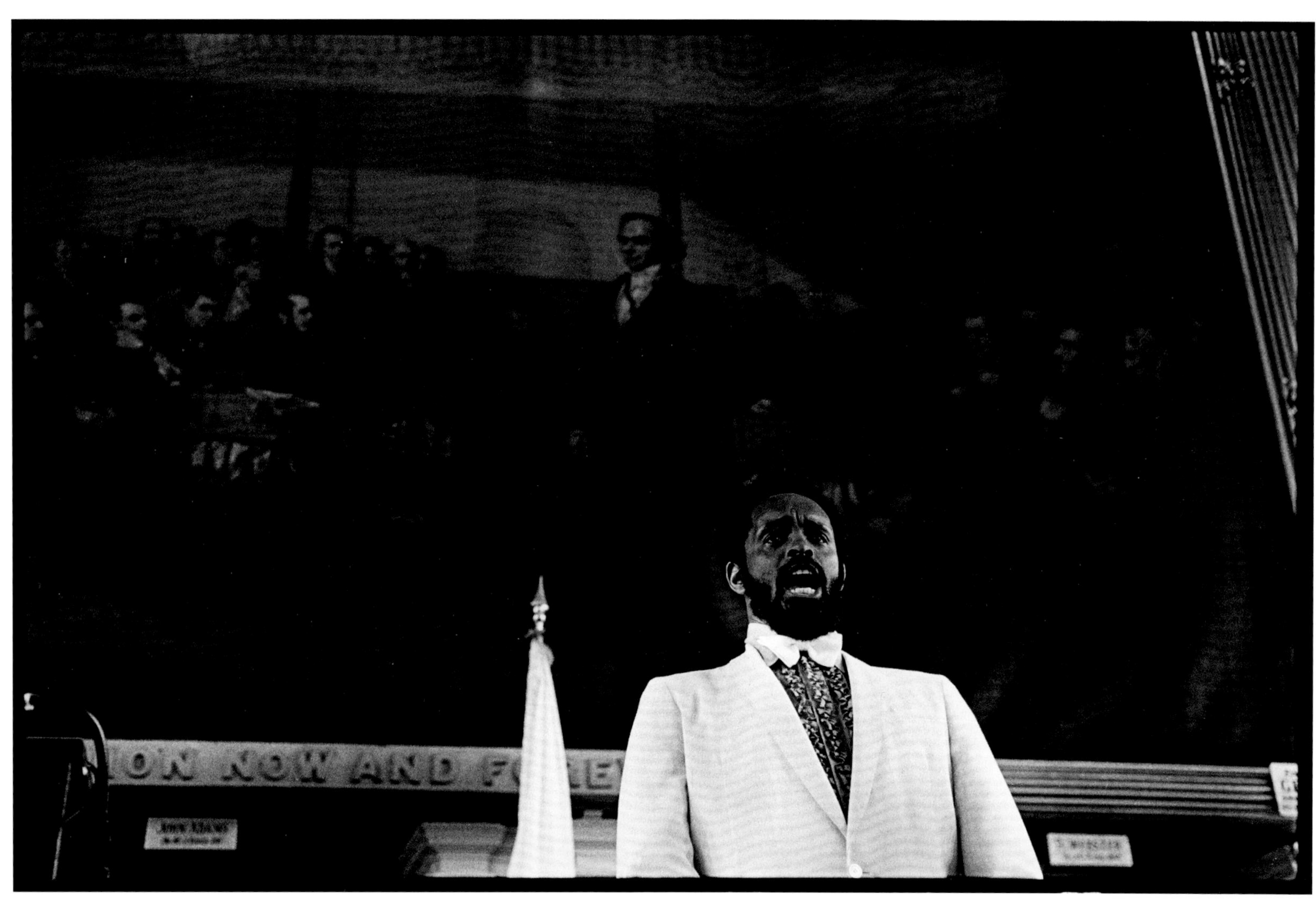

Singing of National Anthem at July
Fourth ceremonies, Faneuil Hall

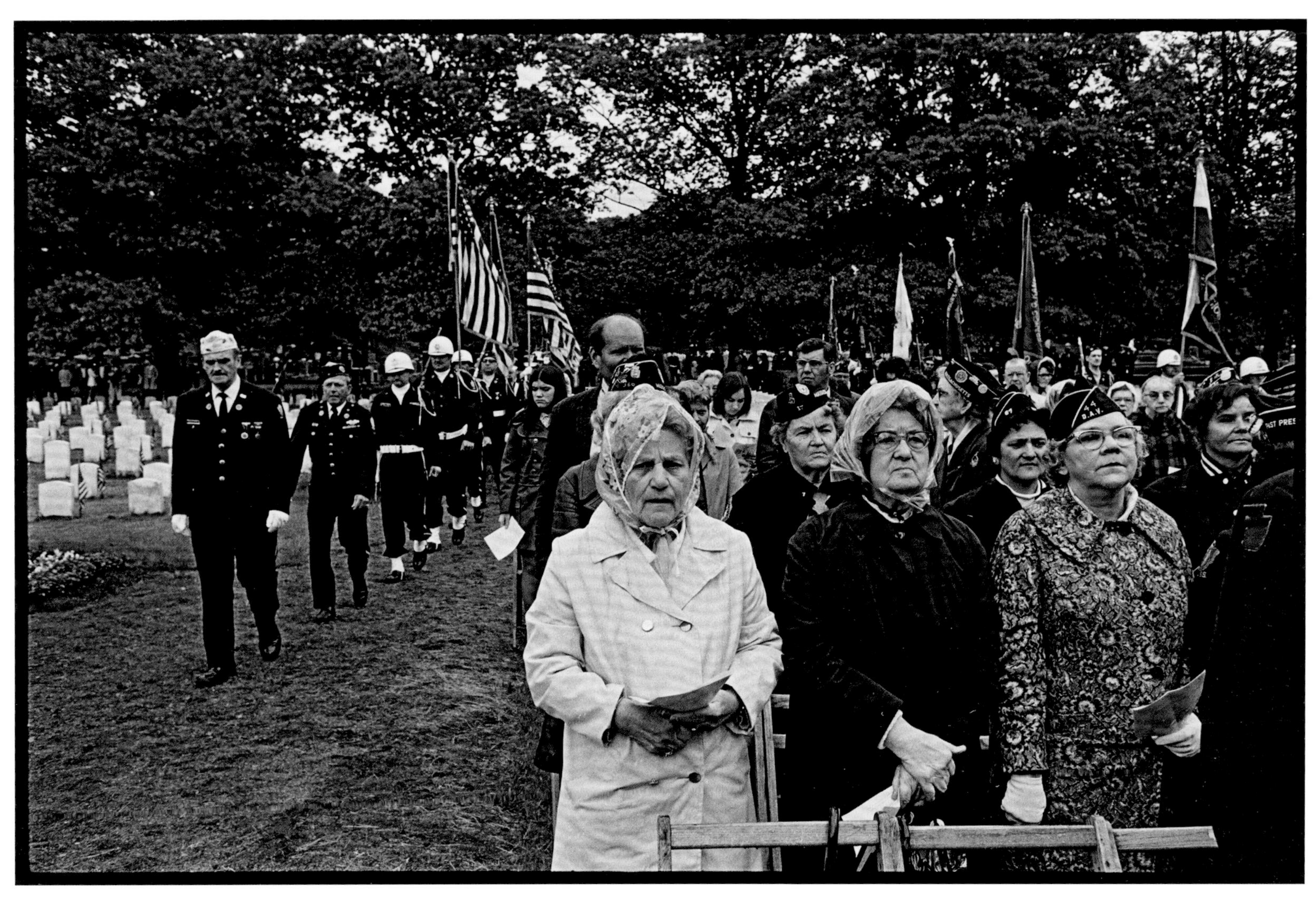

American Legion Memorial Day
Services, Mattapan

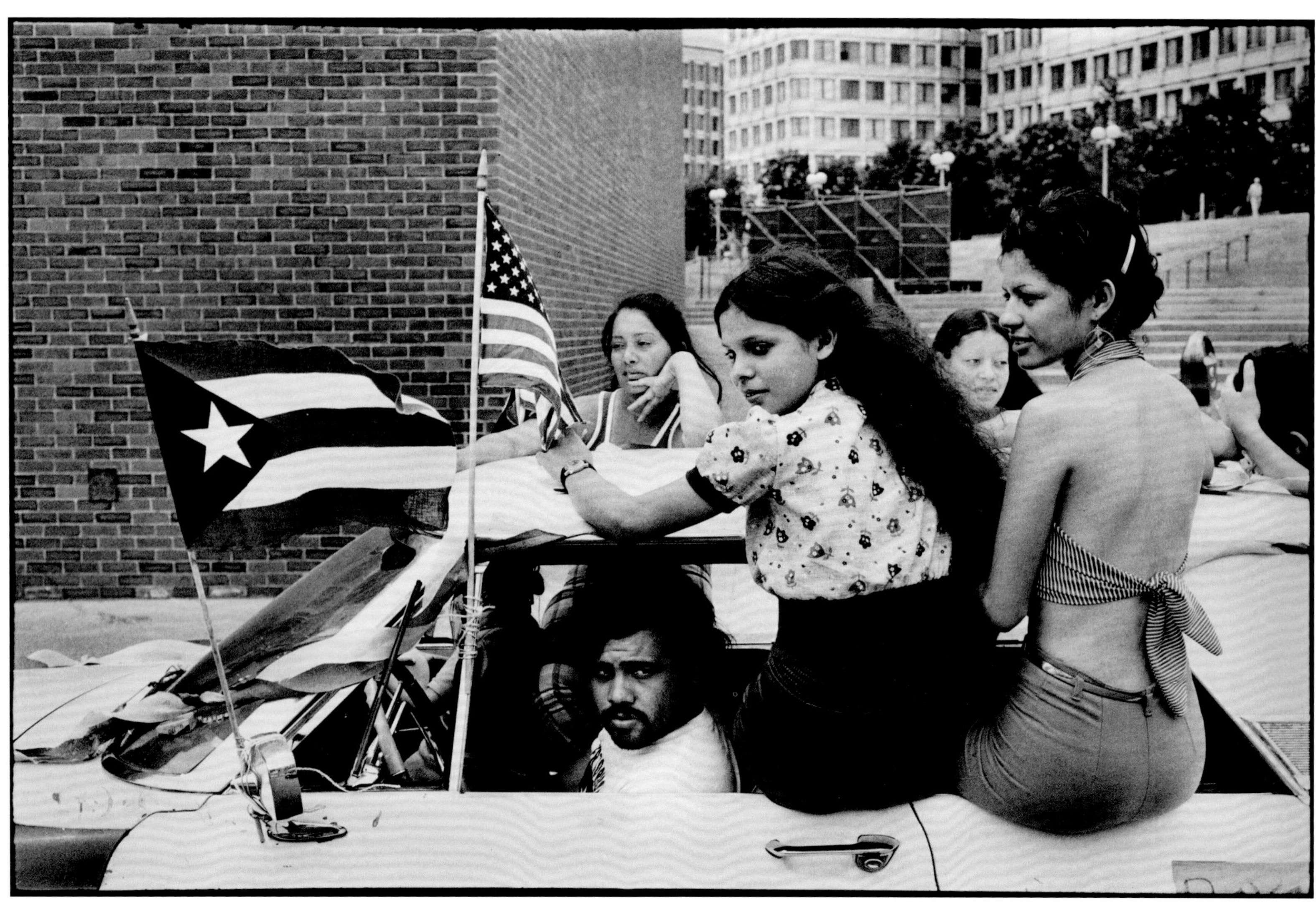

Parade inaugurating Puerto Rican
Festival, City Hall

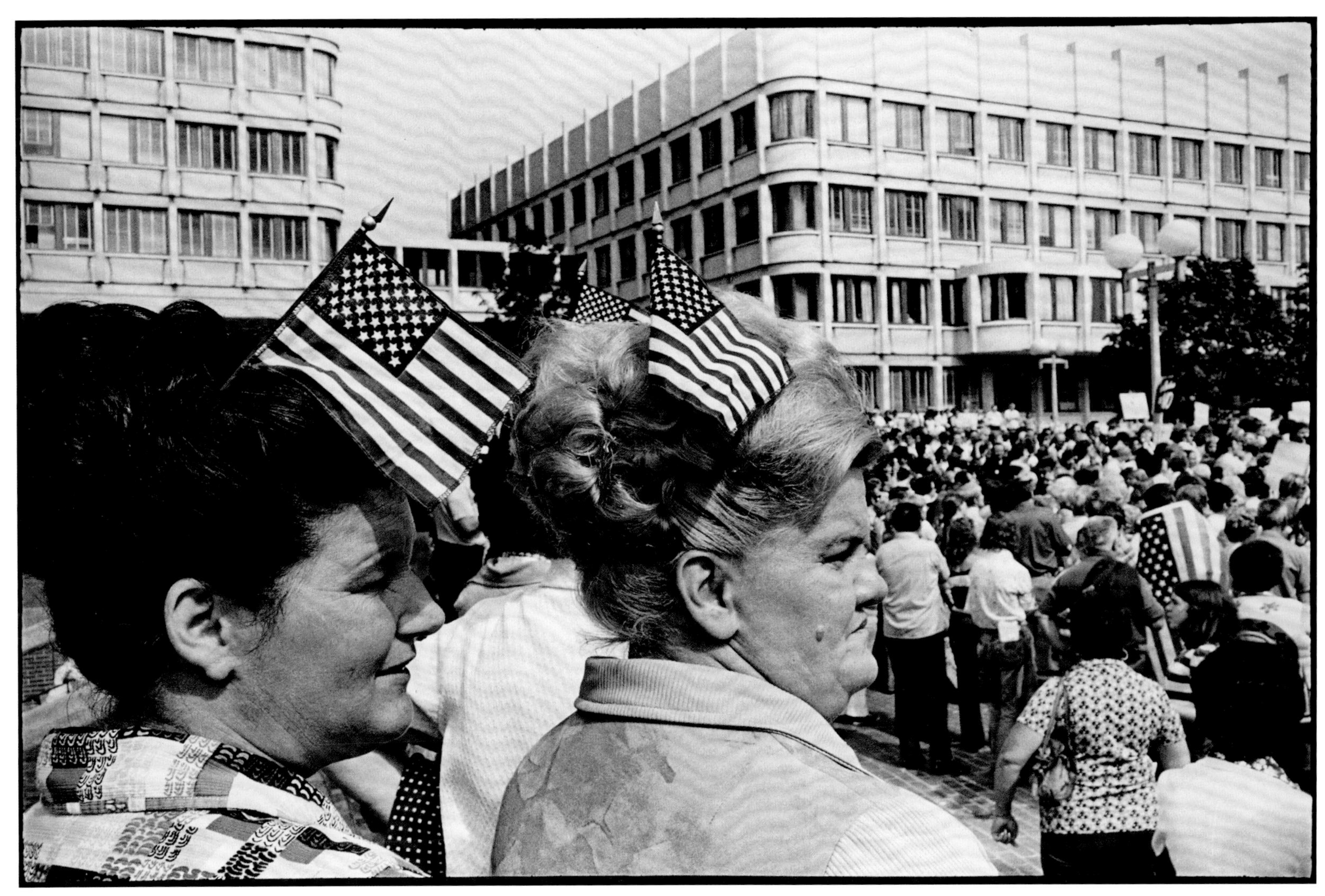

Busing demonstration at Federal Building, Government Center

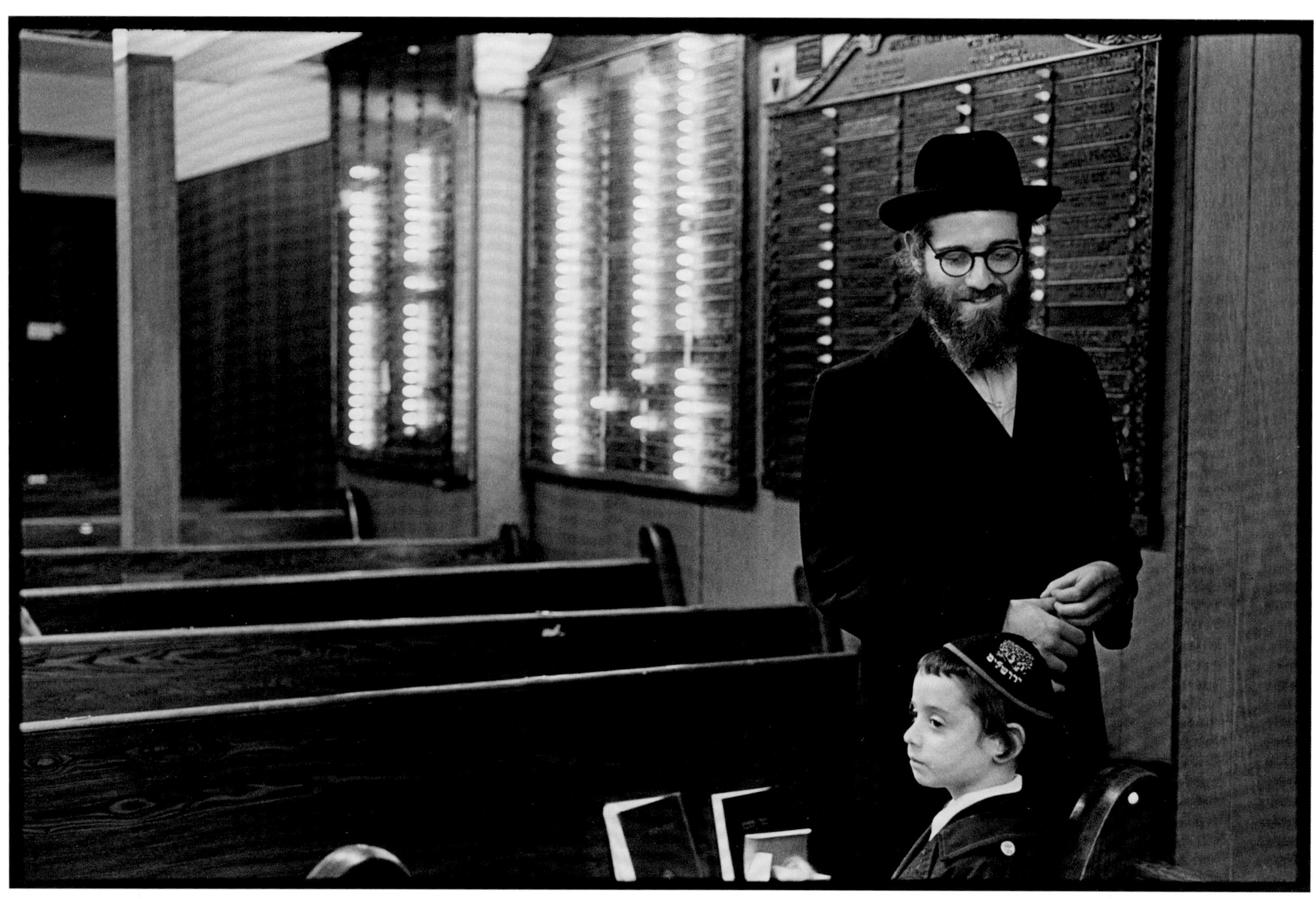

Father and son before service at
Boston Hasidic Center, Brookline

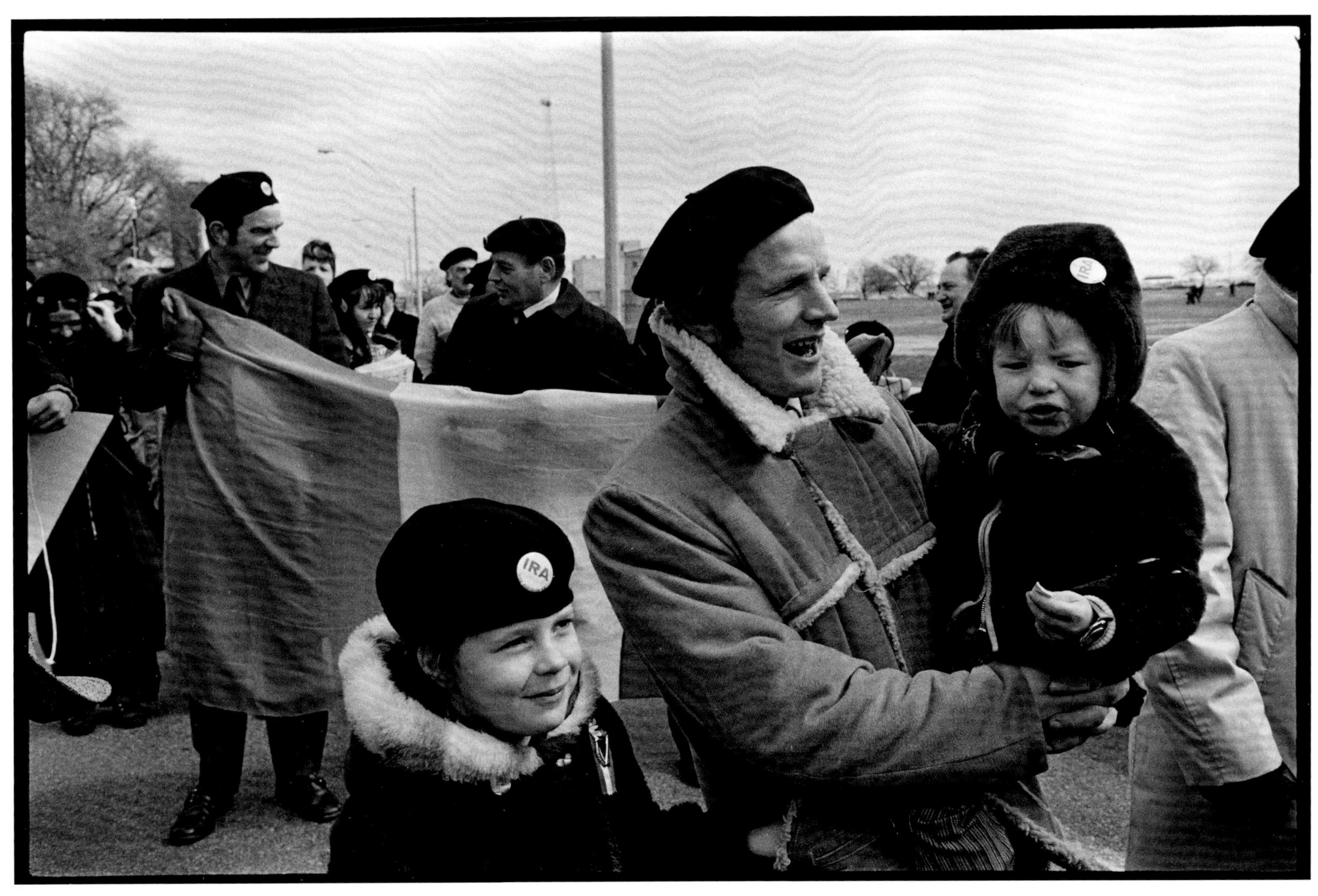

Marchers in St. Patrick's Day parade,
South Boston

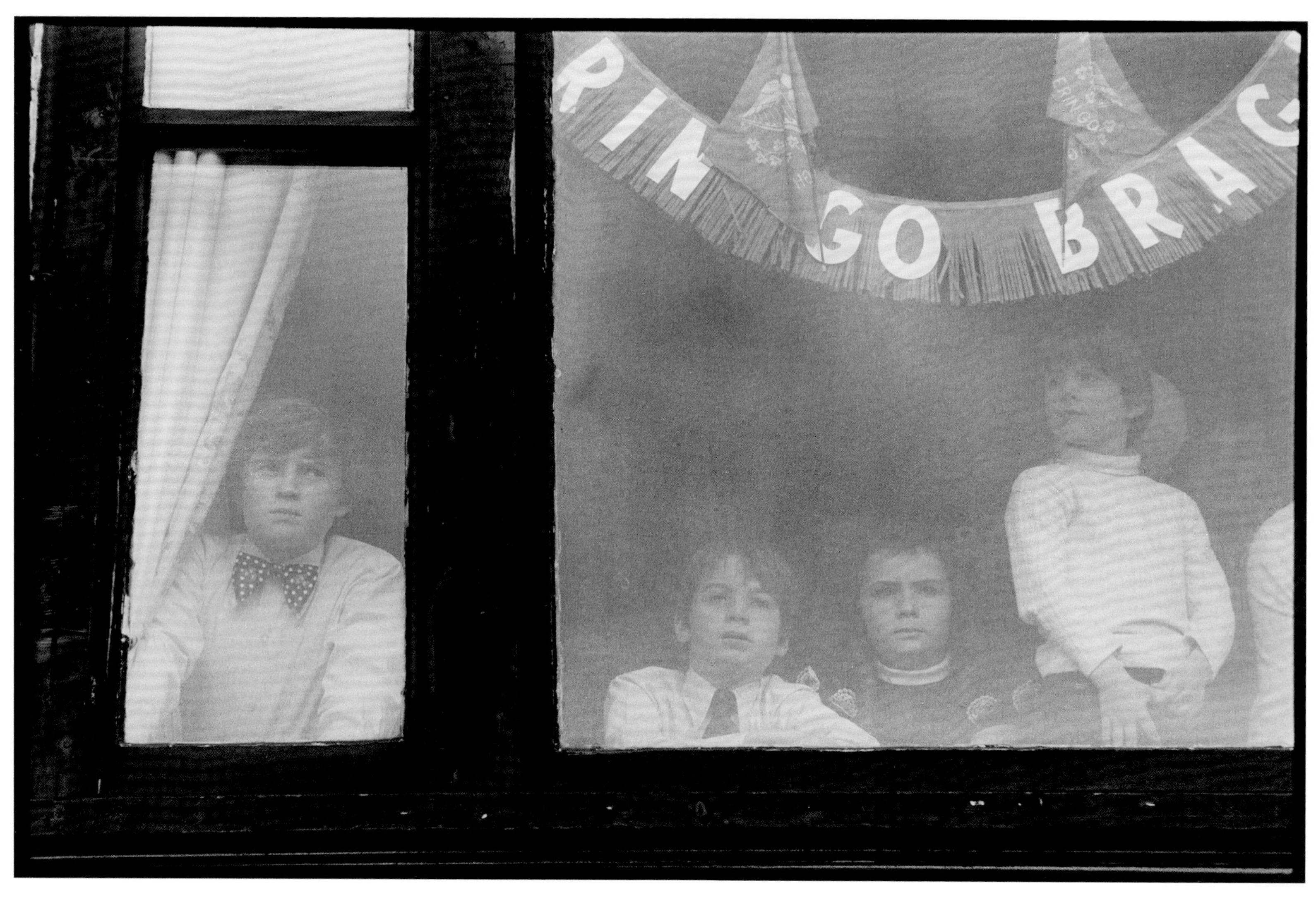

Spectators at St. Patrick's Day parade, South Boston

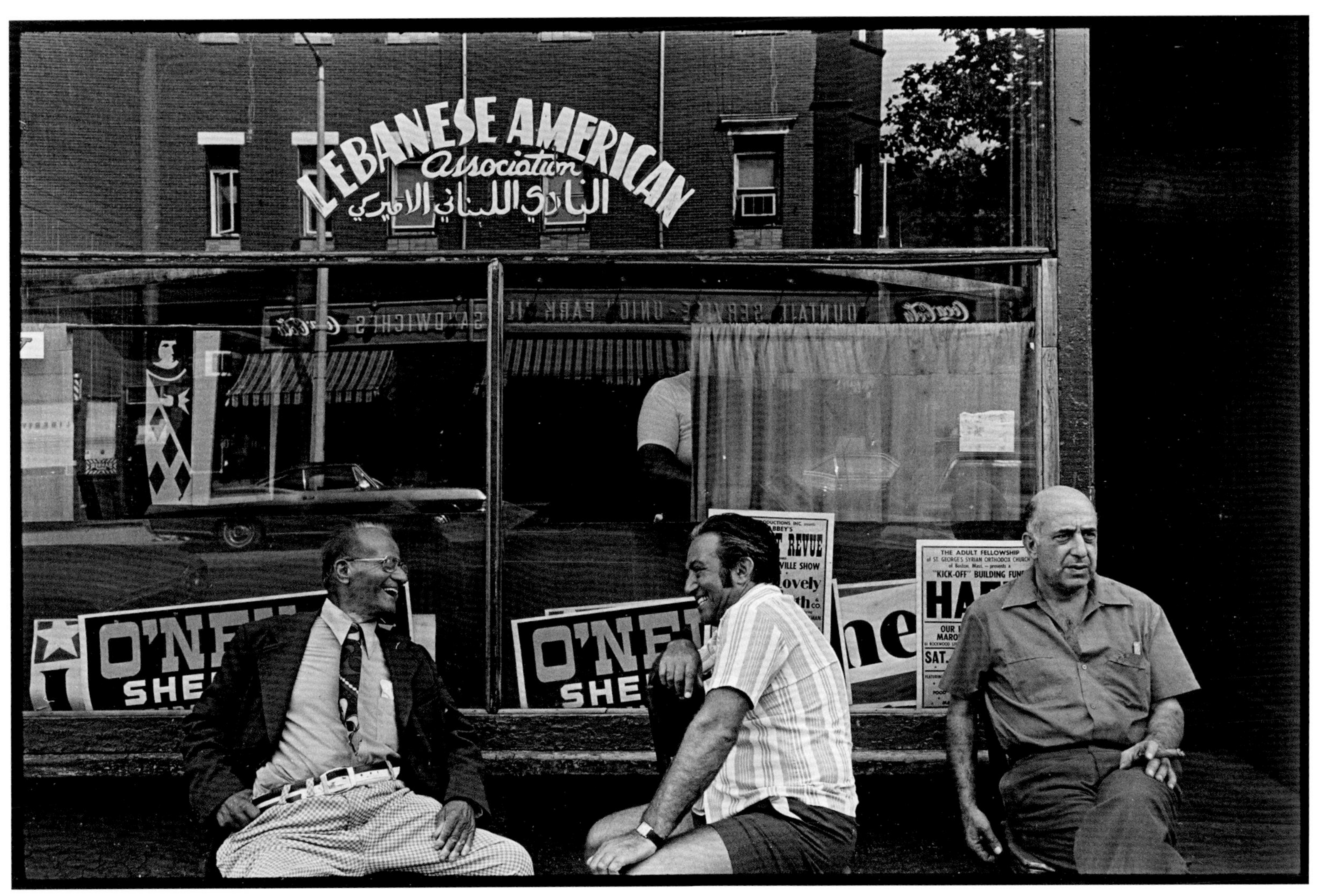

Summer day at Lebanese American Association, South End

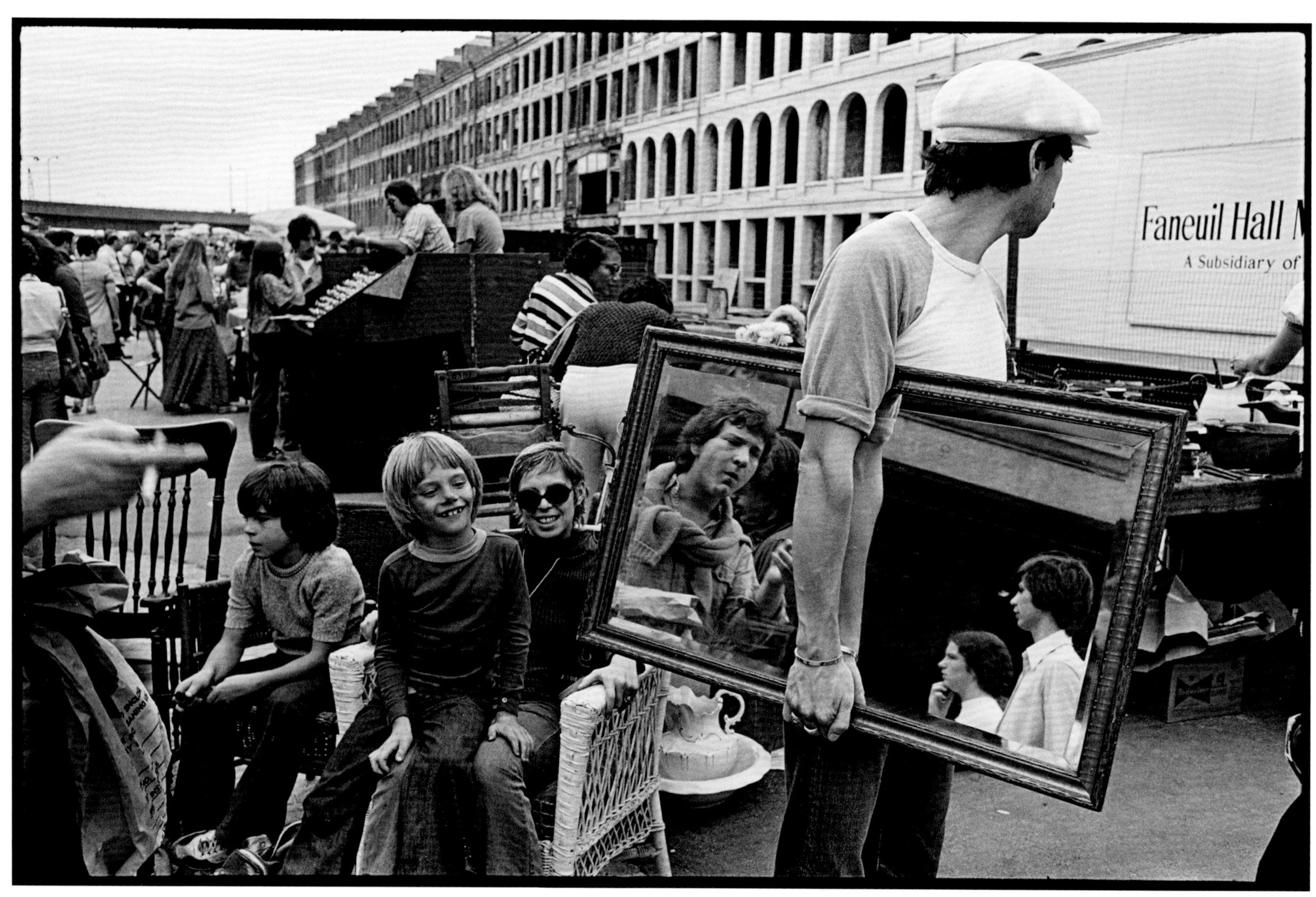

Sunday morning flea market,
Faneuil Hall

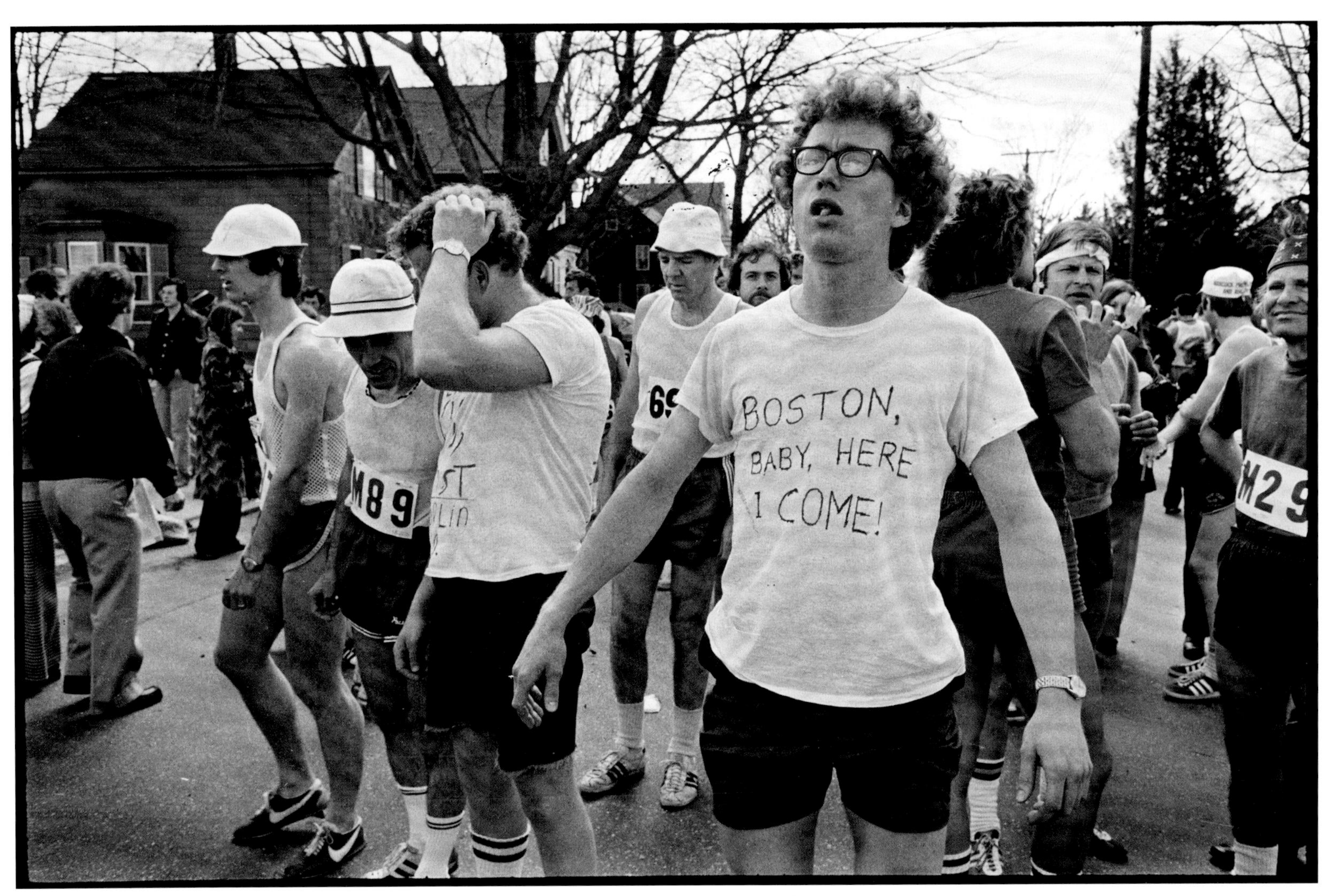

Beginning of Boston Marathon,
Hopkinton

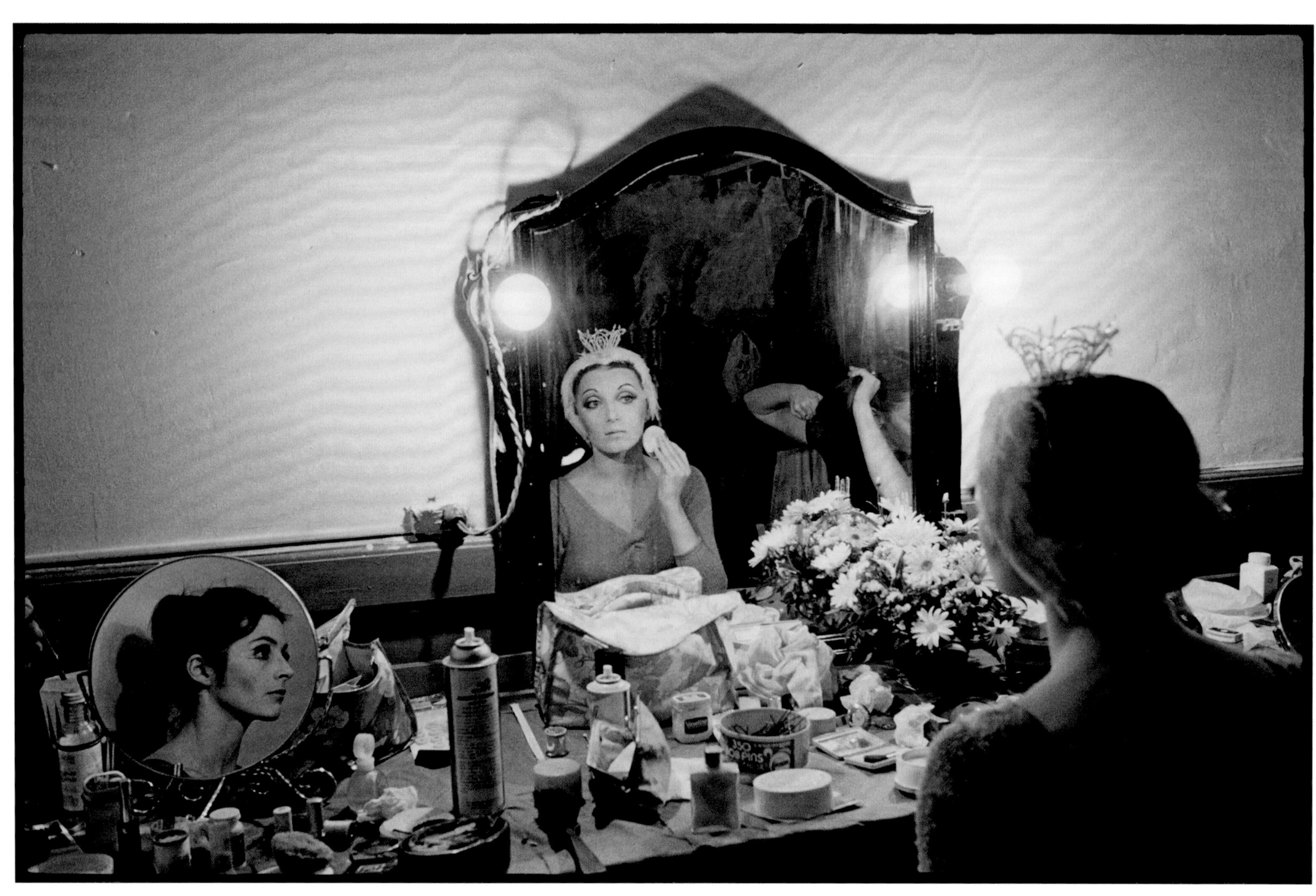

Backstage at Boston Ballet
performance, Music Hall

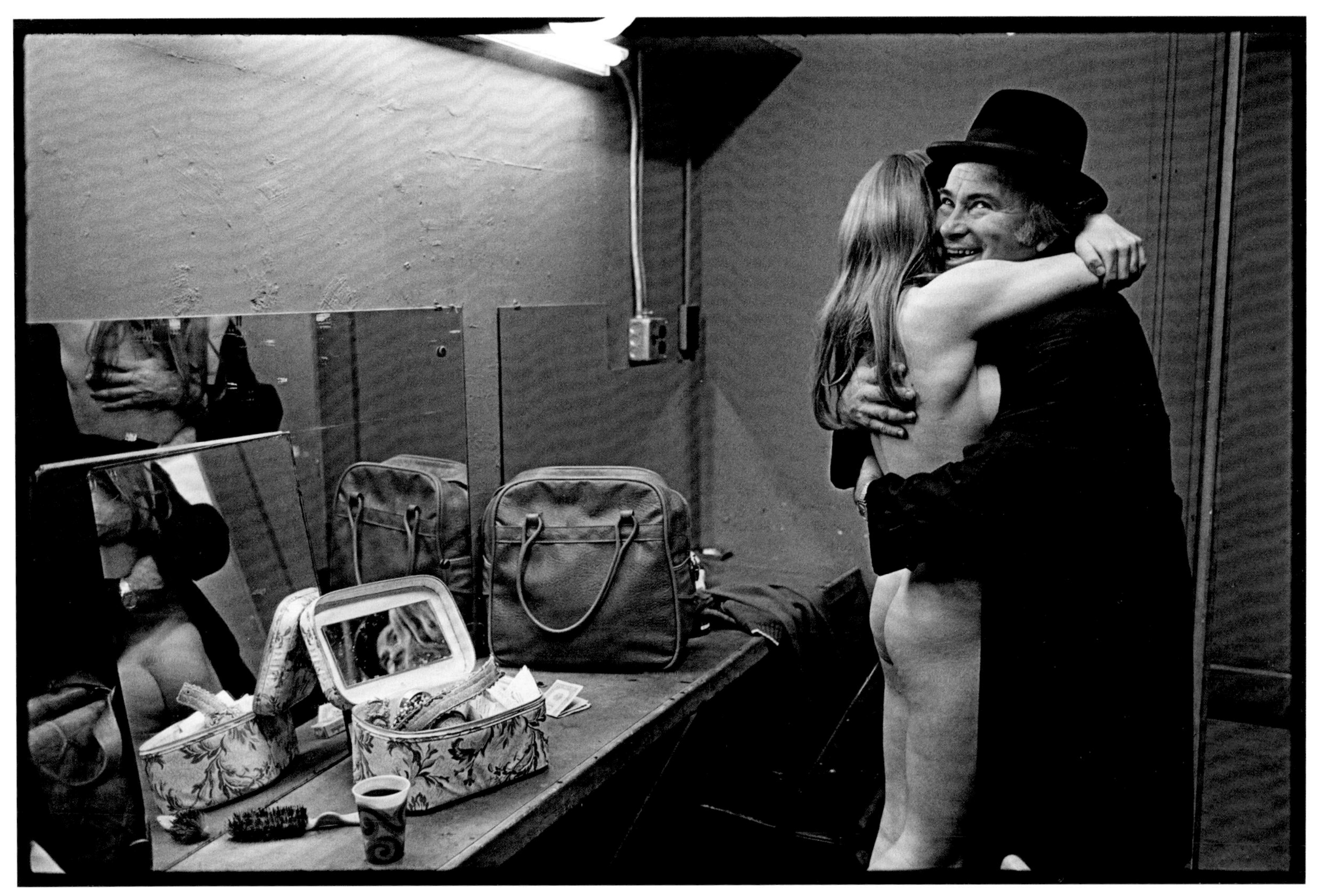

Comedian greeting stripper backstage, Pilgrim Theatre

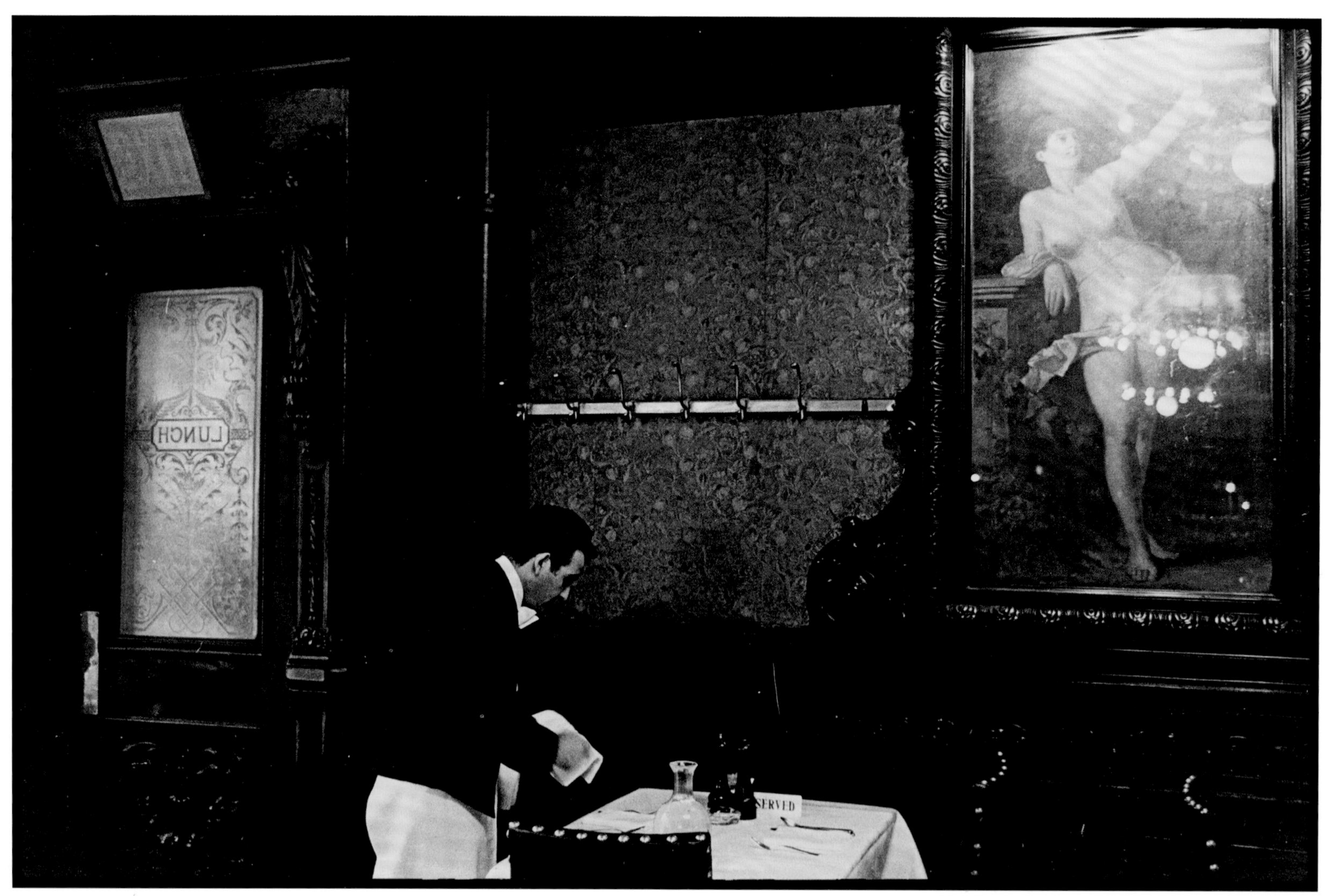

Waiter setting table,
Locke-Ober restaurant

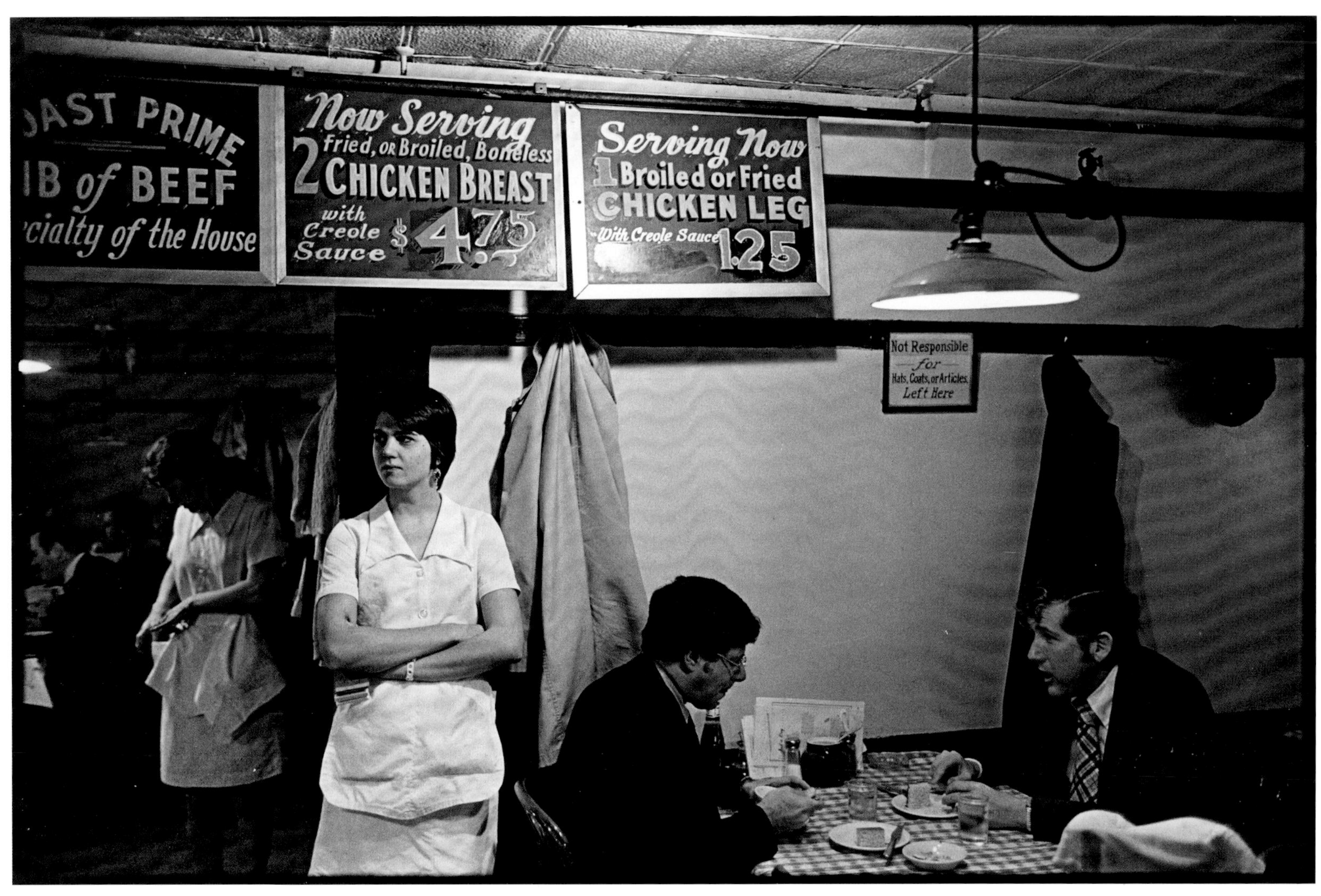

Waitress and diners at lunchtime,
Durgin Park Restaurant

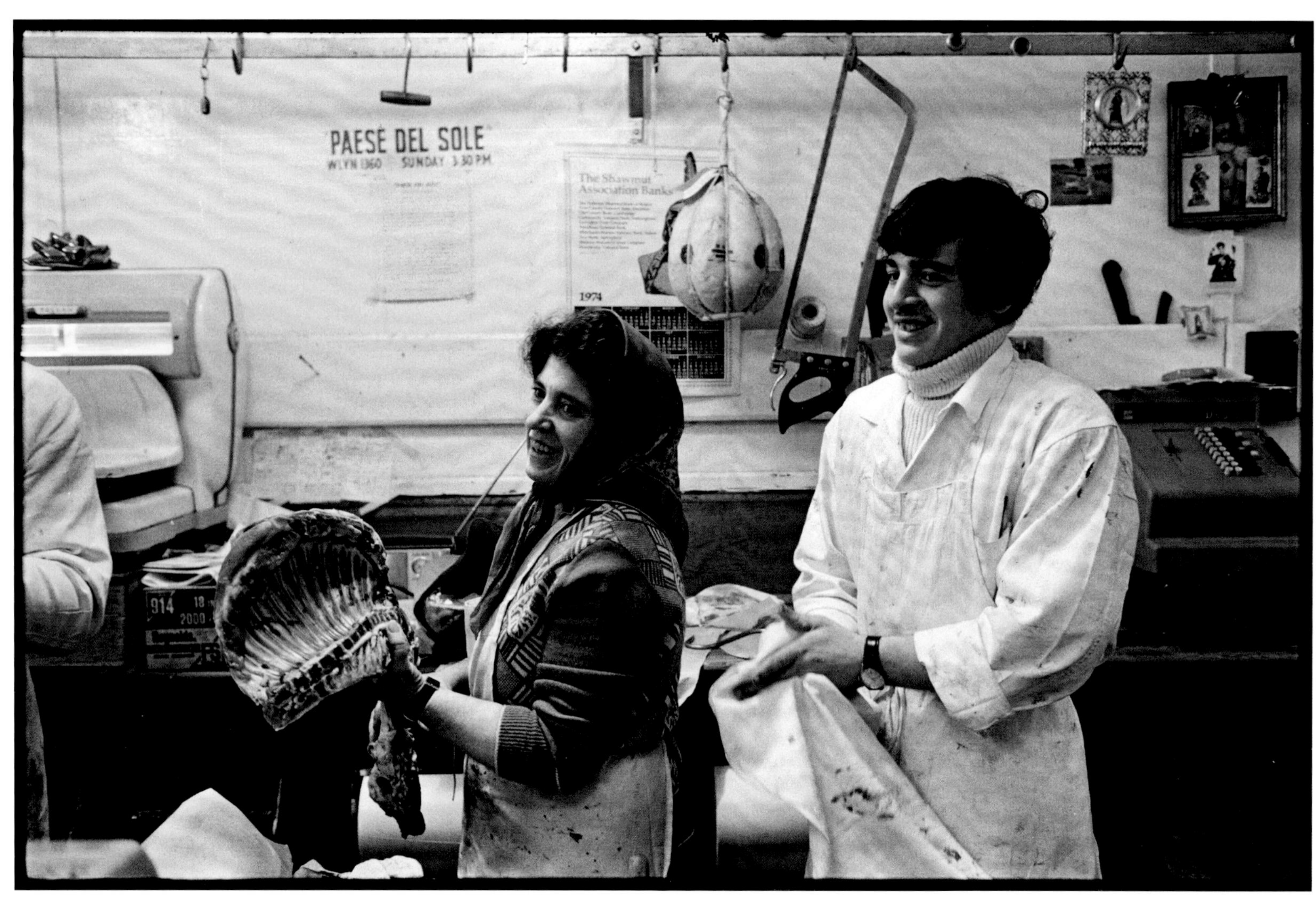

Italian butcher shop at Easter,
North End

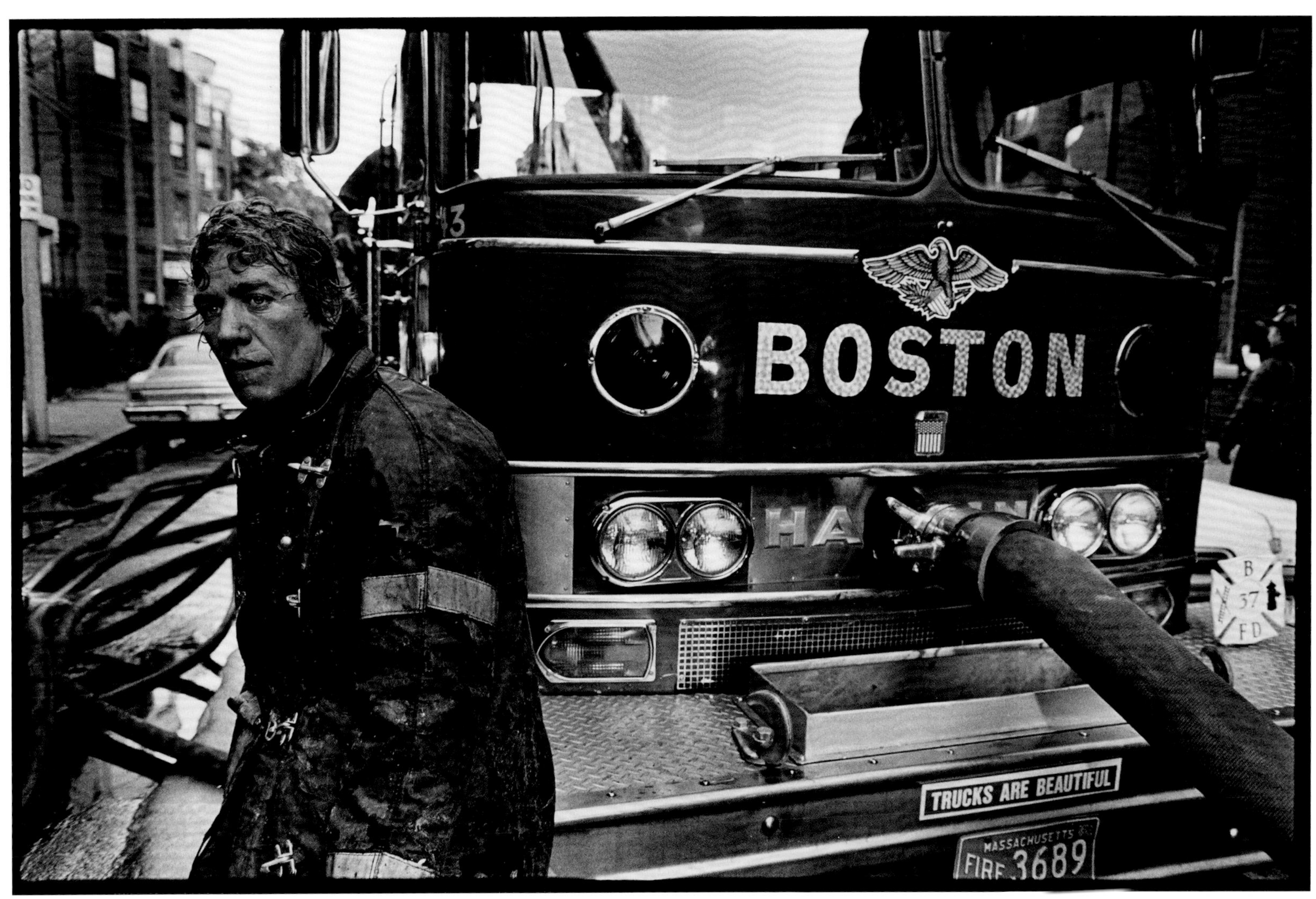

Fireman resting after blaze,
Symphony Road

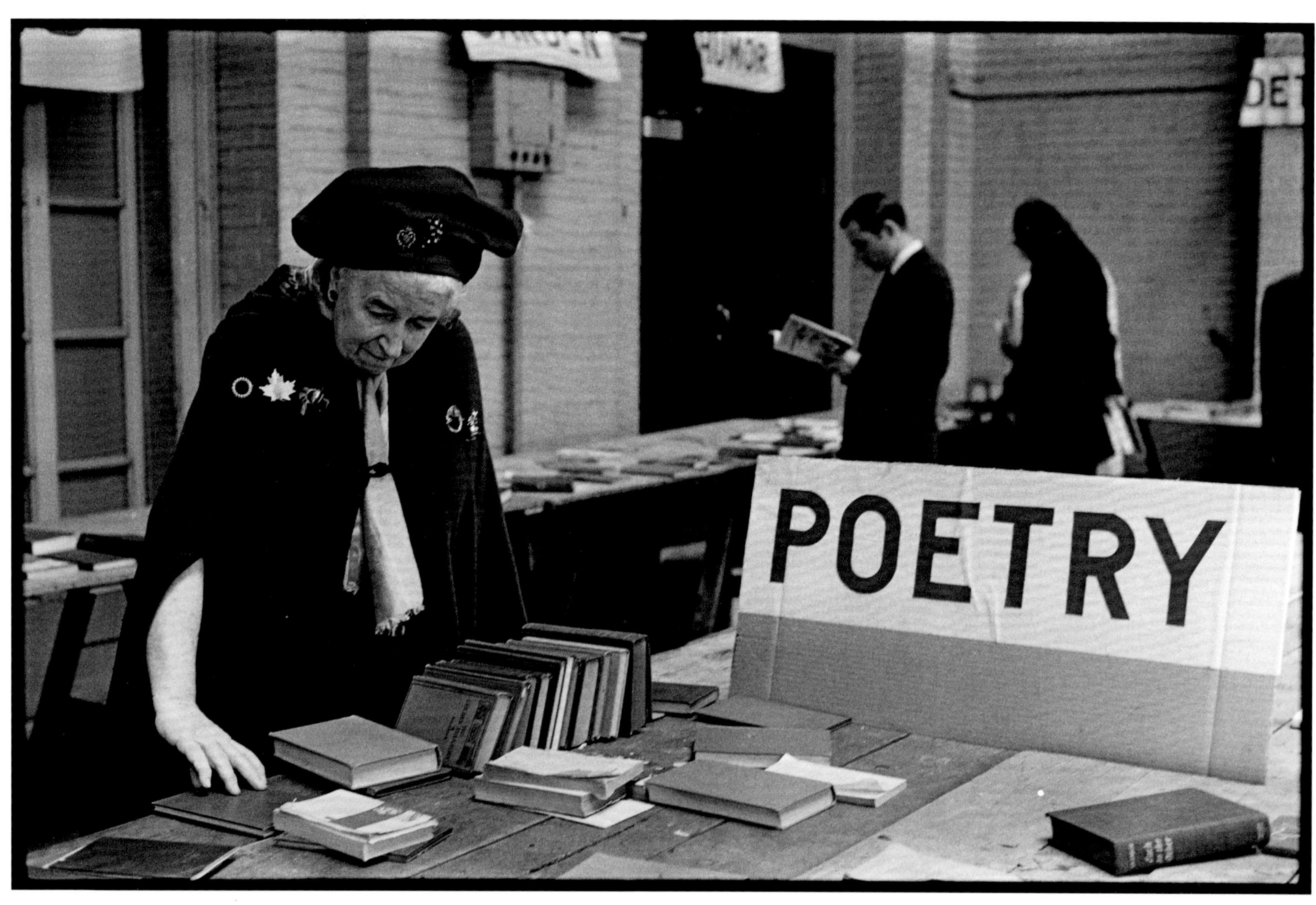

Lady at annual book sale,
Massachusetts Horticultural Society

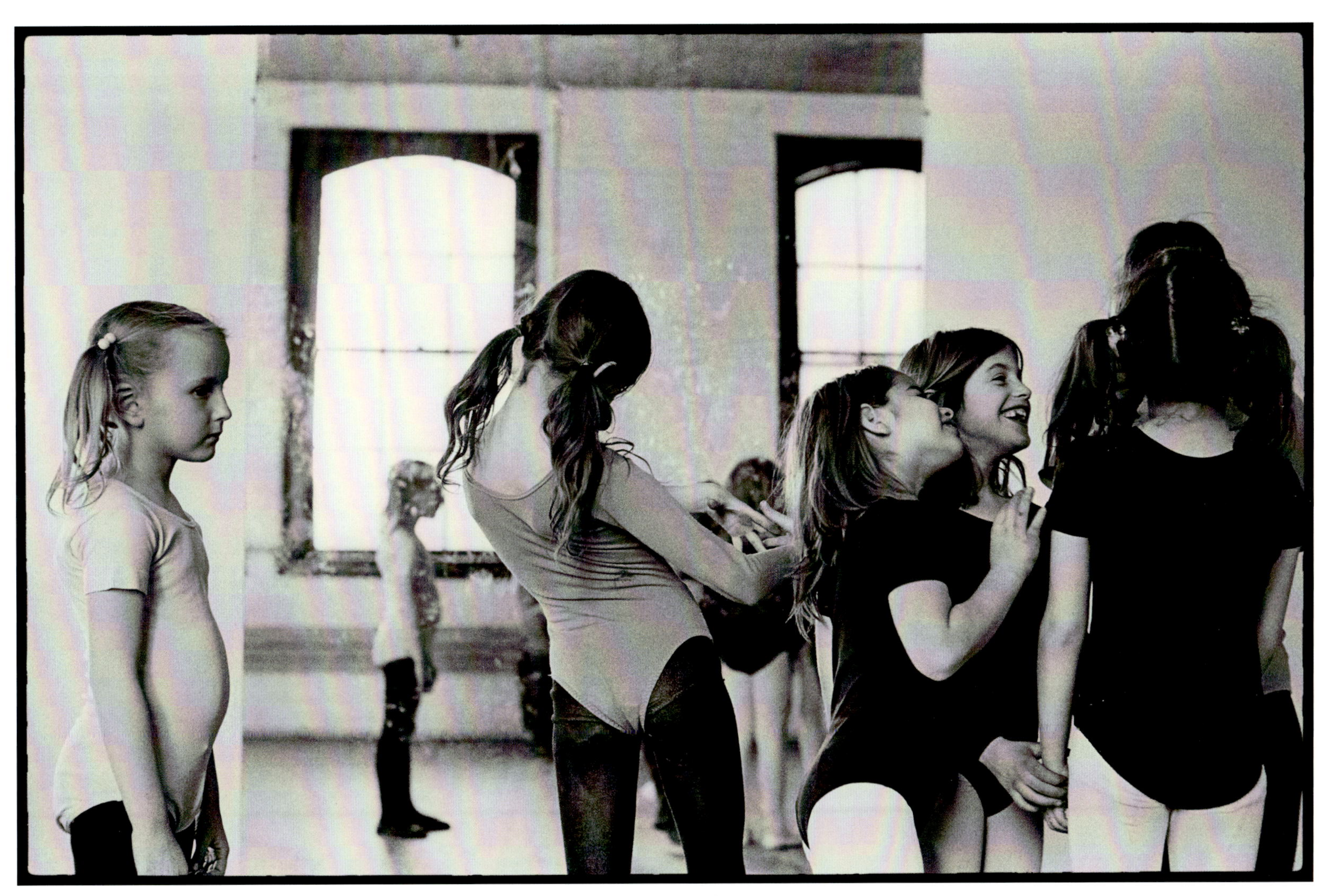

Boston ballet dance class,
Boston Center for the Arts

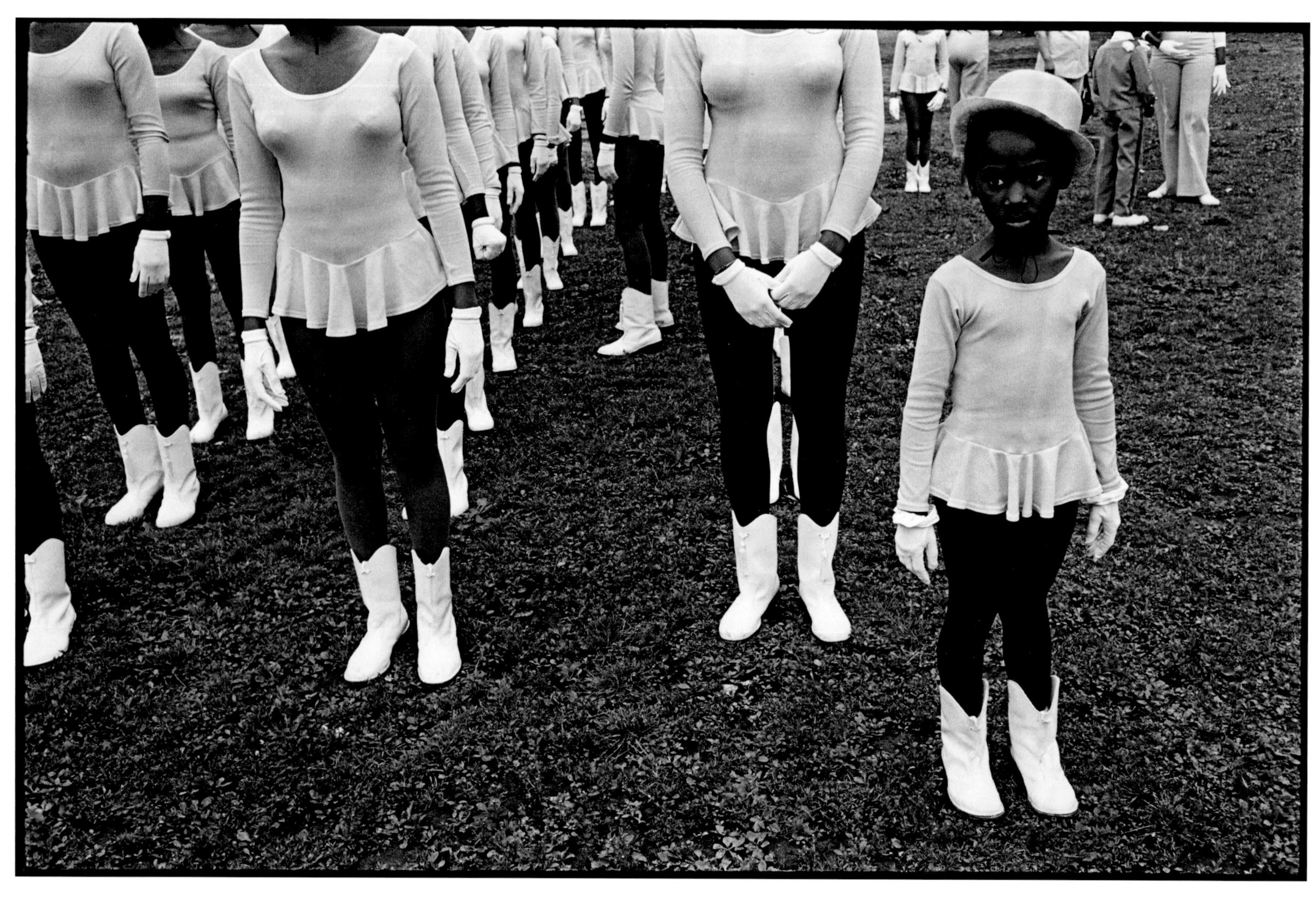

Lining up for Shriners' Parade,
South End

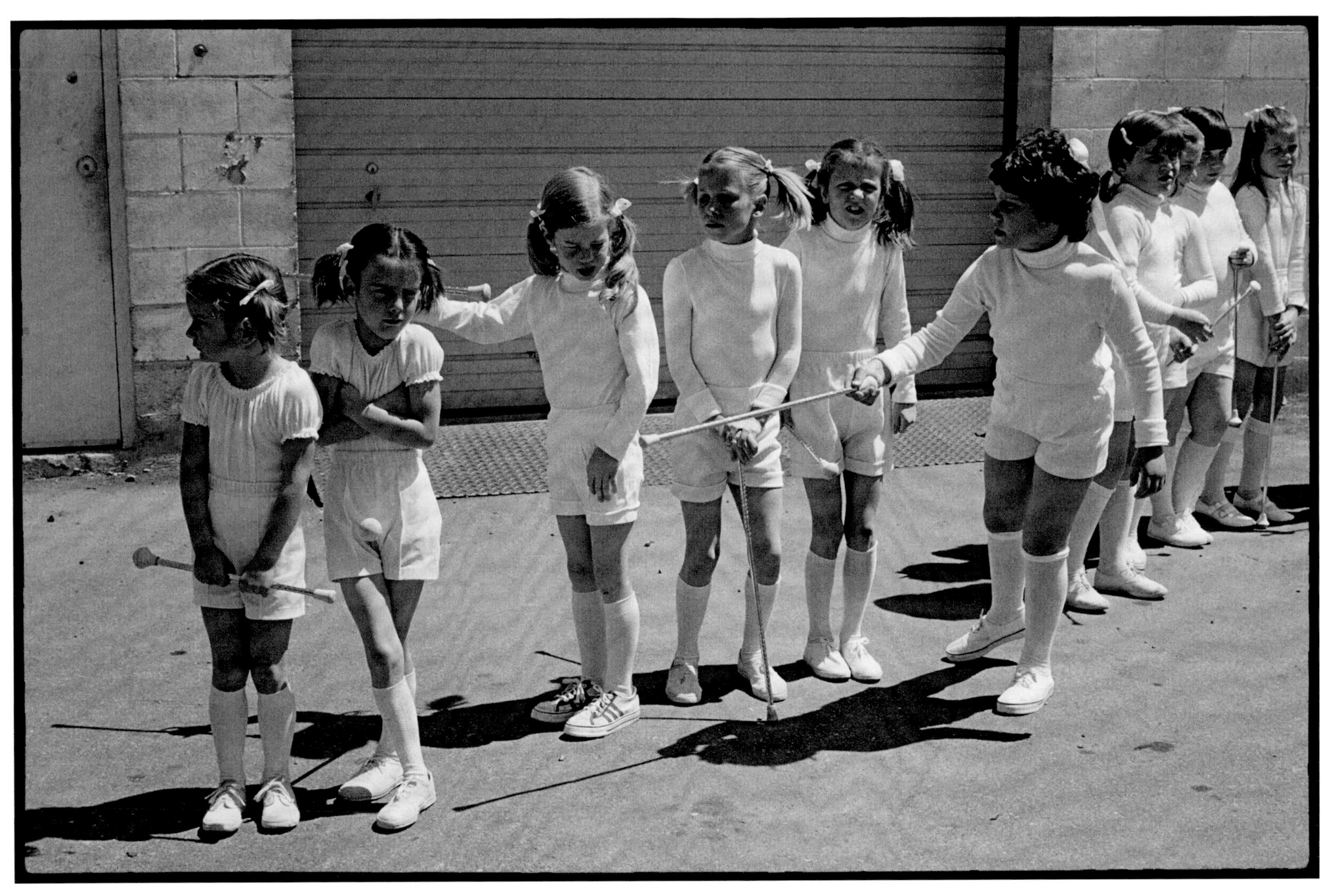

Boston Parks & Recreation girls
gym class, Brighton

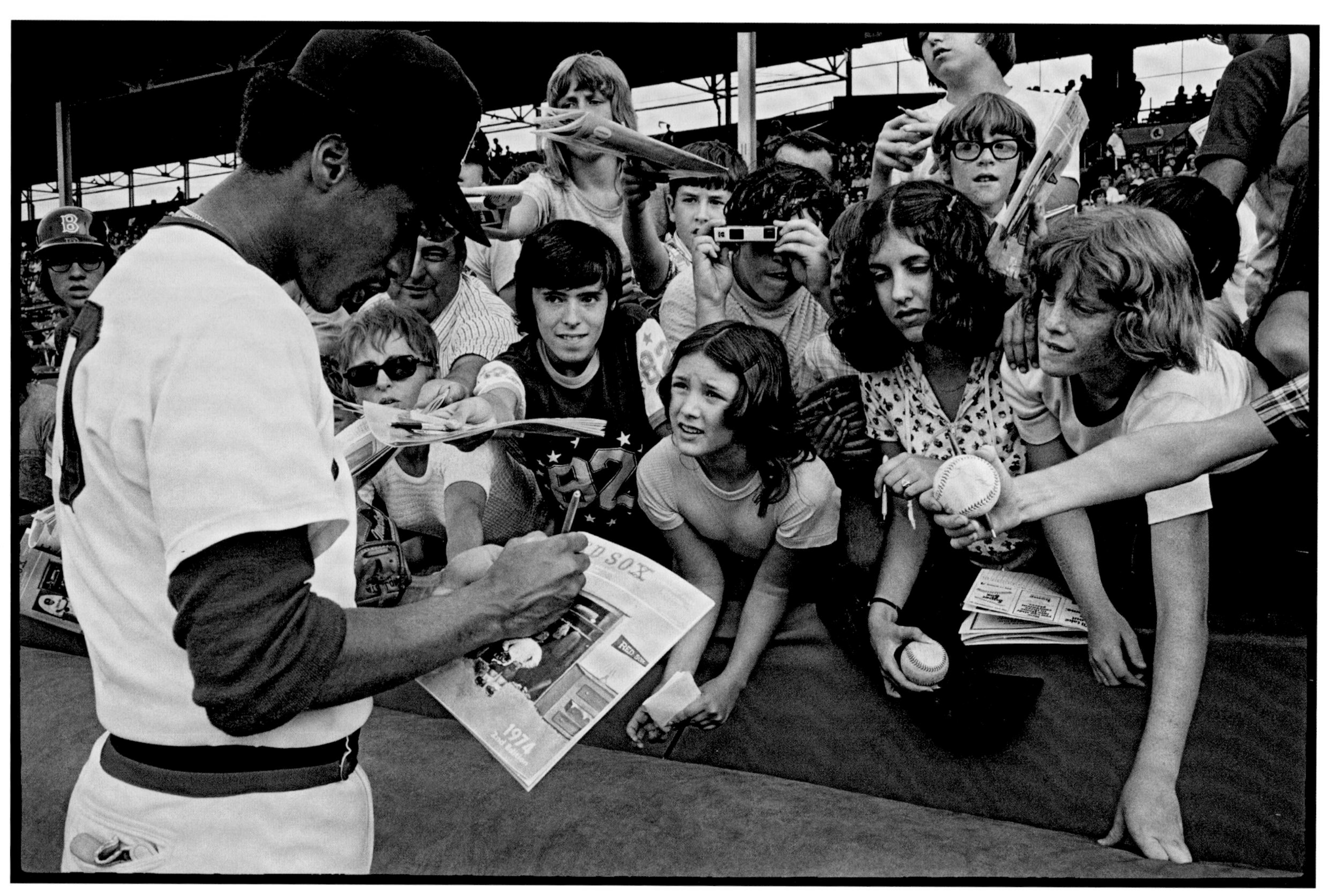

Autograph seekers at Red Sox game,
Fenway Park

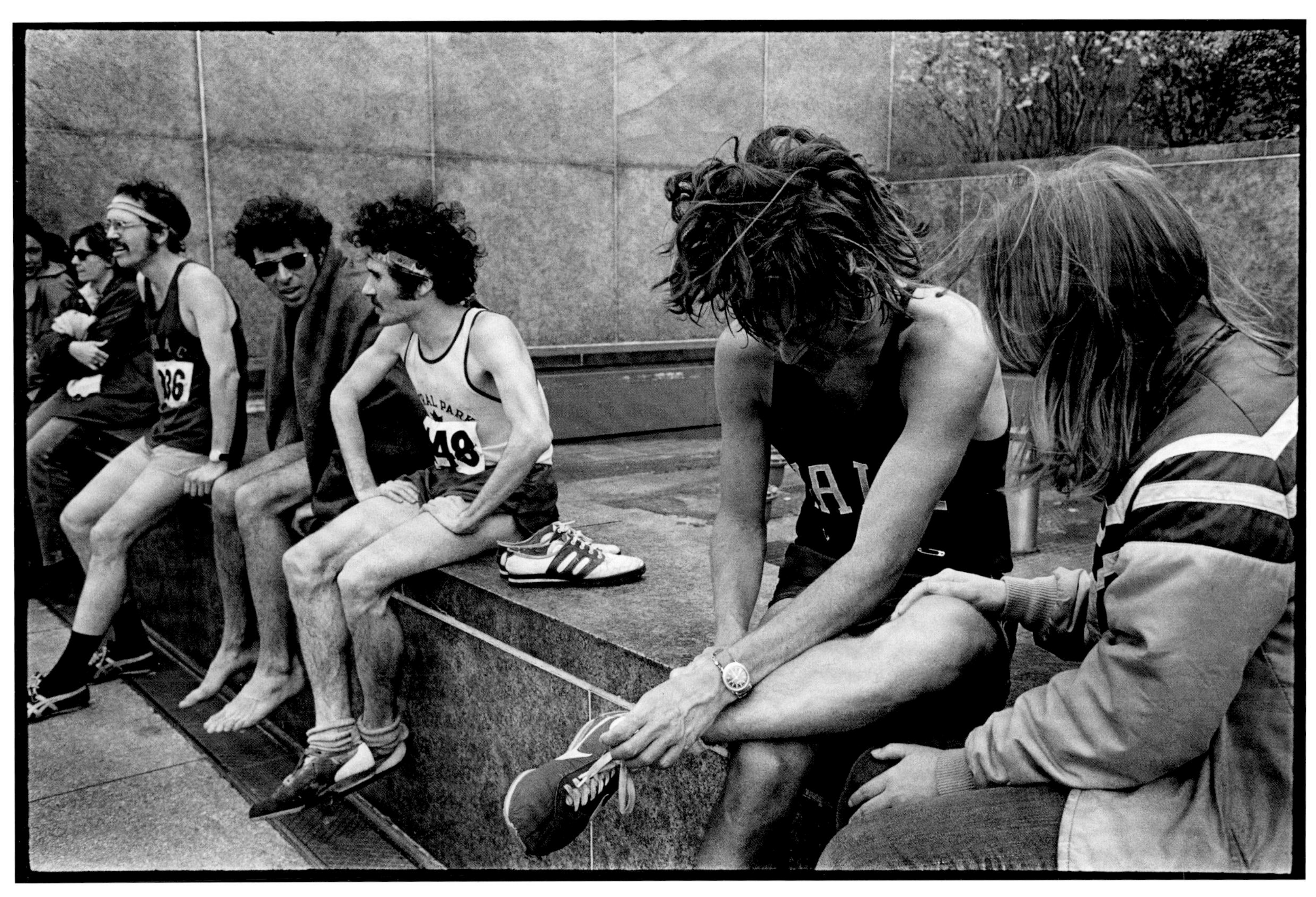

At the finish line of the Boston Marathon, Prudential Center

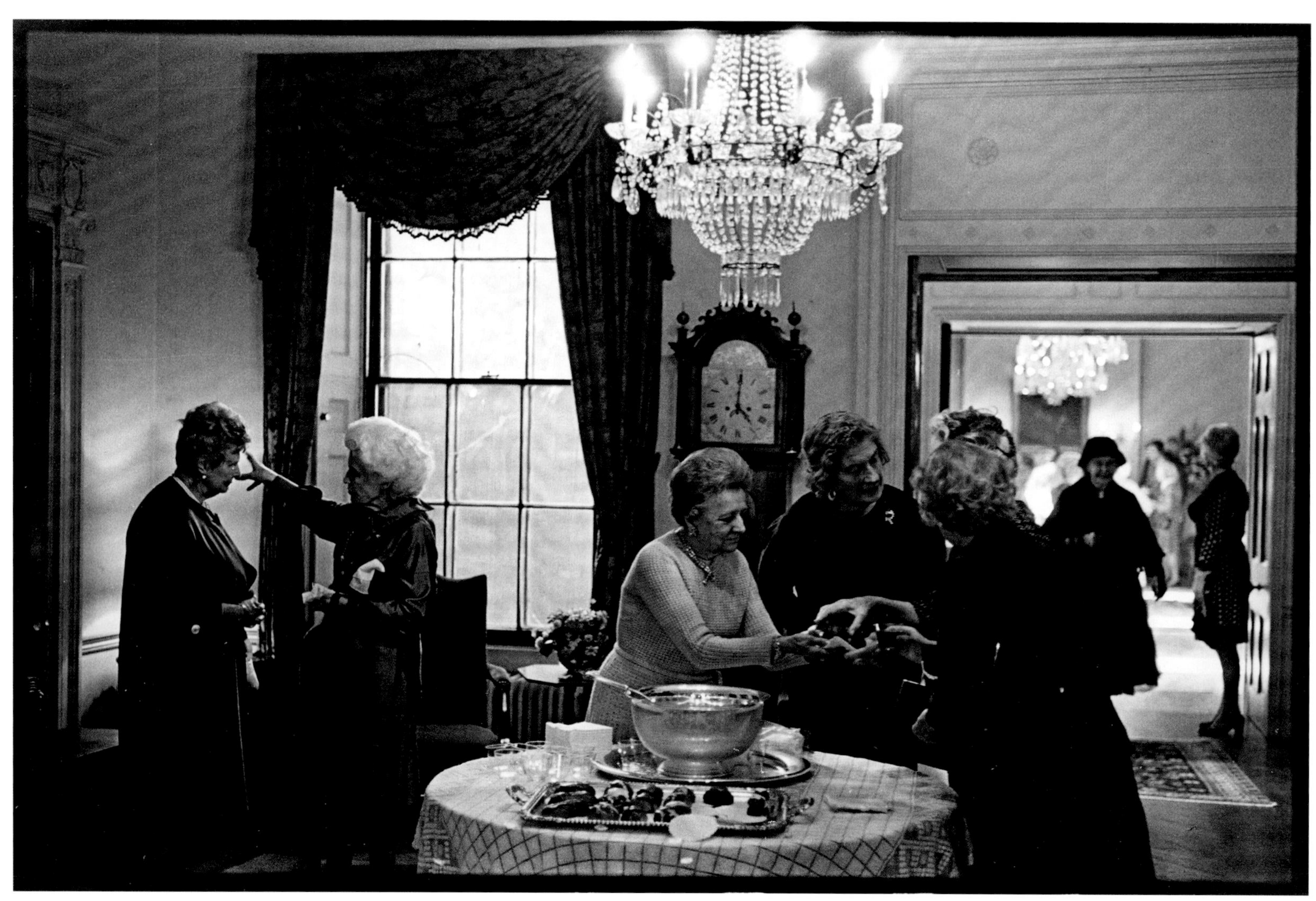

Tea at the Women's City Club,
Beacon Hill

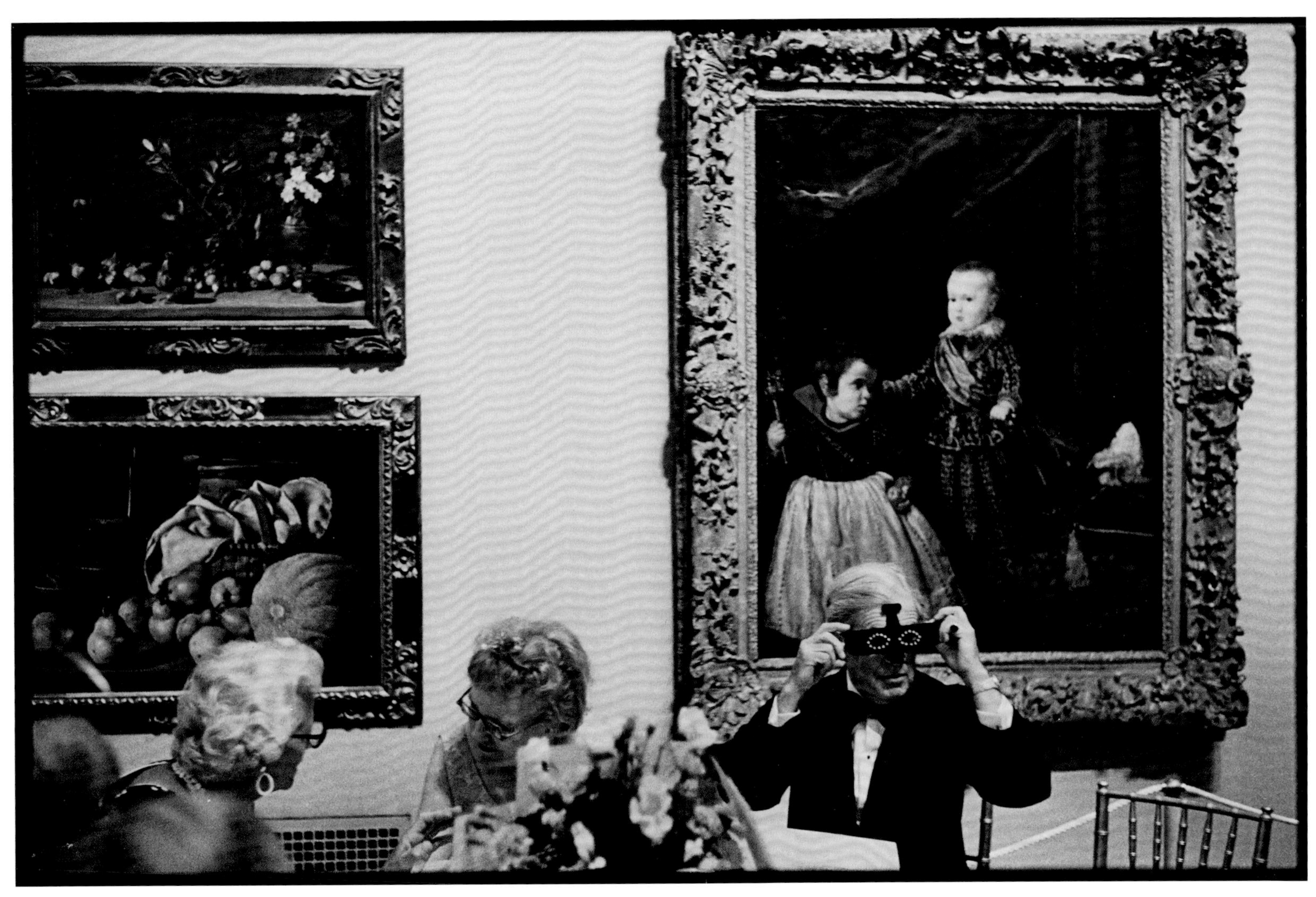

Fête Galante fundraising evening,
Museum of Fine Arts

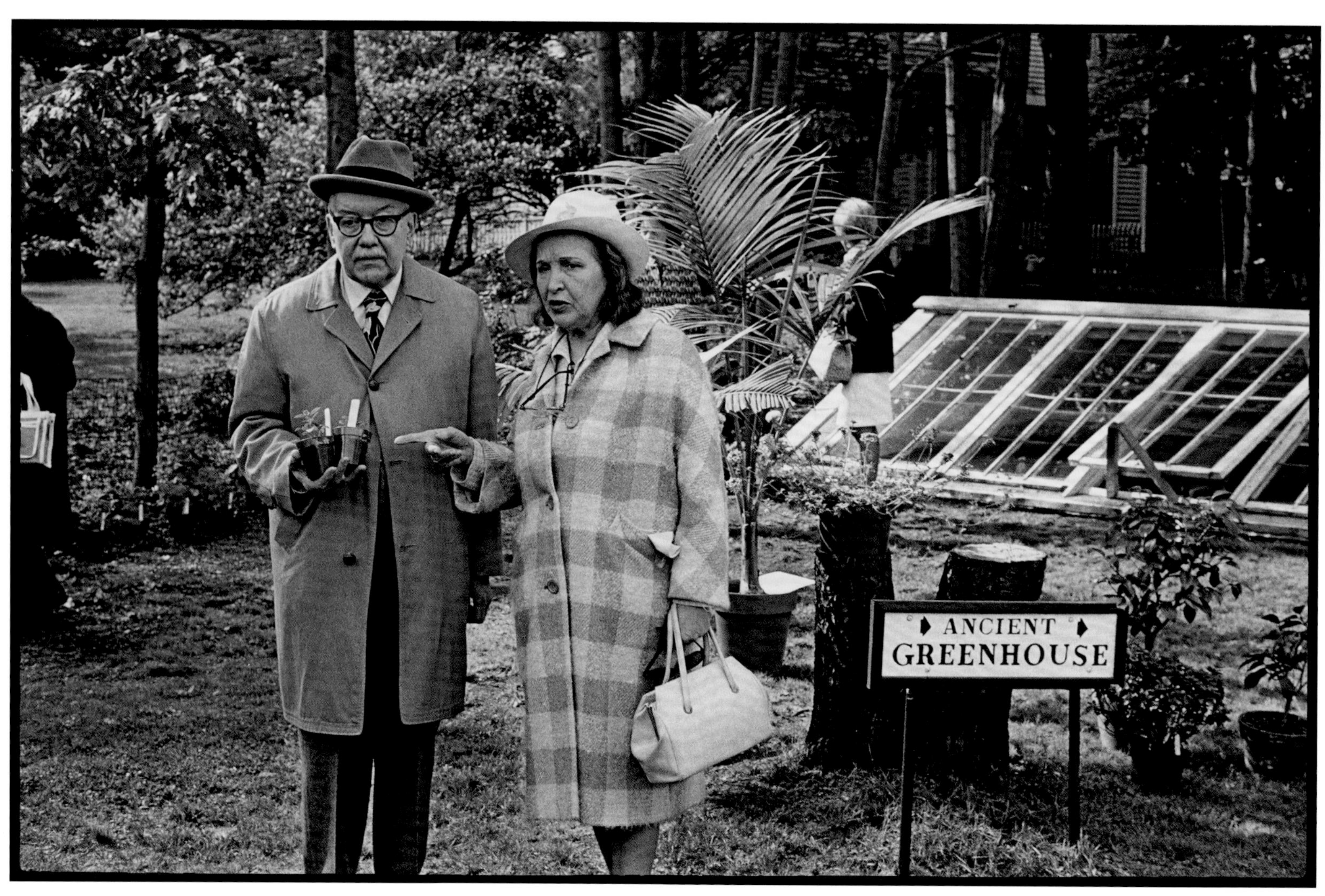

Plant sale of Massachusetts
Horticultural Society, Waltham

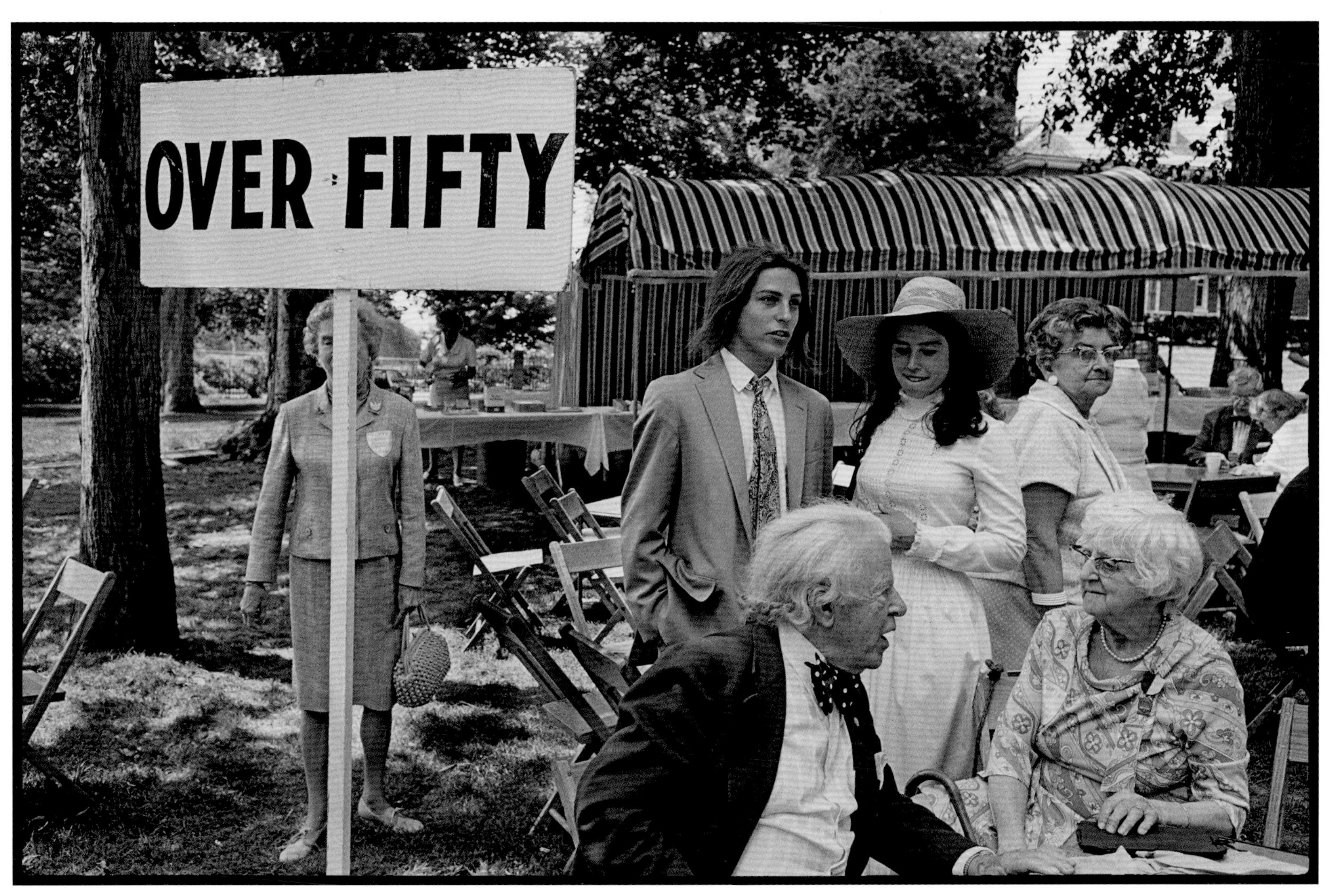

Reunion at Tufts University, Medford

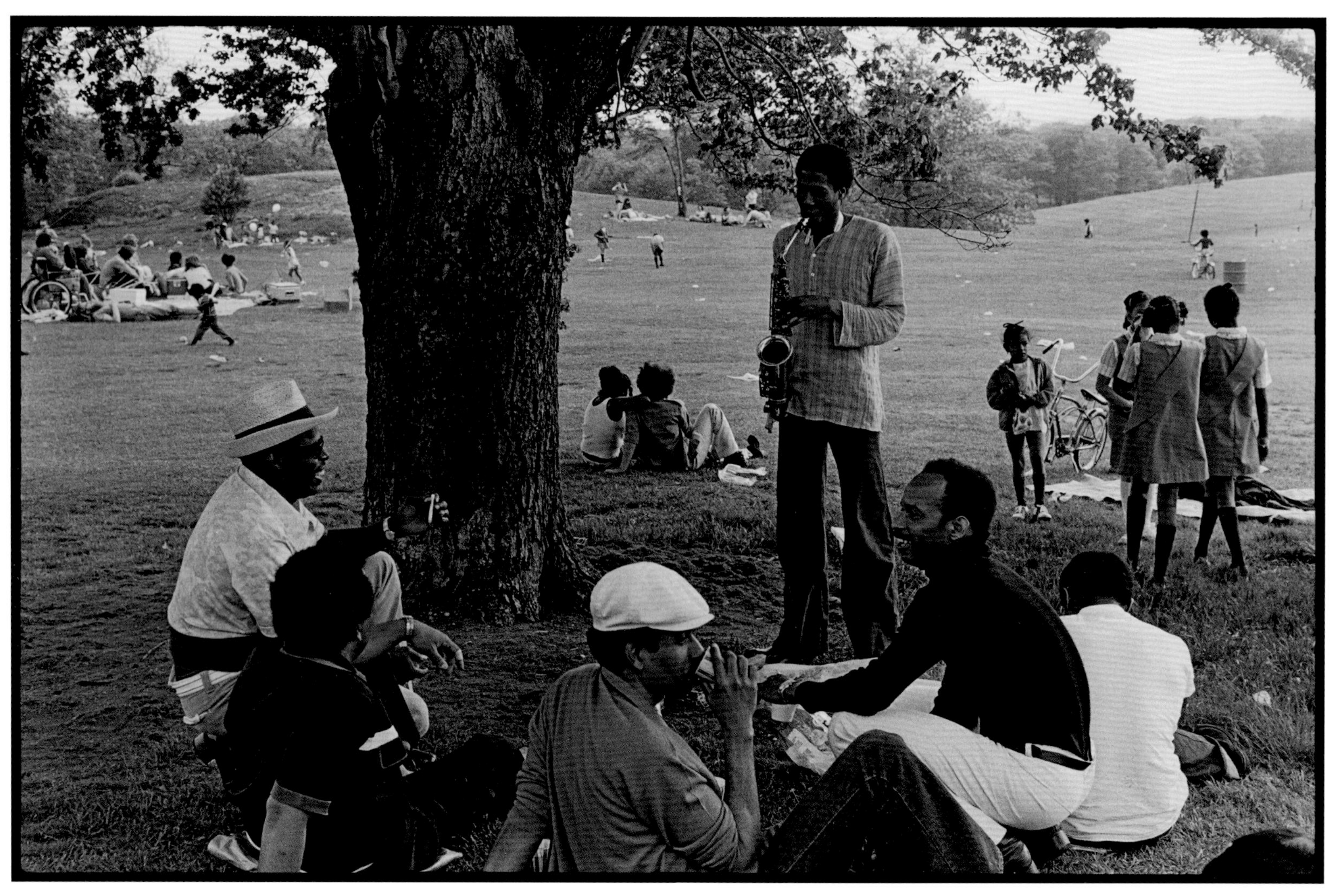

Sunday afternoon gathering of friends, Franklin Park

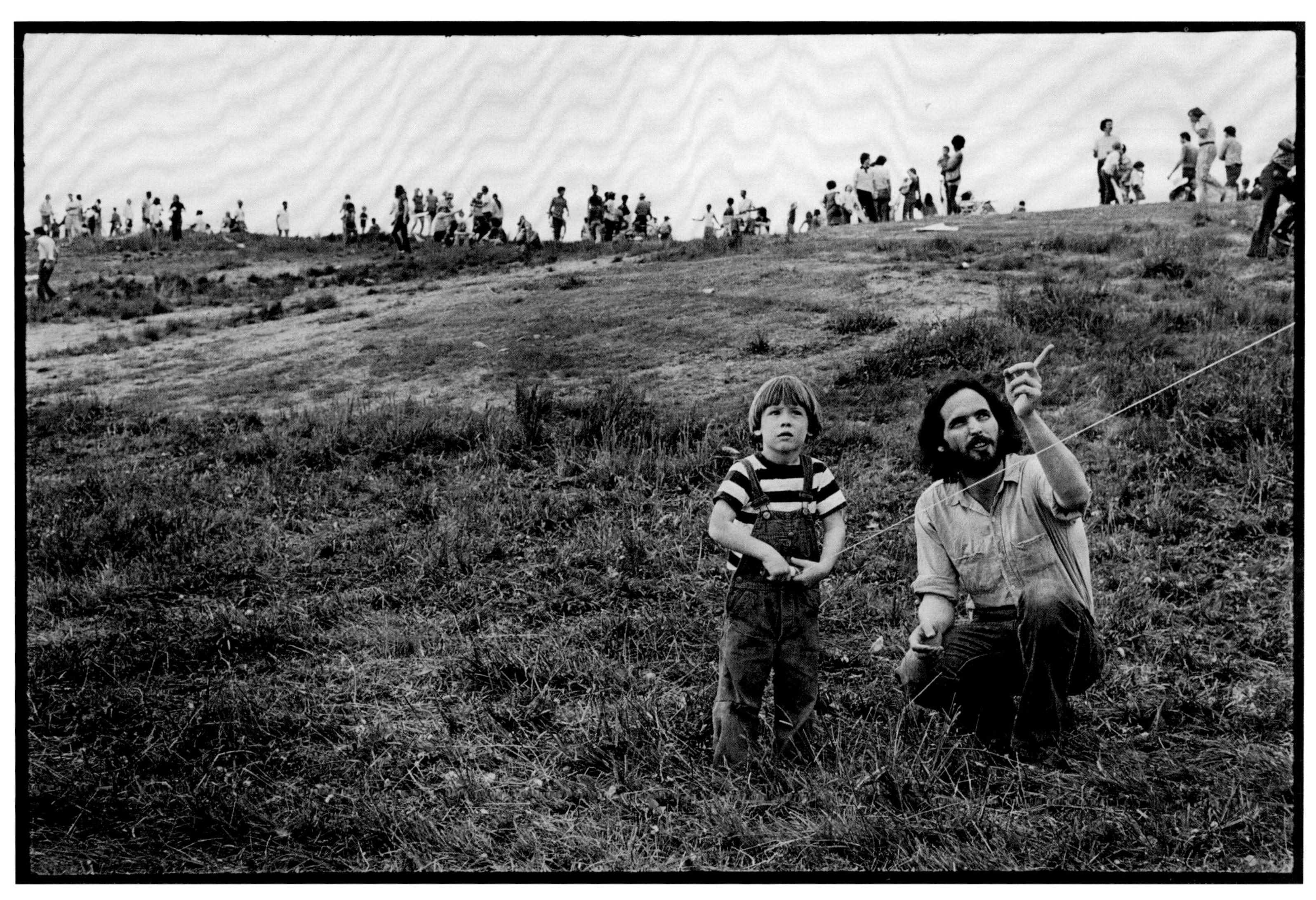

Father and son at Kite Day,
Franklin Park

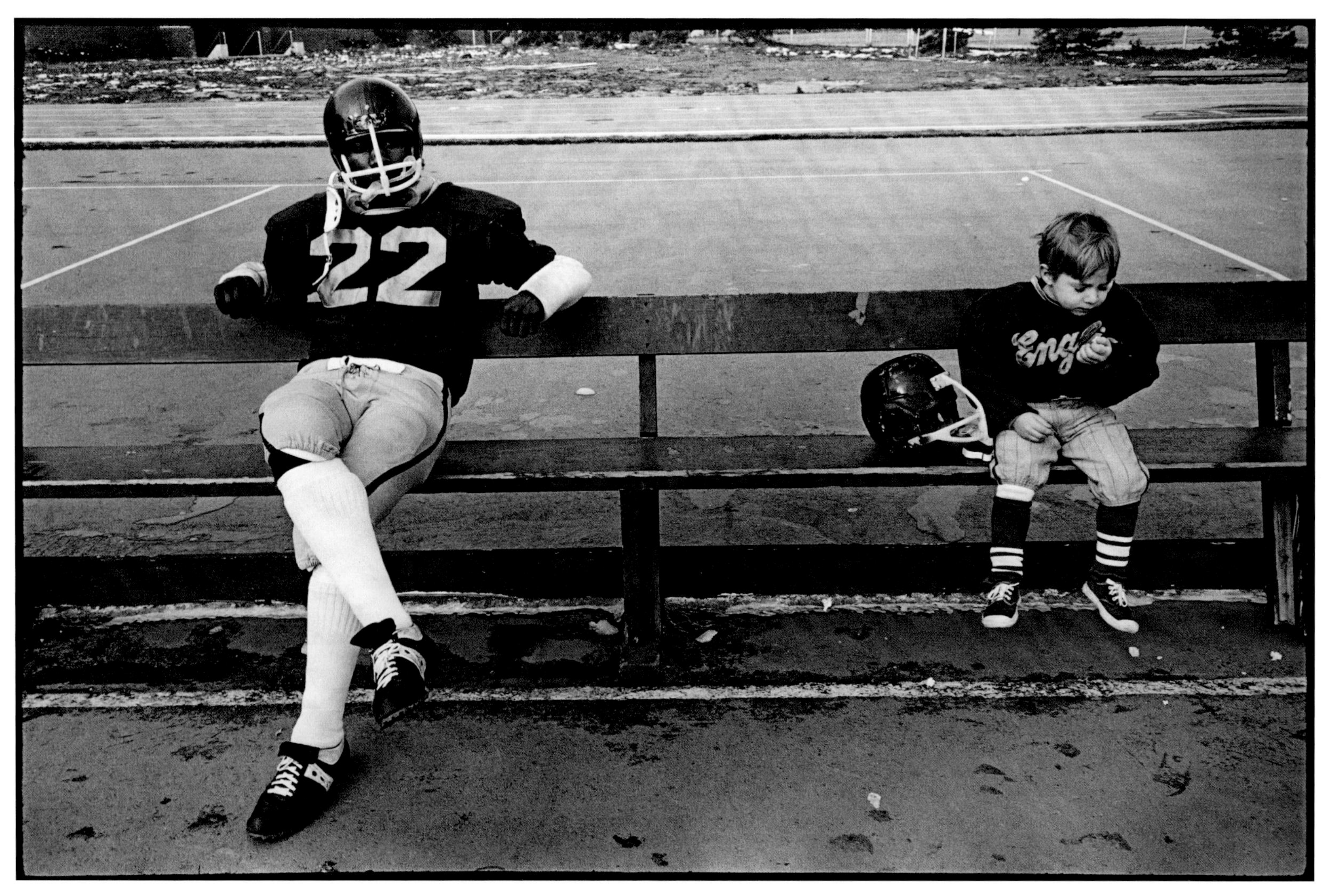

Team mascot and player,
English High School

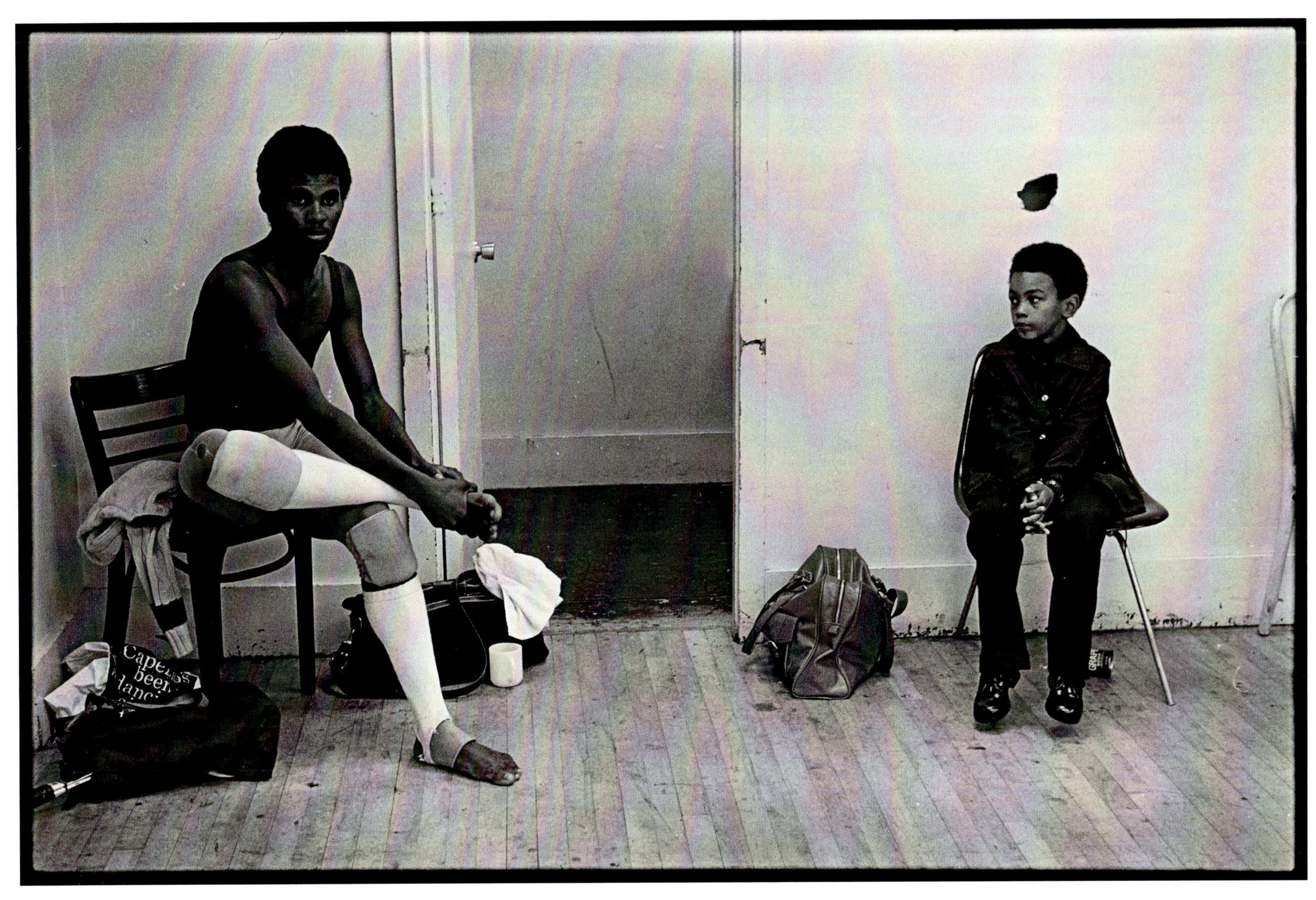

Dancer and admirer at rehearsal,
Elma Lewis School

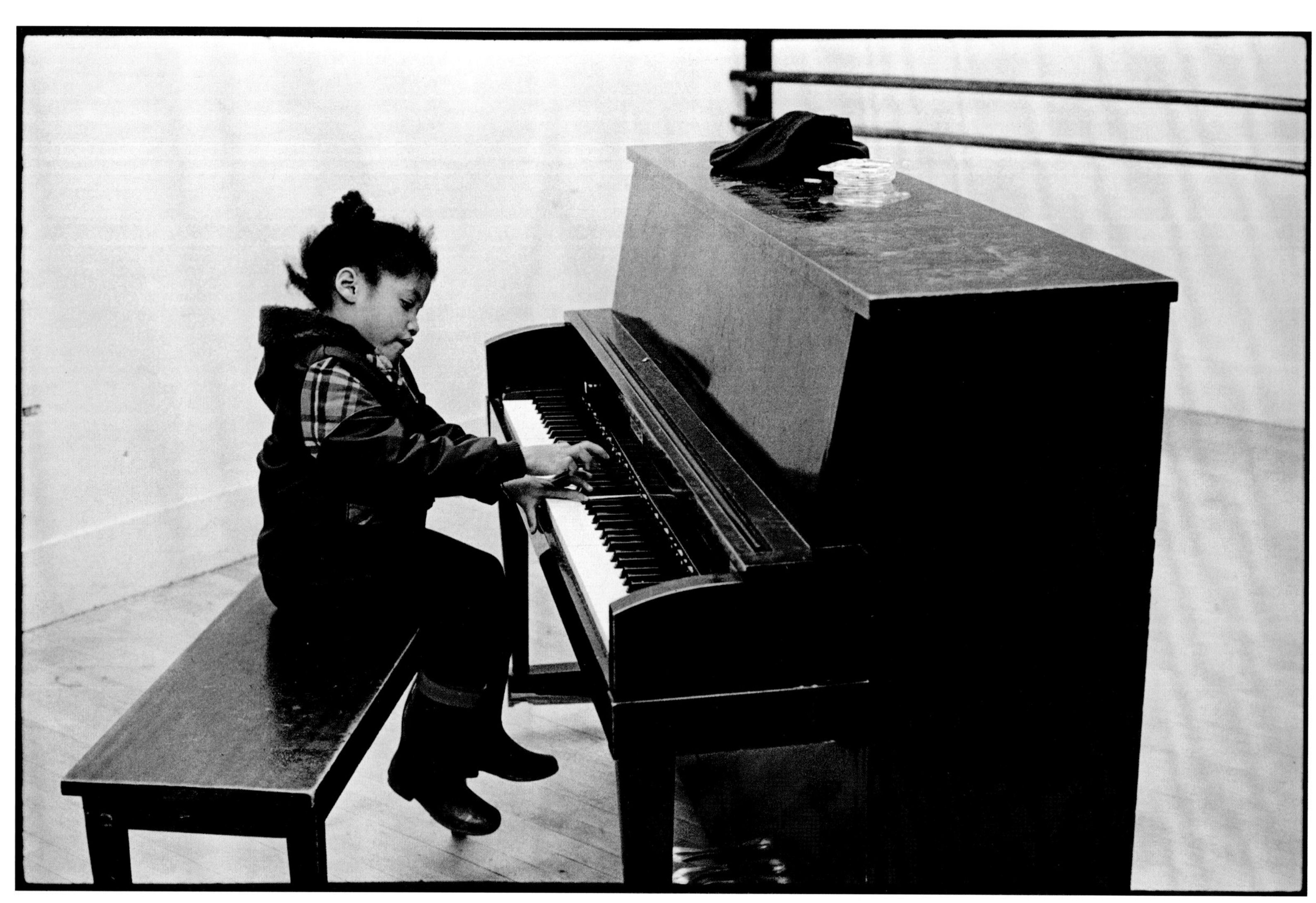

Piano student waiting for lesson,
Elma Lewis School

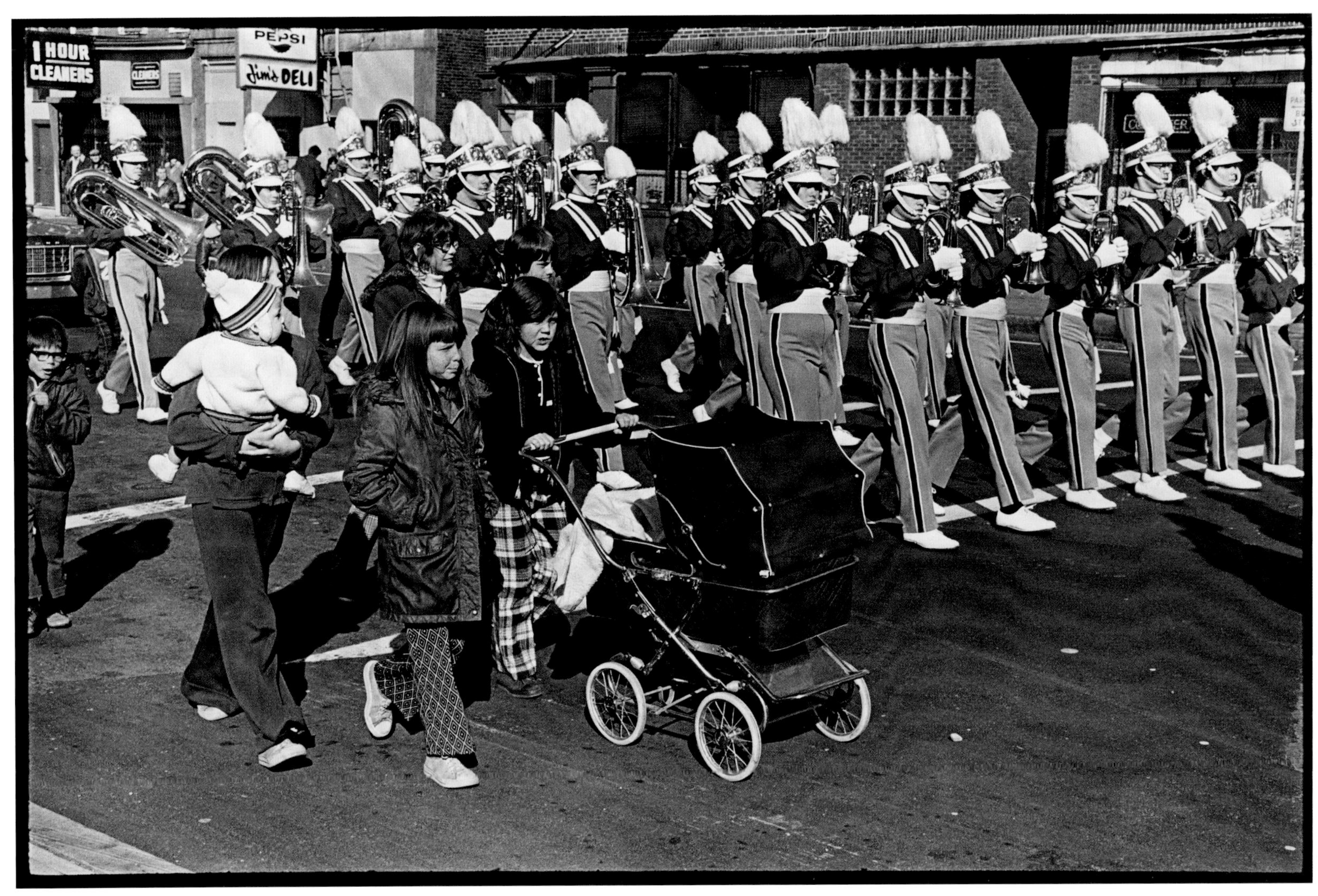

Marching band and parade,
South Boston

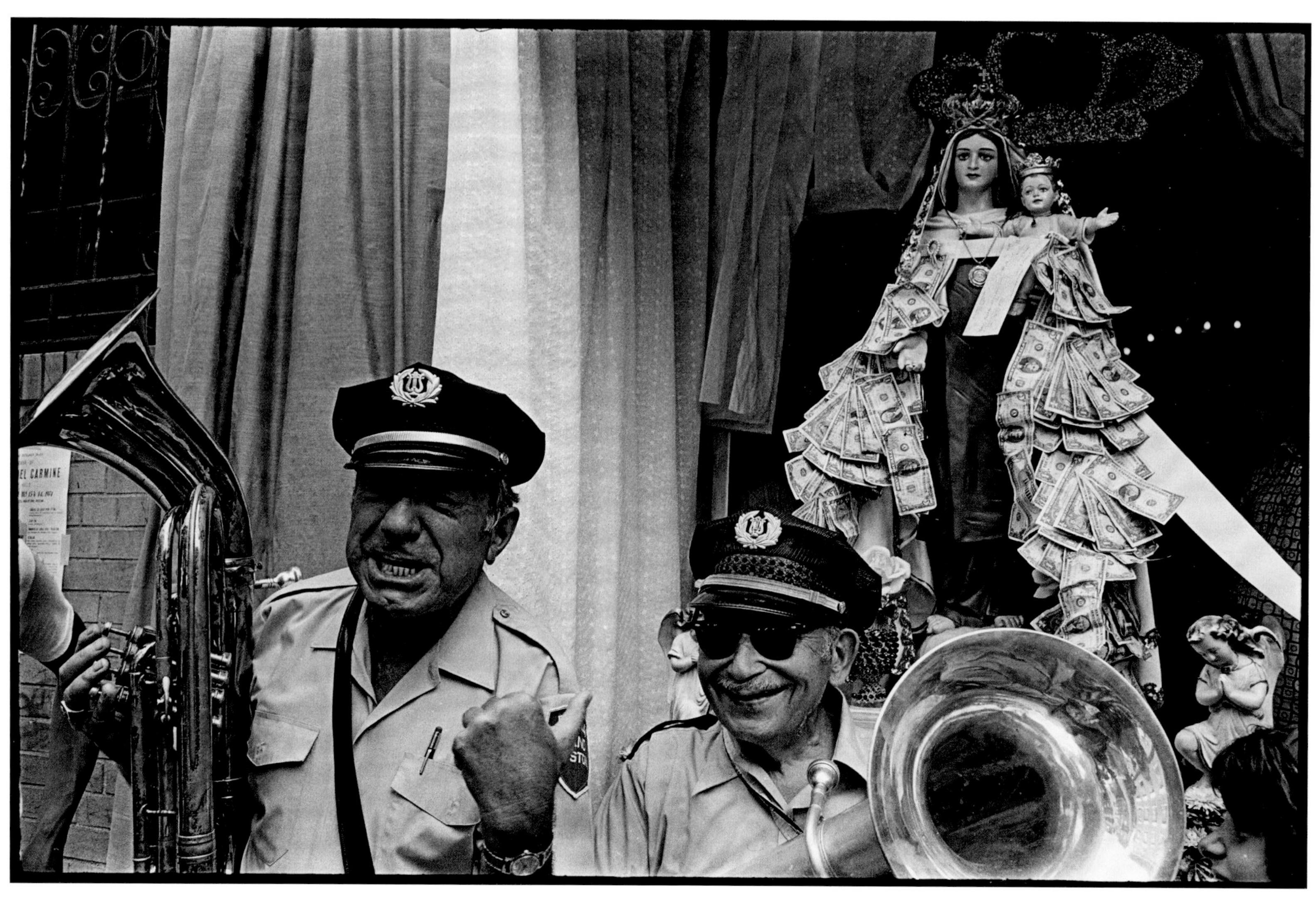

Italian religious street procession,
North End

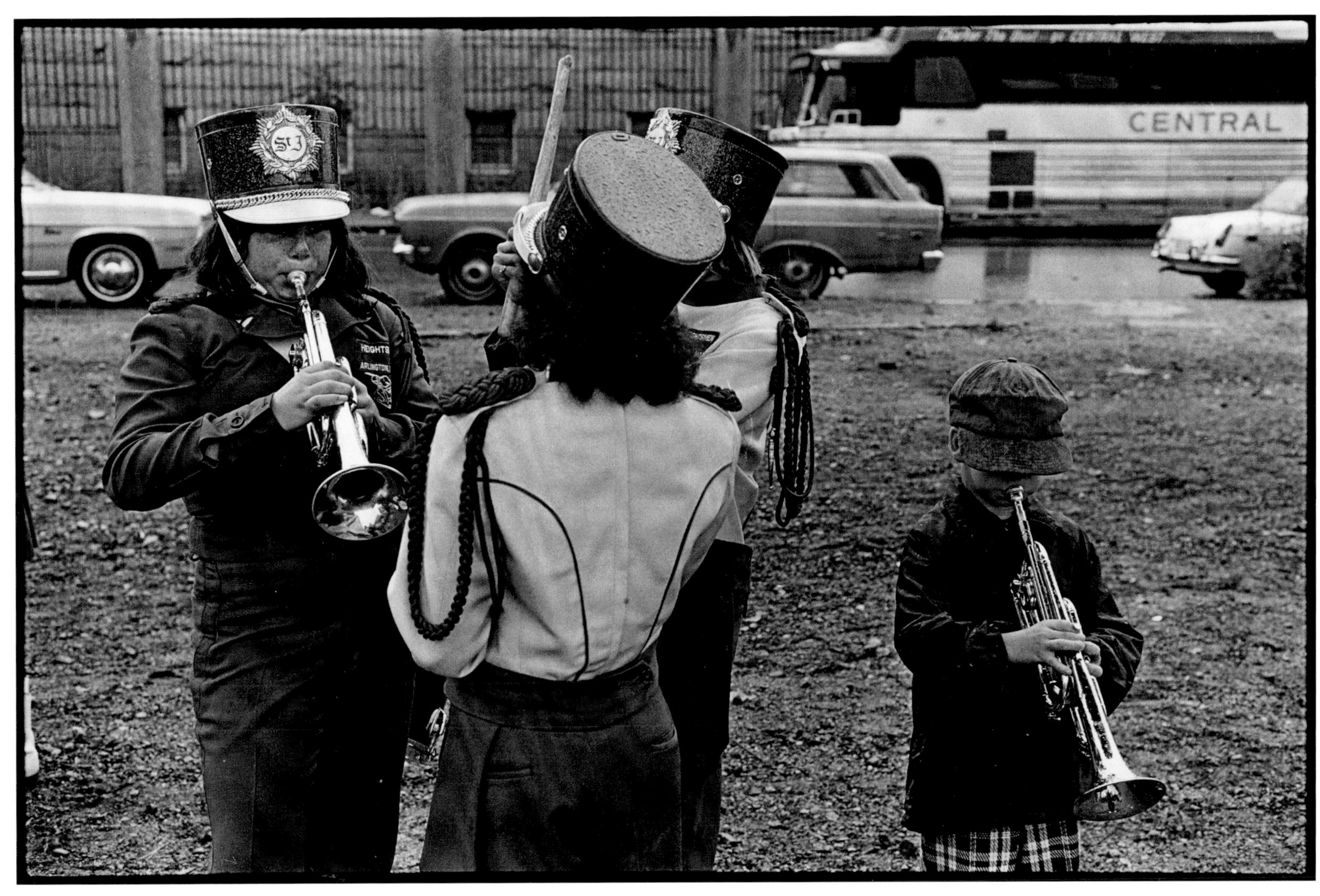

Arlington High School band warming up for parade, Charlestown

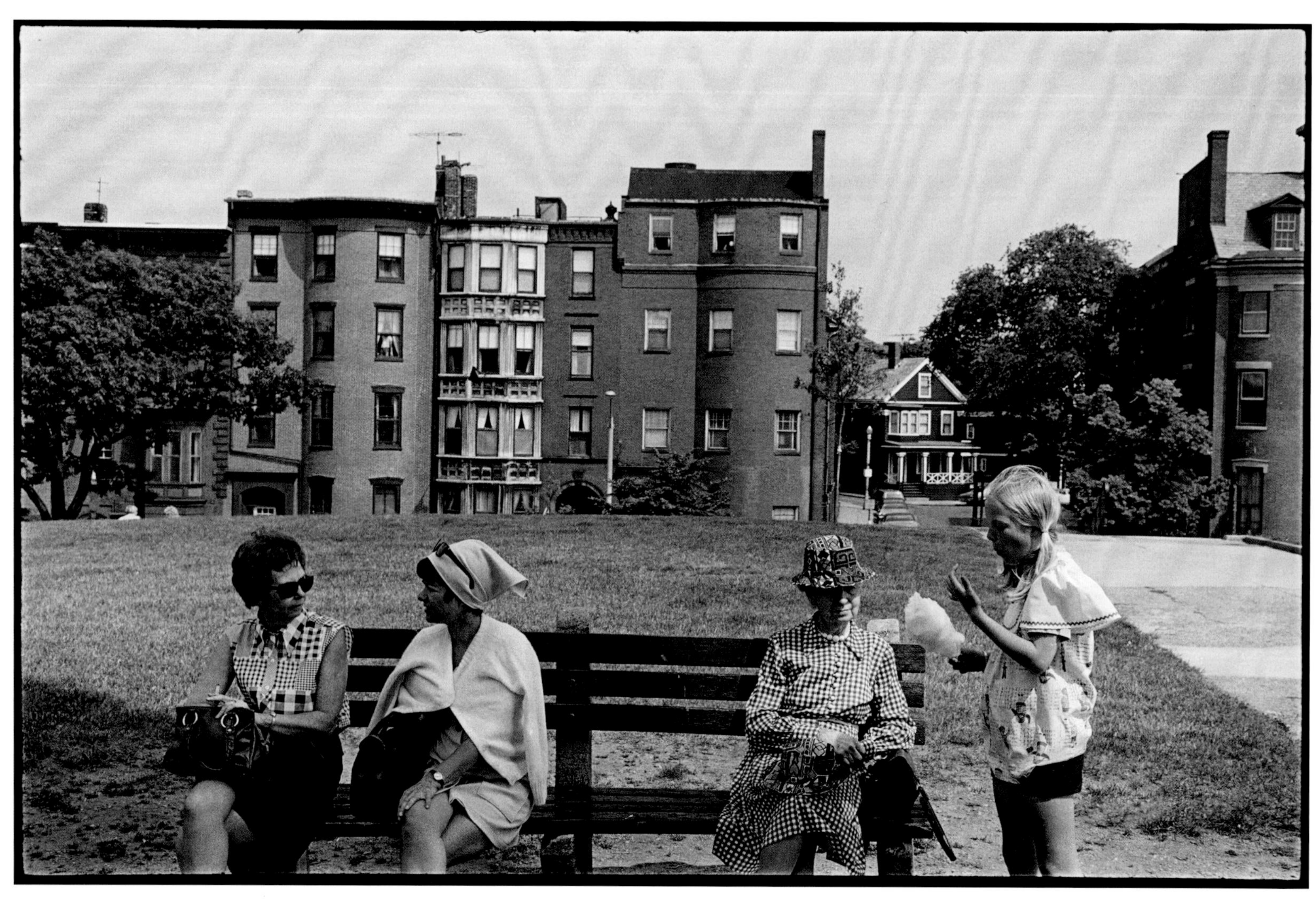

Sunday afternoon on Monument Hill,
Charlestown

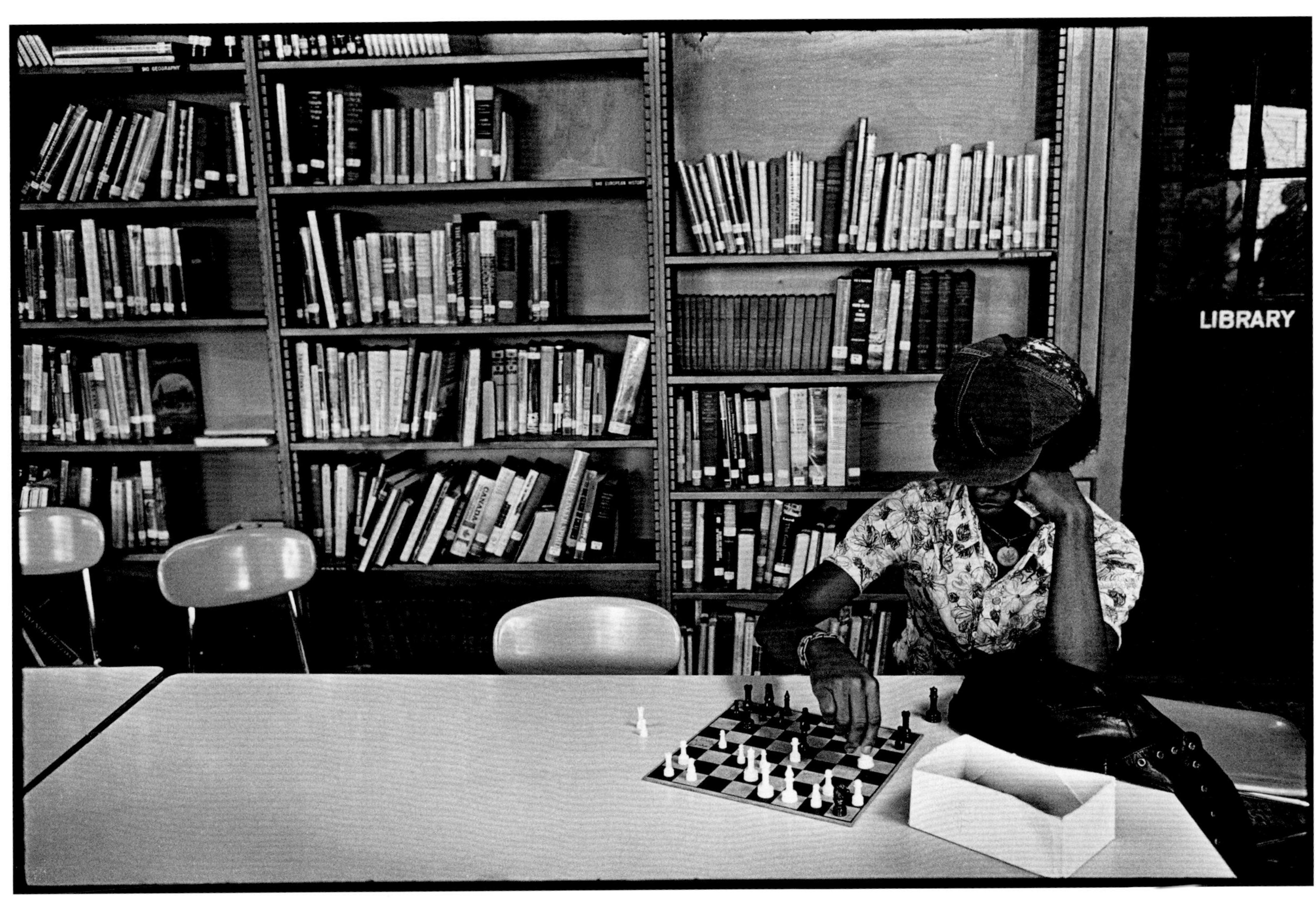

Student with a chess set, Boston

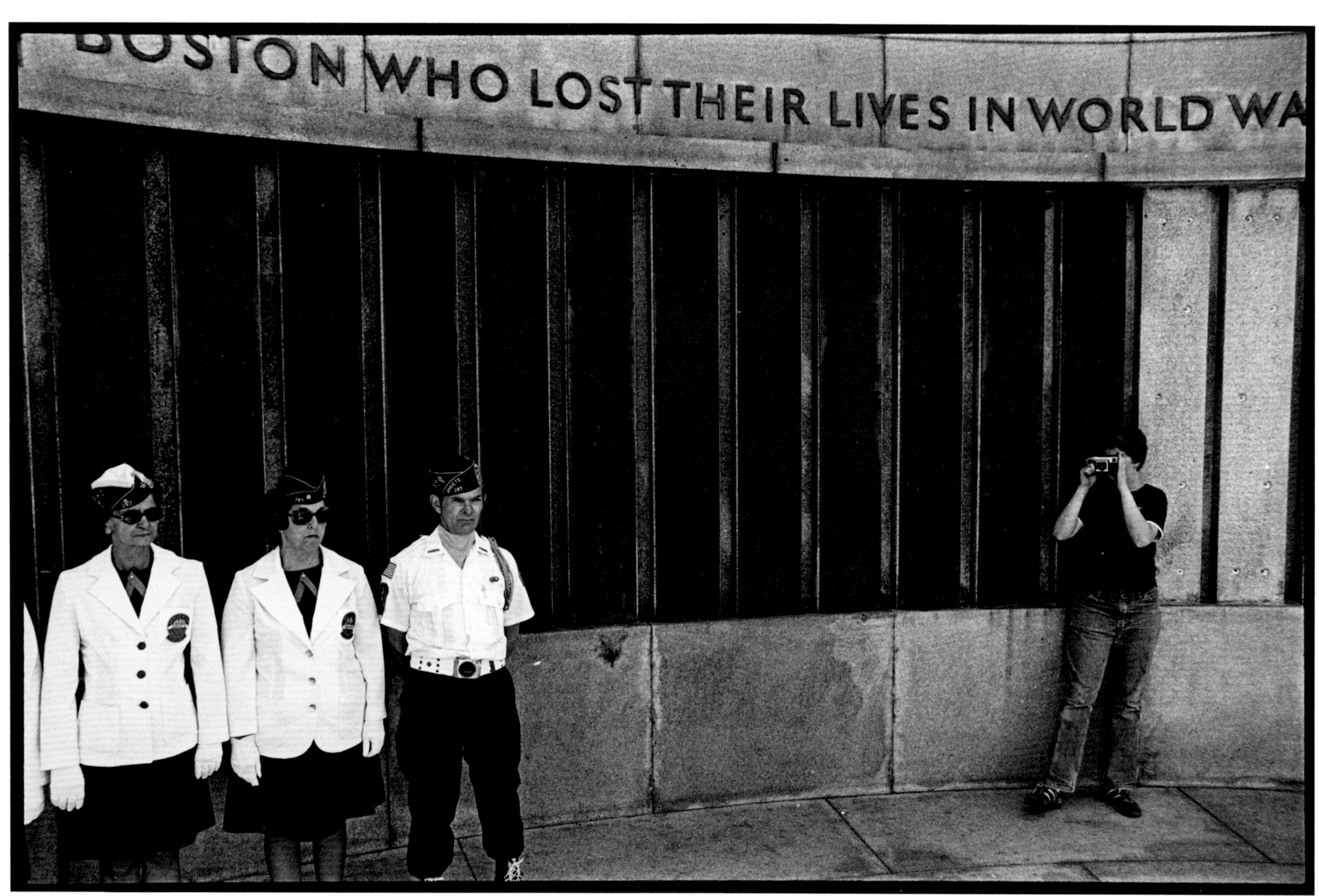

World War II Memorial, Fenway

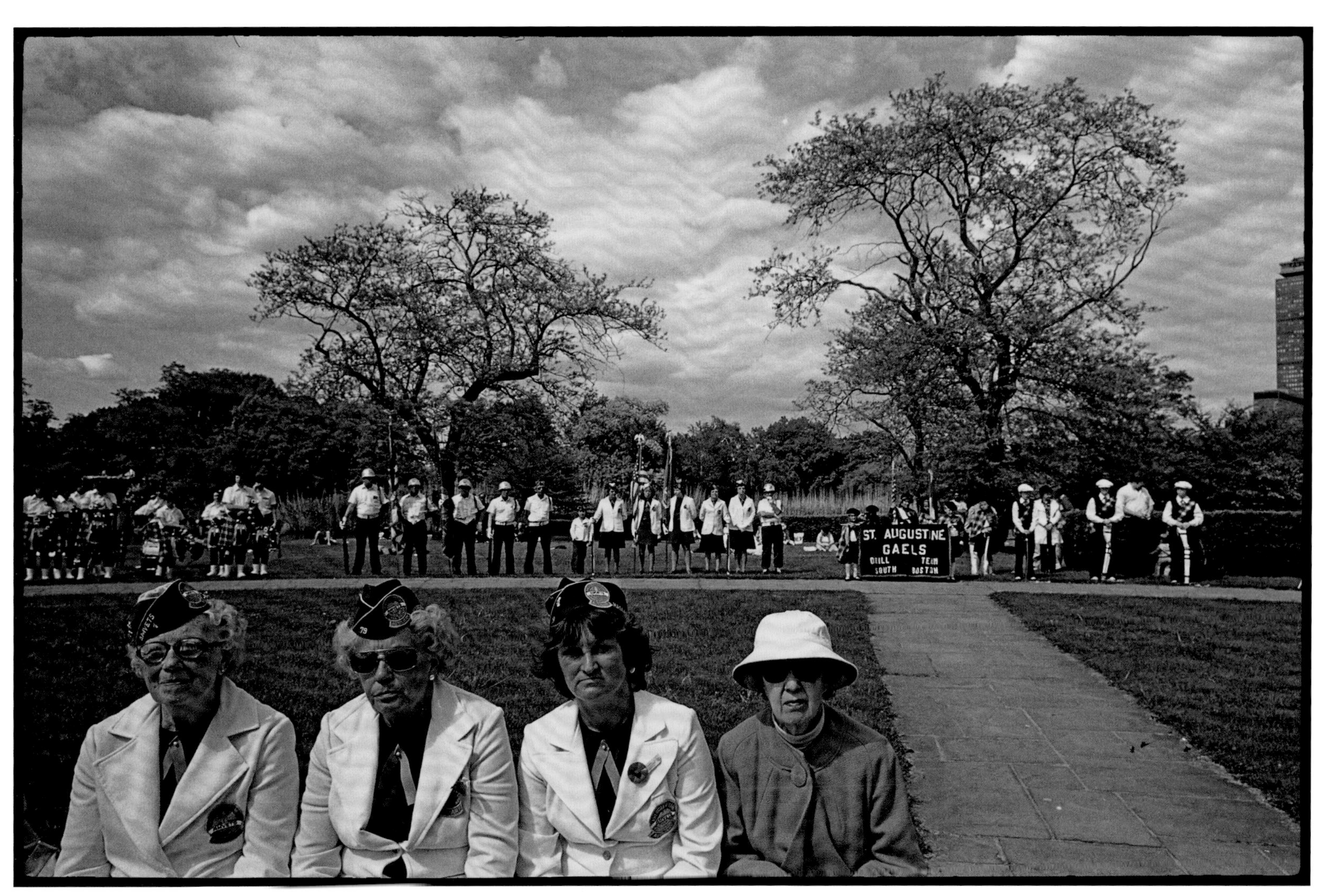

Veteran memorial ceremony, Fenway

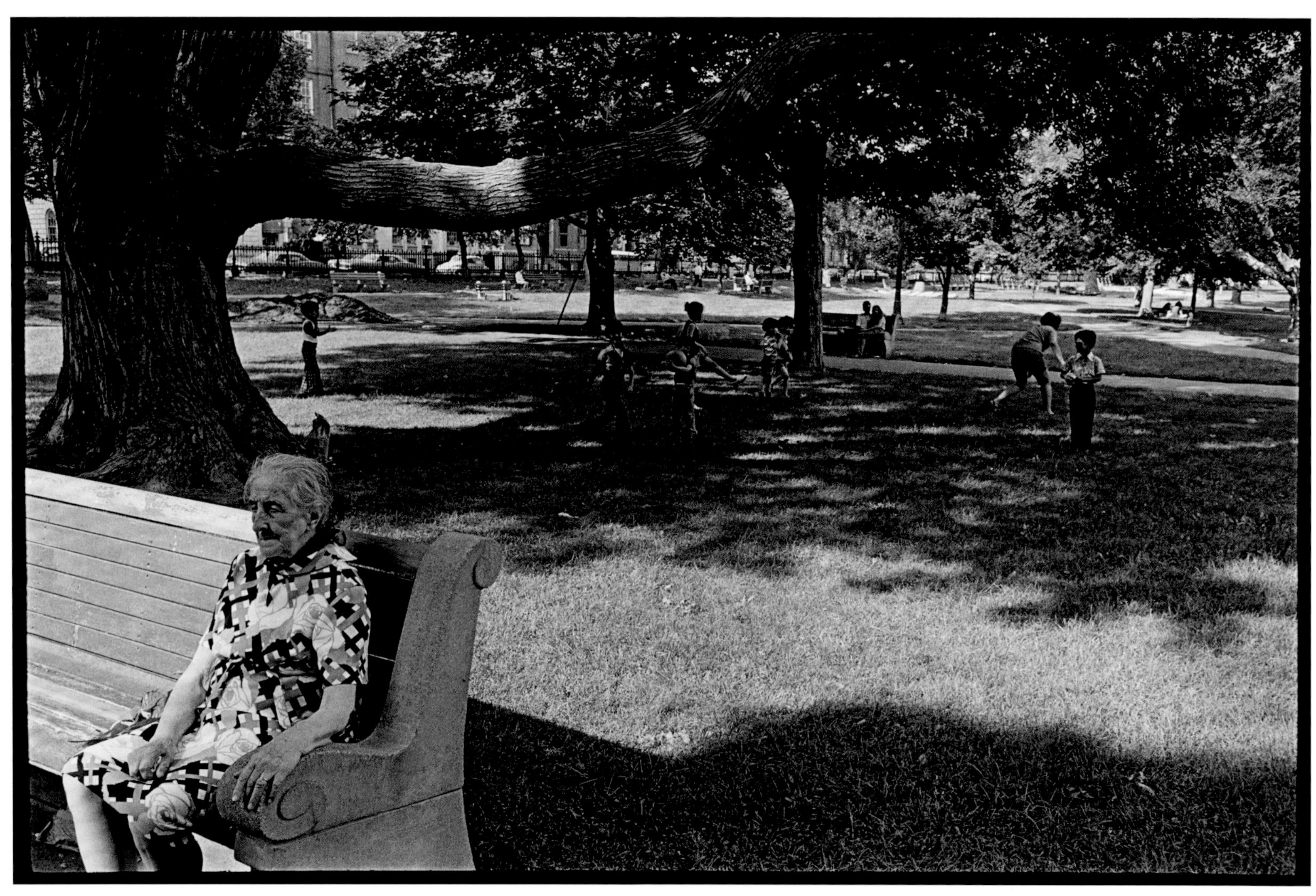

Elderly lady on a park bench,
Public Garden

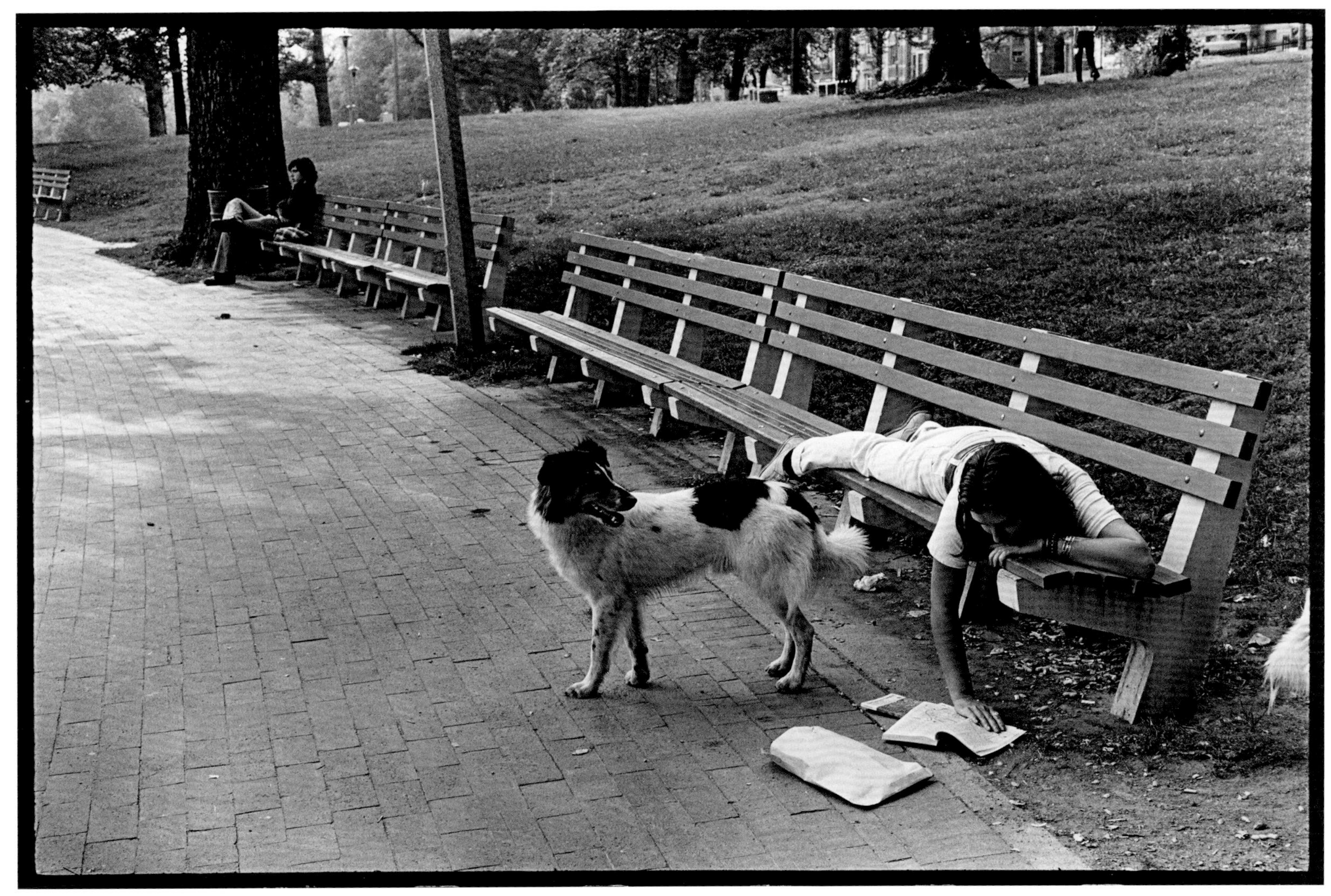

Young girl on a park bench,
Boston Common

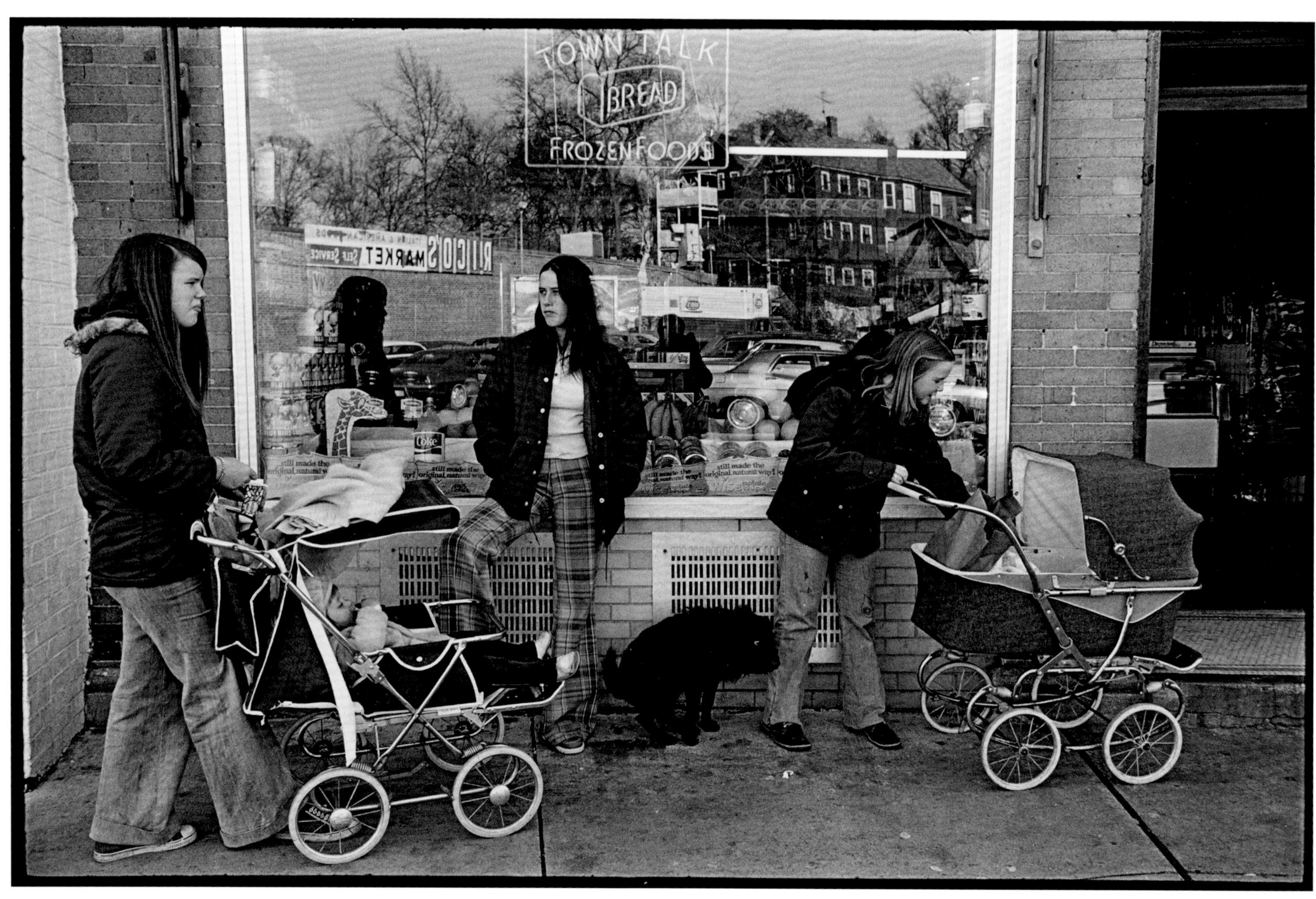

Girls with baby carriages at
neighborhood grocery, Mattapan

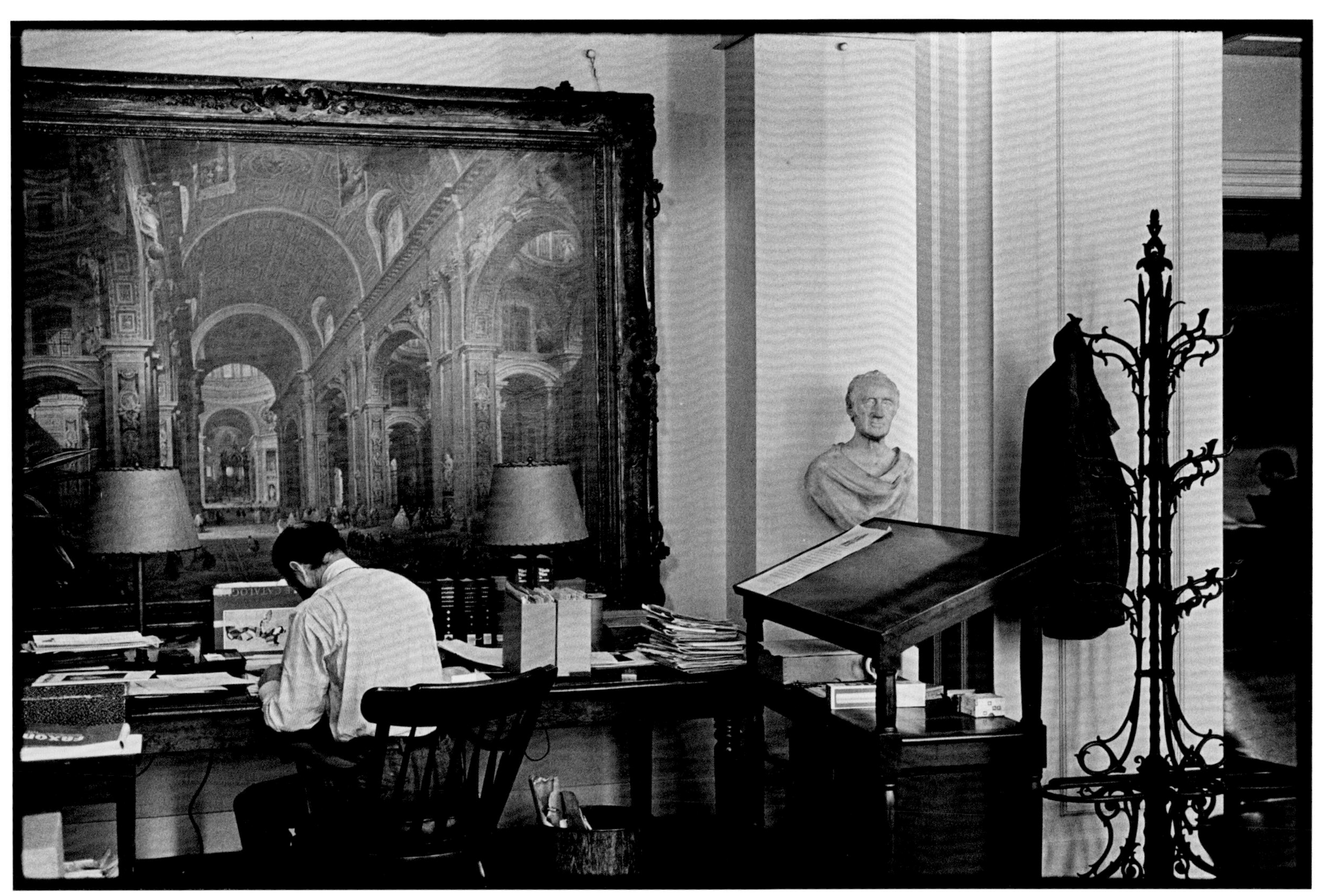

Librarian at work, Boston Athenaeum

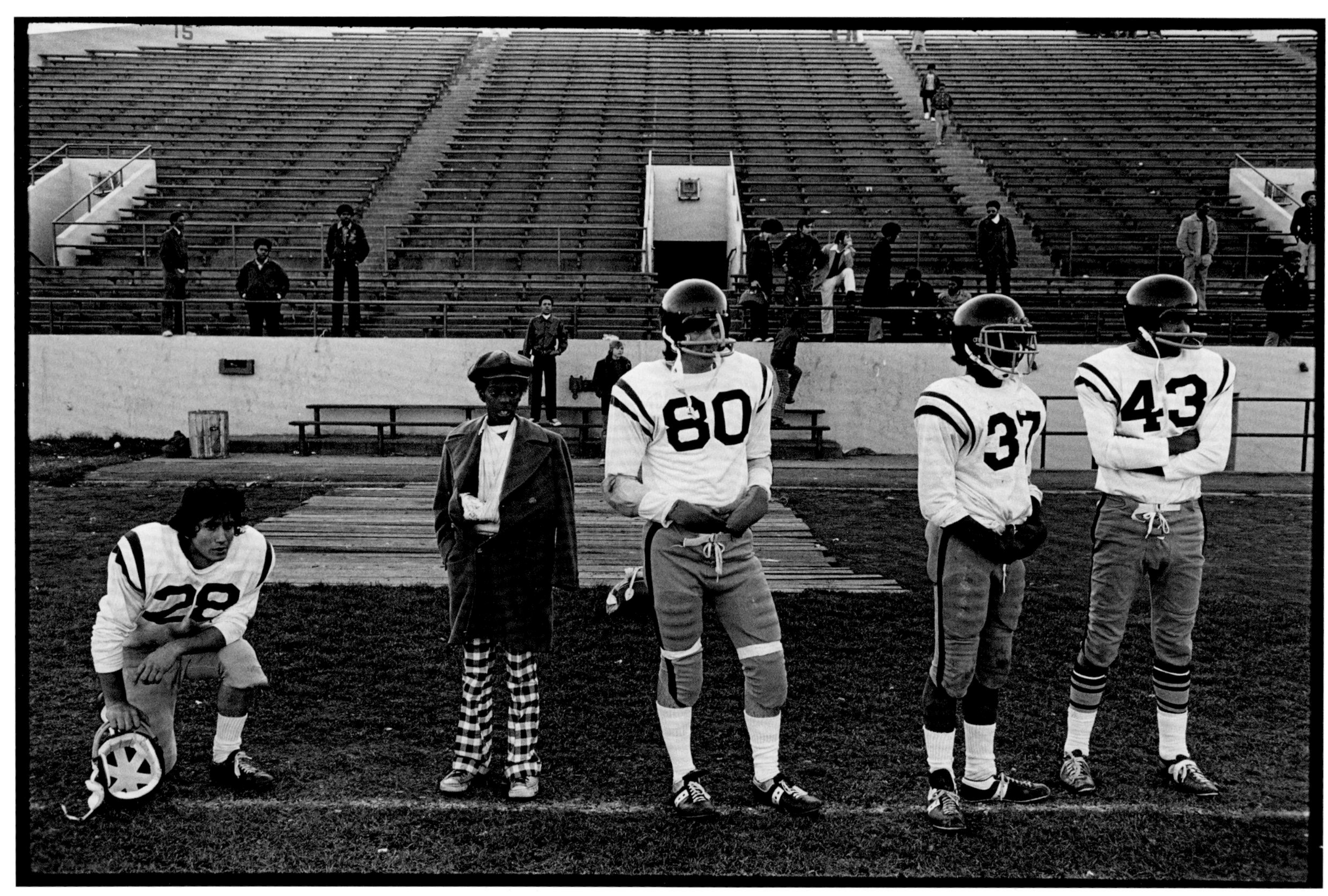

High school football game,
White Stadium

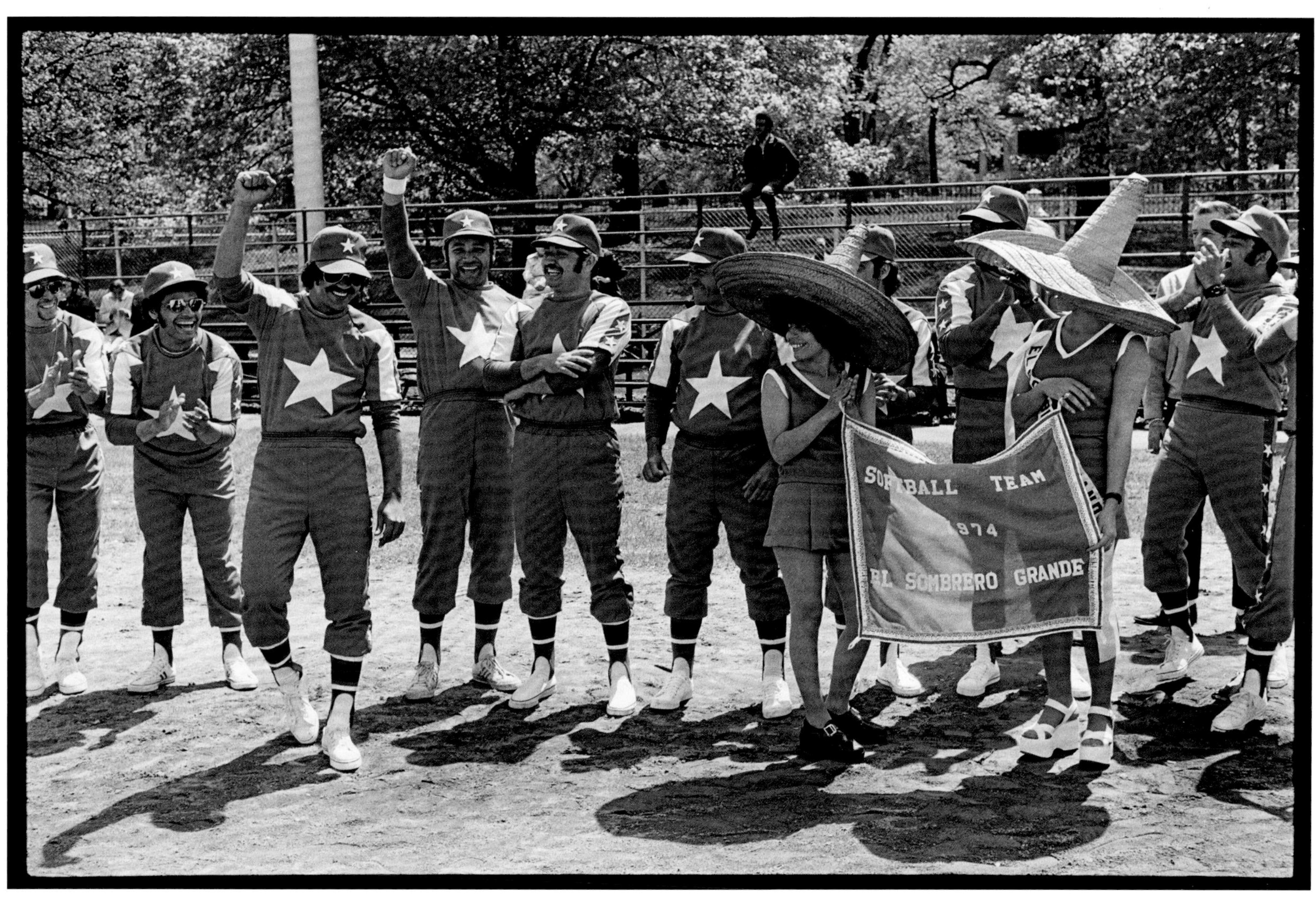

Opening game of Puerto Rican softball league, Boston Common

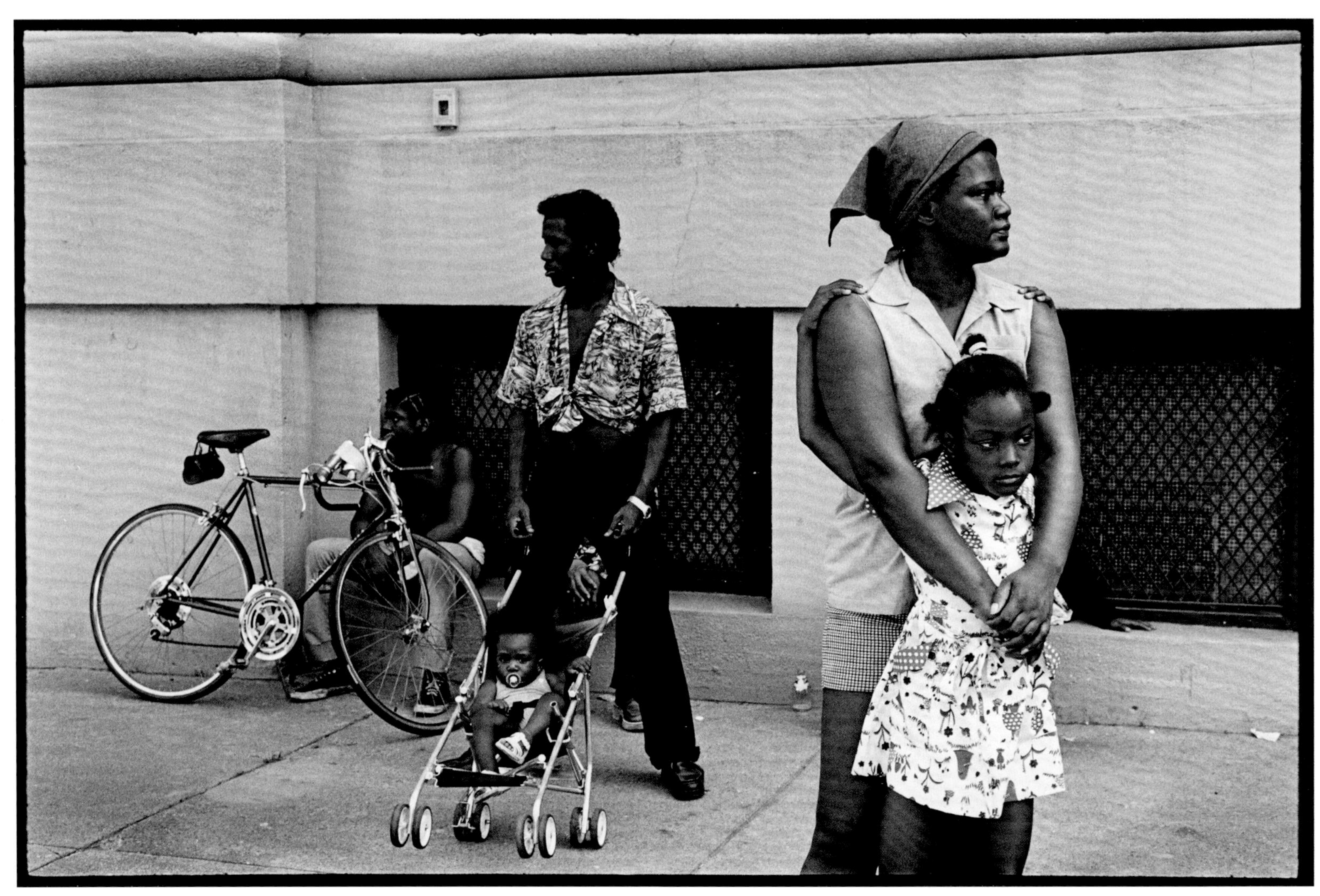

Street scene along parade route,
South End

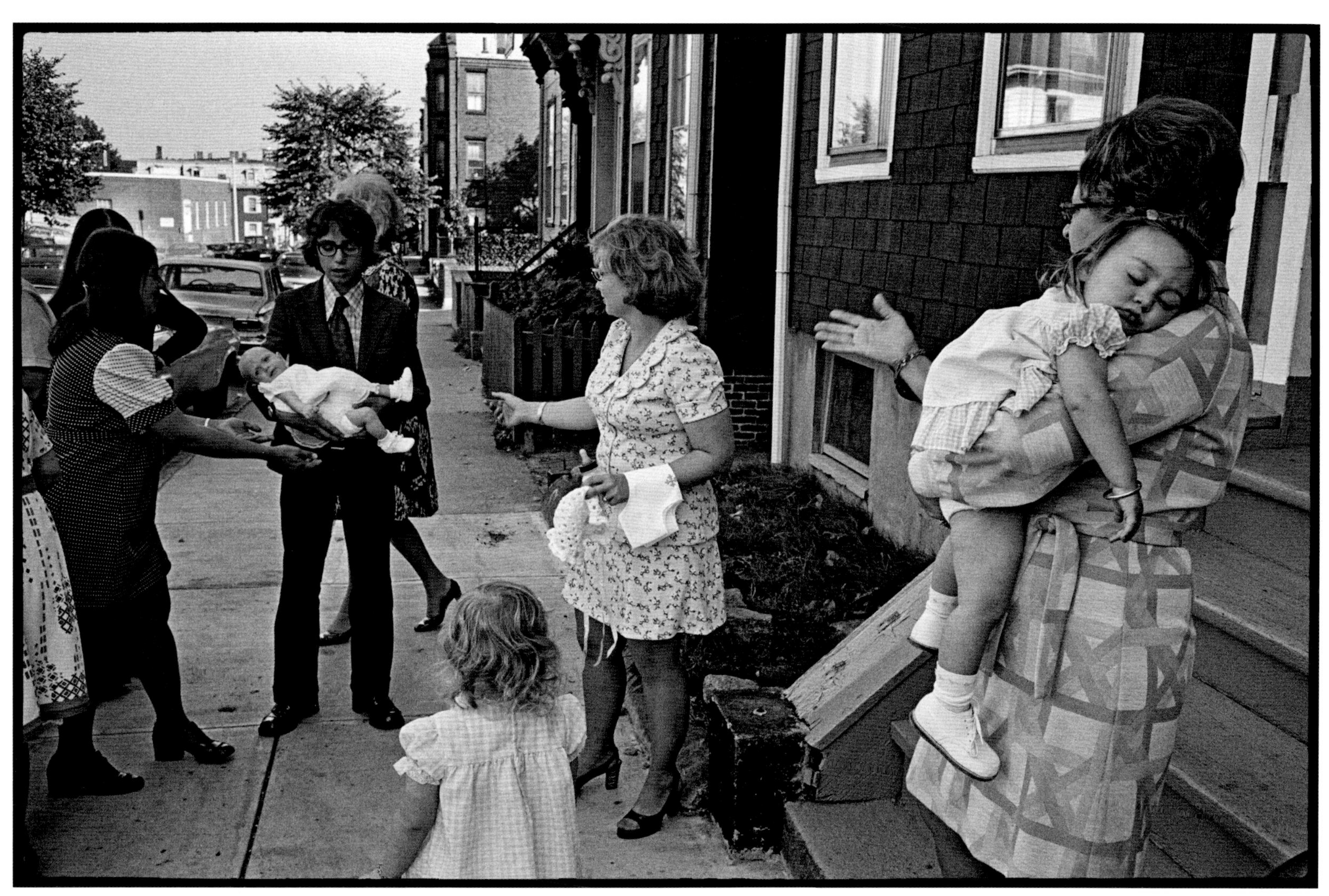

Moran family baptism, South Boston

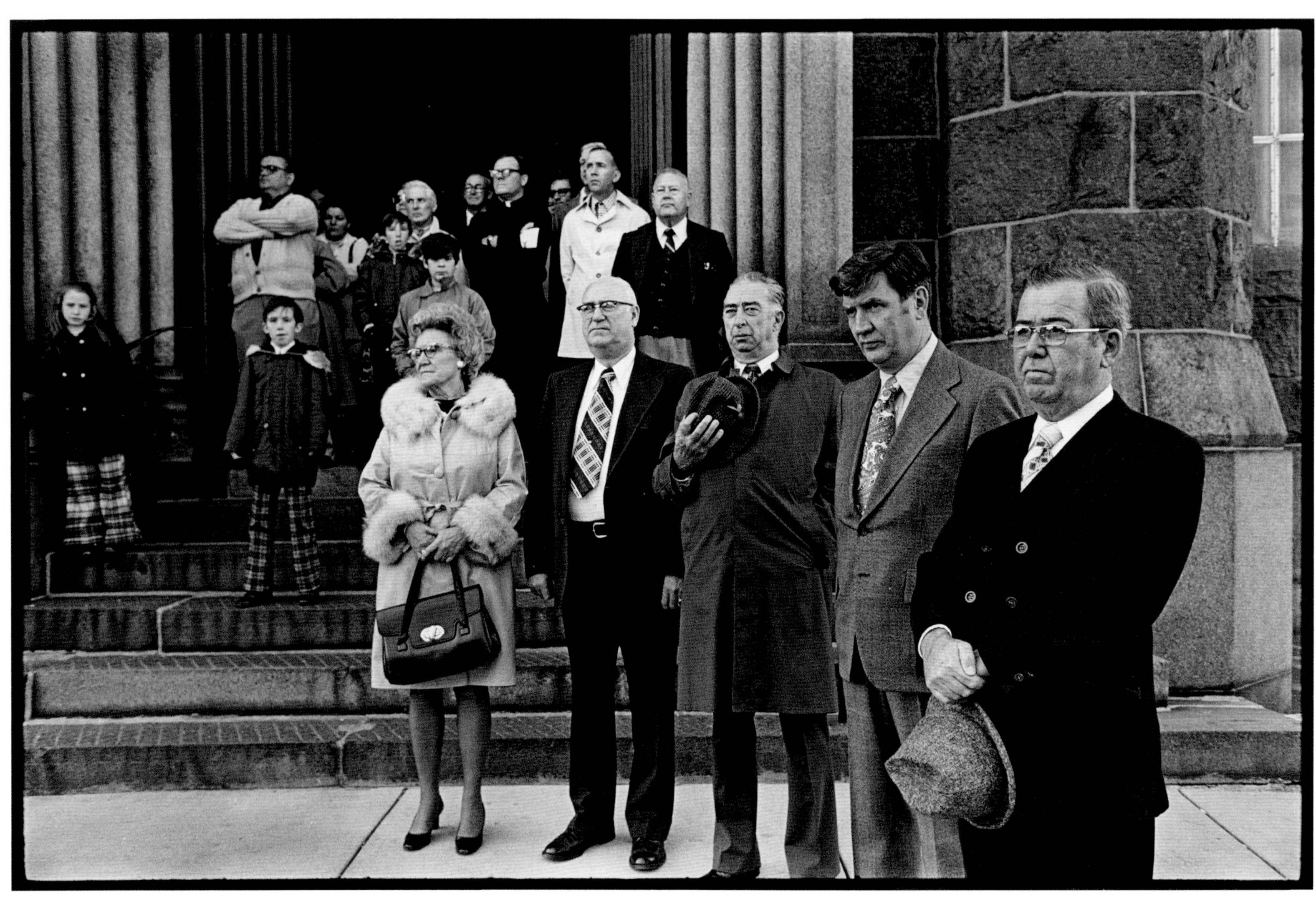

V.F.W. memorial mass at St. Peters
and Paul Church, South Boston

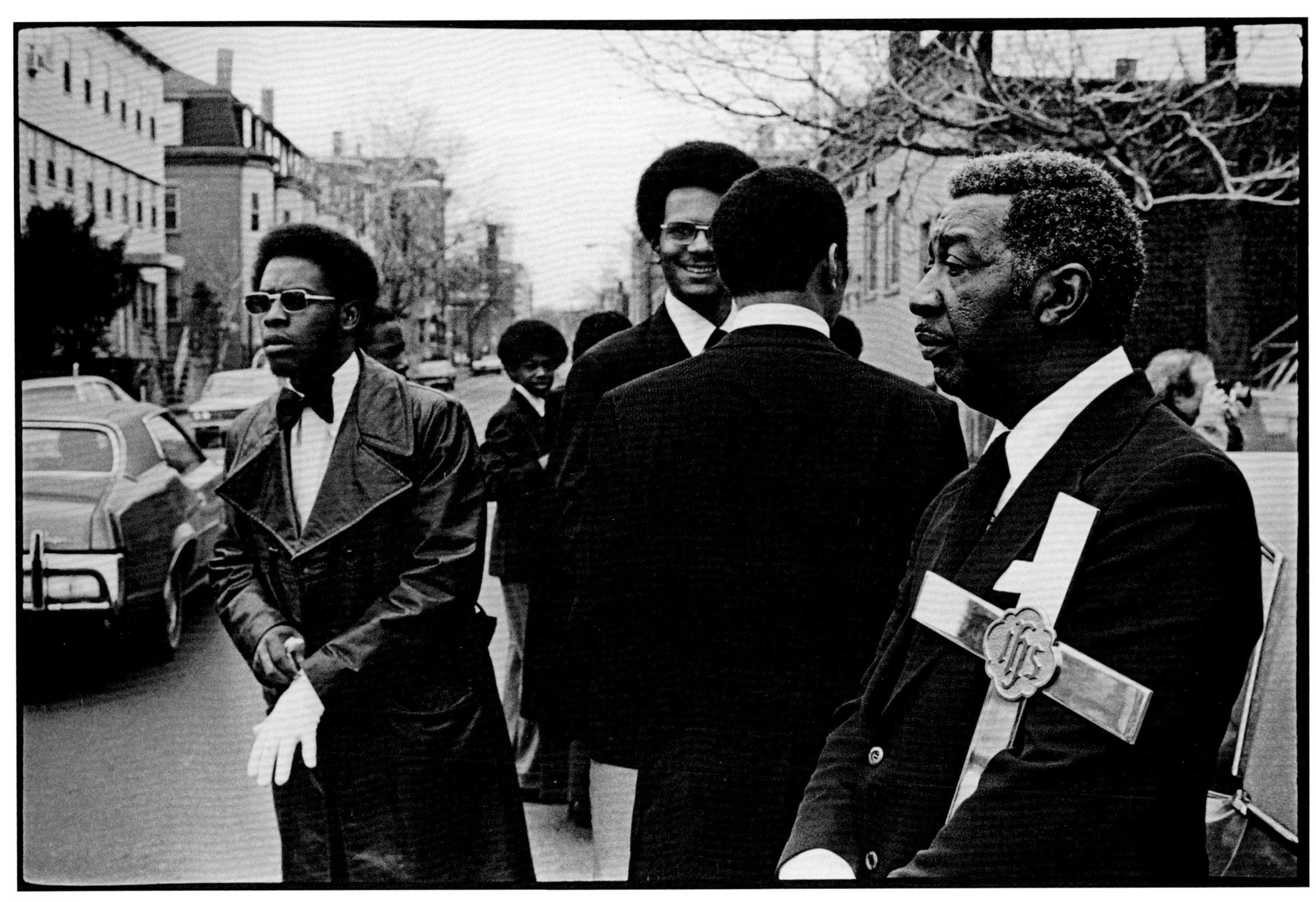

Easter Sunday procession at St. Paul's A.M.E. Church, Cambridge

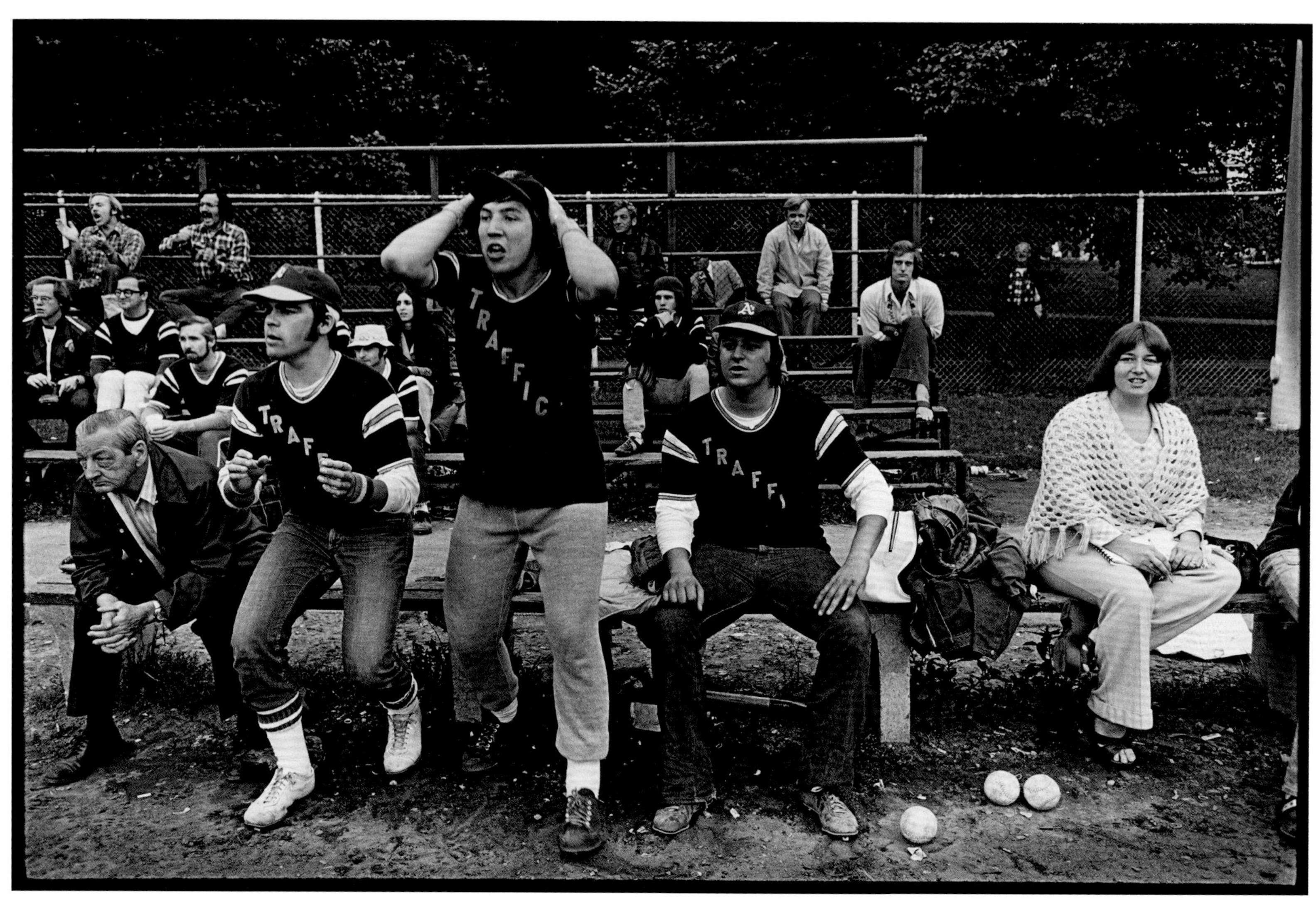

Softball players and spectators at
a game, Boston Common

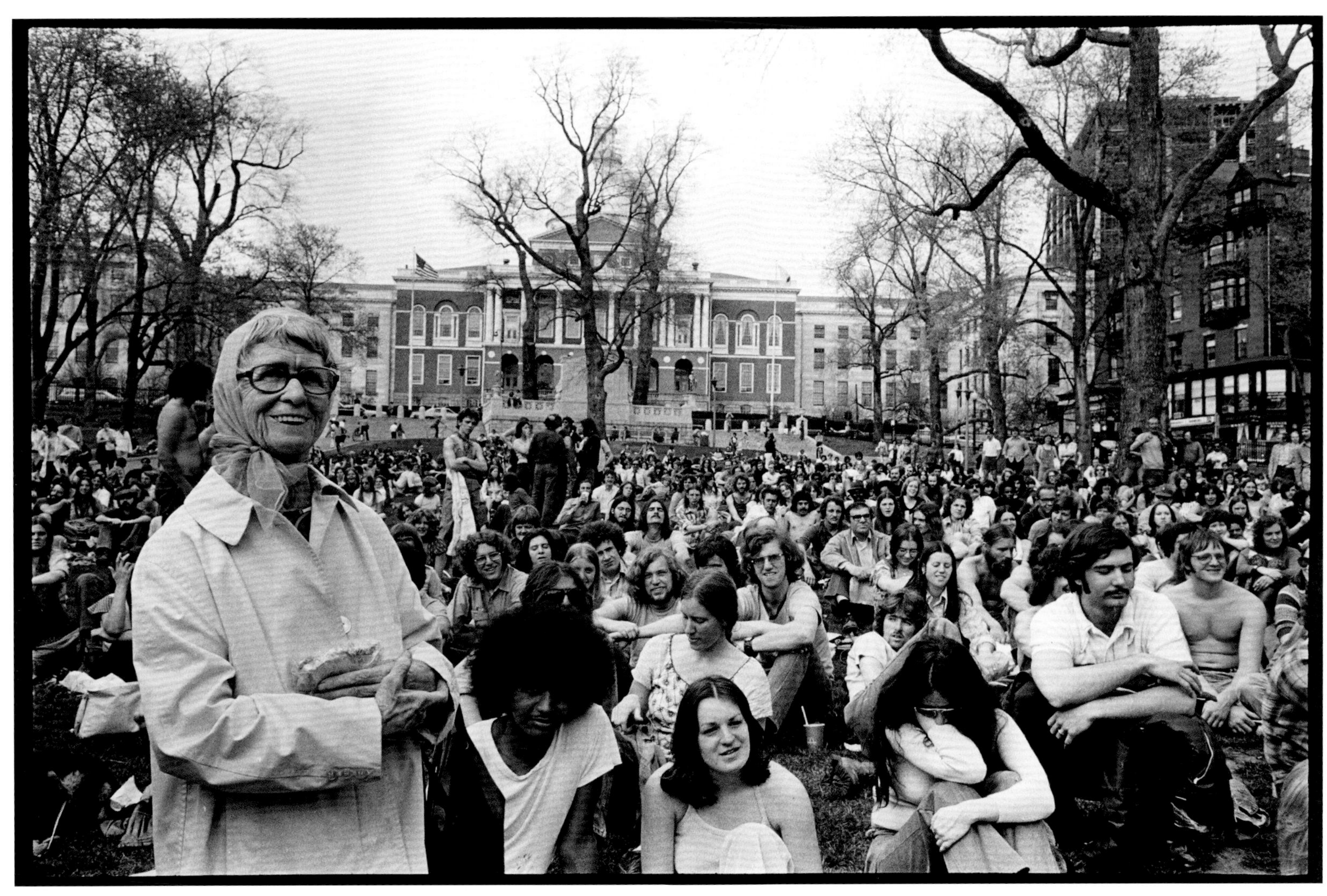

Crowd gathered by State House,
Boston Common

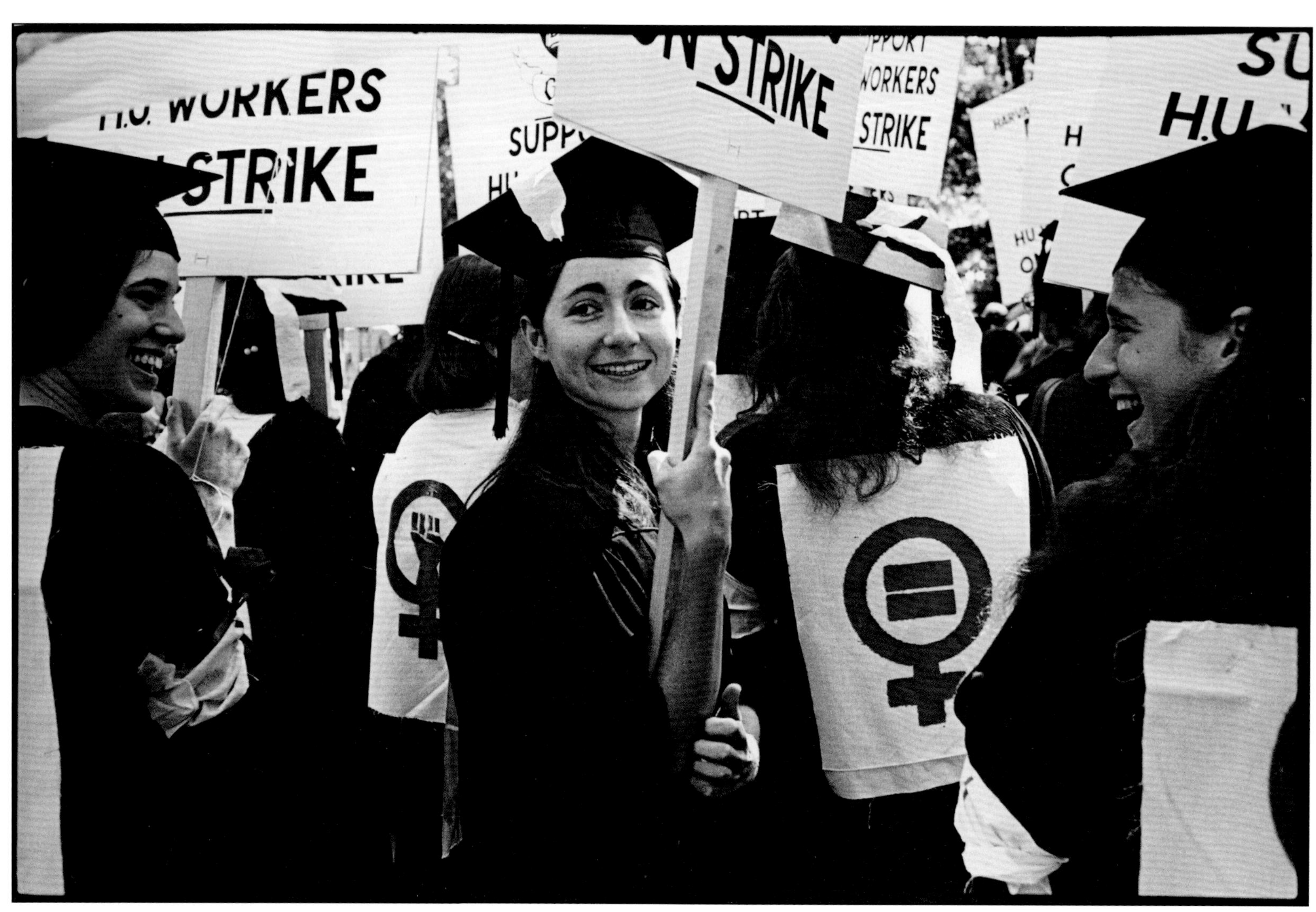

Commencement day procession at
Harvard University, Cambridge

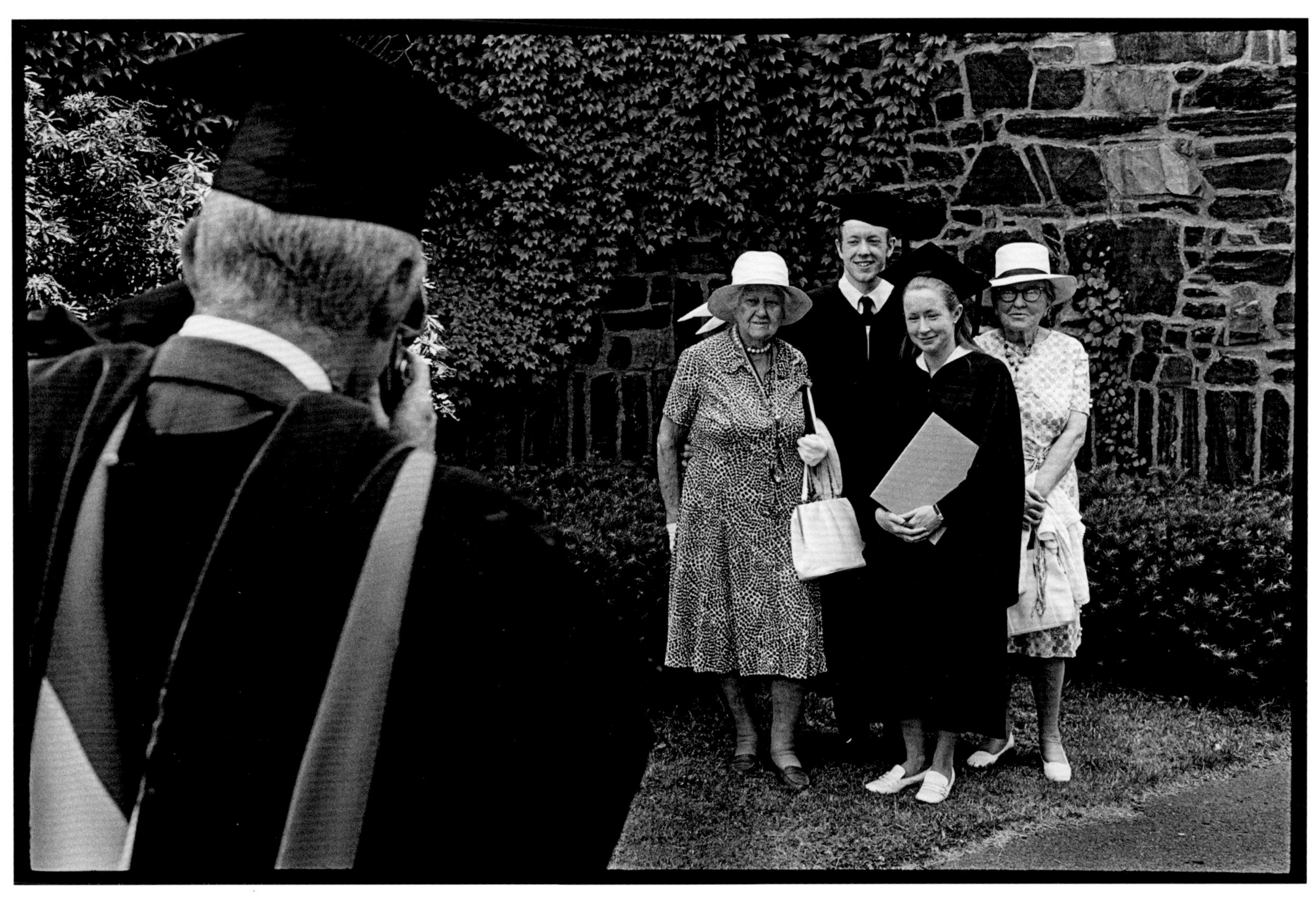

Commencement day at Tufts
University, Medford

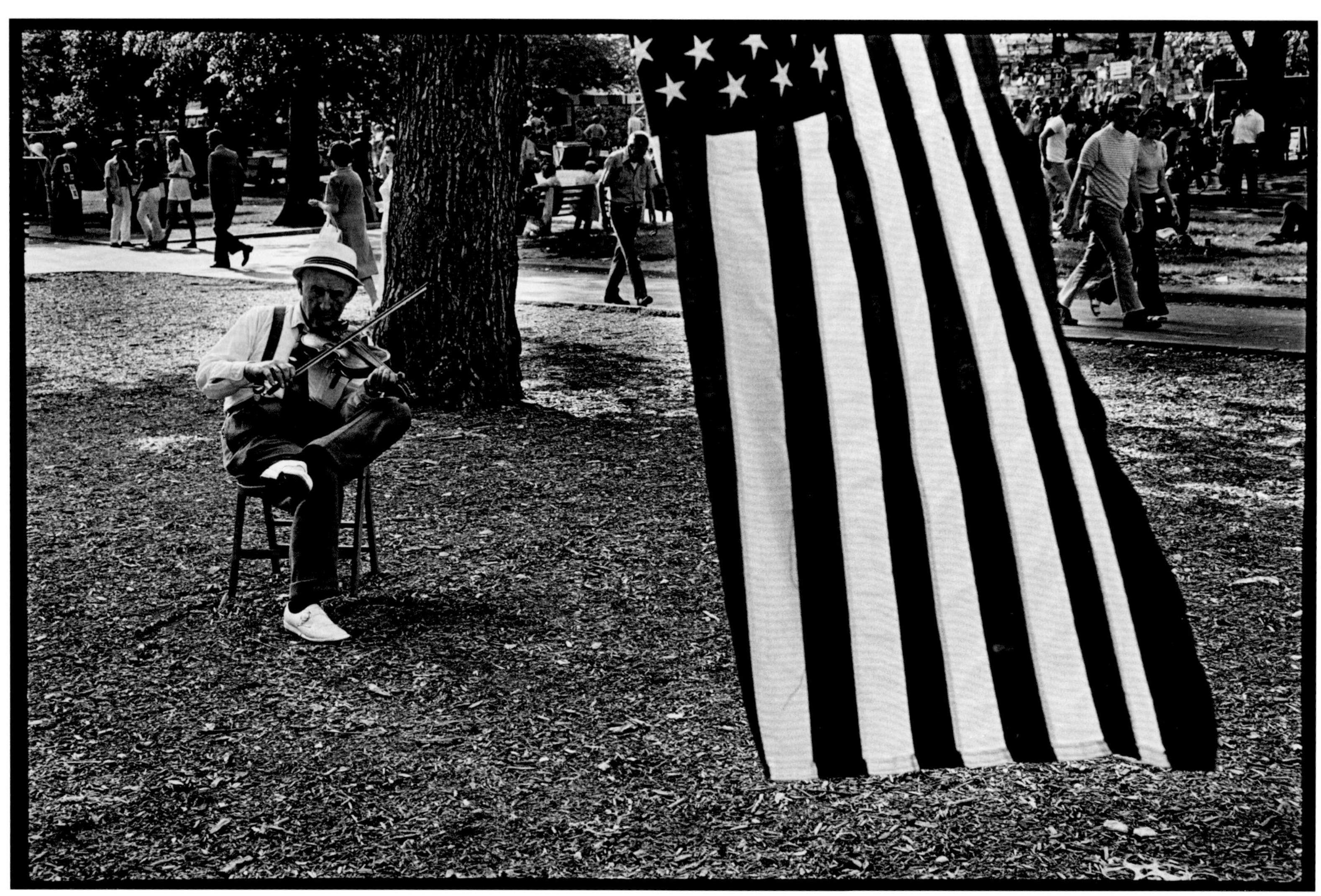

Fiddler and flag, Boston Common

Oral Histories

50 Years Later: The Community Reflects

In 2025, the Boston Athenaeum commenced a citywide outreach project to spread the *Bostonians* series. Community members were invited to help identify individuals depicted in the images. When matches were made, those individuals shared their stories, memories, and reflections about the moment captured and the time period it represented. In cases where specific names could not be connected, we turned to politicians, artists, educators, and activists—figures tied to the institutions, neighborhoods, events, and public spaces represented in the series—to provide reflections that spoke to the broader context of the 1970s. The excerpts that follow, beginning with contextual reflections and moving to personal responses, draw from these oral histories, layering the photographs with a chorus of voices that expand their meaning and situate them within the lived histories of Boston. The oral histories were collected and edited by Lauren Graves and Lilly Havstad.

Barney Frank

Barney Frank was a state representative for Boston's Ward 5 from 1972 to 1980. During his tenure at the State House, Frank championed a liberal agenda. Notably, he was an early and outspoken advocate for gay and lesbian rights and pushed for redistricting the state senate to ensure more diverse and equitable representation. These commitments continued to define his decades-long career in Congress.

The '70s start with me leaving the mayor's office, going to work in Congress for a year, then coming back up in '72, so for most of the '70s, I'm a state representative evolving to wanting to come out. By process of elimination, I became one of the leading gay-rights advocates in America, complicated by the fact that I'm a closeted gay man. And I didn't do this—you know, it's kind of like in the barbershops, you always have these mirrors, and the mirror reflects the mirror. Goes like, all right now, I'm gay. Should I sponsor the Gay Rights Bill? If I do, will people think I'm gay? Or they'll think I wouldn't have done it if I was gay, so therefore I must not be. This is '72, post-Stonewall, no gay activity in Boston before that. I know that because working for the mayor, I did interest groups as part of my job. And I was hoping to find a gay group. I didn't know any gay people . . .

In fact, the first gay-pride parade in Boston was '71. I was in Washington when it happened. But two groups formed in 1972, separately: the Homophile Union of Boston, which was men, and the Daughters of Bilitis, who I guess was Sappho's girlfriend. I wonder where that name came from. And I began to work with both of them. One of the leaders of the Daughters of Bilitis was Ann McGuire. . . . I said, if the gay community had a different structure, she would have been Saint Ann of Lesbos.

The first parade I marched in was '72—very small. The first one was '71; I rode in '72. But I began to work with them in my campaign. And I remember one of the first things I learned was—I was asked by the gay men to intervene with the police department. Not because of brutality, but because they were under-policed. The problem was gay men, closeted gay men, would get themselves in a position where they were assaulted or robbed but couldn't go to the cops because they would have to go public. And they were unprotected. And I worked with the cops, and we worked out a procedure whereby a gay man who had been assaulted or robbed in those circumstances could tell the cops everything but not come forward as a witness. The cops would then begin to get a pattern of information about the bad guys and were able to try to catch some of them that way.

Clara Wainwright

Cambridge-based artist Clara Wainwright, along with a group of young creatives, formed the Committee for the Better Use of Air, which organized Boston's first kite festival at Franklin Park in 1969. They ran the festival for 13 years and the tradition continues today.

The day of the festival, the weather was beautiful, and, you know, this was the first really huge thing I'd ever done. And you just never know if there'll be anybody there. But a lot of people showed up, particularly from Dorchester to Roxbury. . . . You know, people did amazing kites. There was one man, who was an architect, who built this huge kite that must have taken him days, all made out of balsam wood or something. And so it was such a mixture of kids who had never seen kites before, who came from very poor families, on up. . . .

Speaking on her community-oriented art practice, Wainwright shared:

I would say I just chase delight. And if I can't come across it, I figure out a way to make it happen.

Jeri Robinson

Jeri Robinson is an educator who experienced the Elma Lewis School across three generations—as a student, a teacher, and later as a parent. Founded in 1950 by activist and educator Elma Lewis, the school provided children in Roxbury and Dorchester with high-quality arts education rooted in cultural pride and discipline. Robinson recalls that even when she was a young child in the 1950s, the school instilled in her a deep sense of self-worth and responsibility, shaping both her identity and her lifelong commitment to education.

Elma Lewis would drum it into us . . . that you don't have to be the smartest person in the room, but you can at least go and behave, take it in. And that you're not going to find that everybody cares about you, or has the intent that you will be successful, so some of this has got to come from within and from your inner community. . . . She would say to you, "Say to yourself, 'You're beautiful.'" Now nobody was saying that to kids back in 1957. [There were] a lot of issues around self-esteem and holding yourself accountable. So that was part of the rest of that message. And I got a similar message from going to church, and our Sunday-school superintendent, who also was a piano teacher, Mrs. Haynes, was similar. These were very strong Black women. . . . So I said, we're the Elma Lewises and the Mrs. Hayneses of now. We need to be those people for these kids.

Pedro Santiago

Pedro Santiago is a Puerto Rican community activist. He grew up in Ciales, Puerto Rico, and came to Boston in the late 1960s after serving in the Vietnam War. In 1969, he began attending the Puerto Rican Festival, organized by Chico Muñoz. By 1974, he was working as an emcee for the festival and as a community organizer, supporting and promoting civic engagement within the Puerto Rican population in Boston.

The festival is a great thing because it gets people together . . . so we can demonstrate what we are, show other people our culture and music. And Puerto Ricans, we are very proud of our small island.

Puerto Rico, I'm not lying, Puerto Rico has more songs and poems dedicated [to it]—maybe a hundred times more—than the whole rest of the world. I include the universe. . . . I don't know why the island has that sense of love. Yeah, the Puerto Ricans, they love the island. Even fourth-generations here, you'll see them at the festival with the flag, and they don't even know what the flag means. But it's transferred from one generation to another, even if they don't know.

The festival right now is run by Boston Ricans. . . . A Boston Rican is a person who moved here as a child or was born in Boston. . . . I was born in Puerto Rico, I grew up in Puerto Rico. They don't know Puerto Rico like I do. So we have to teach these individuals, men and women, to get educated, to be aware of what's going on, run for office, try to get jobs at city hall, at the state house, you know? But obviously to do that they have to get educated first, you know? That's my teaching.

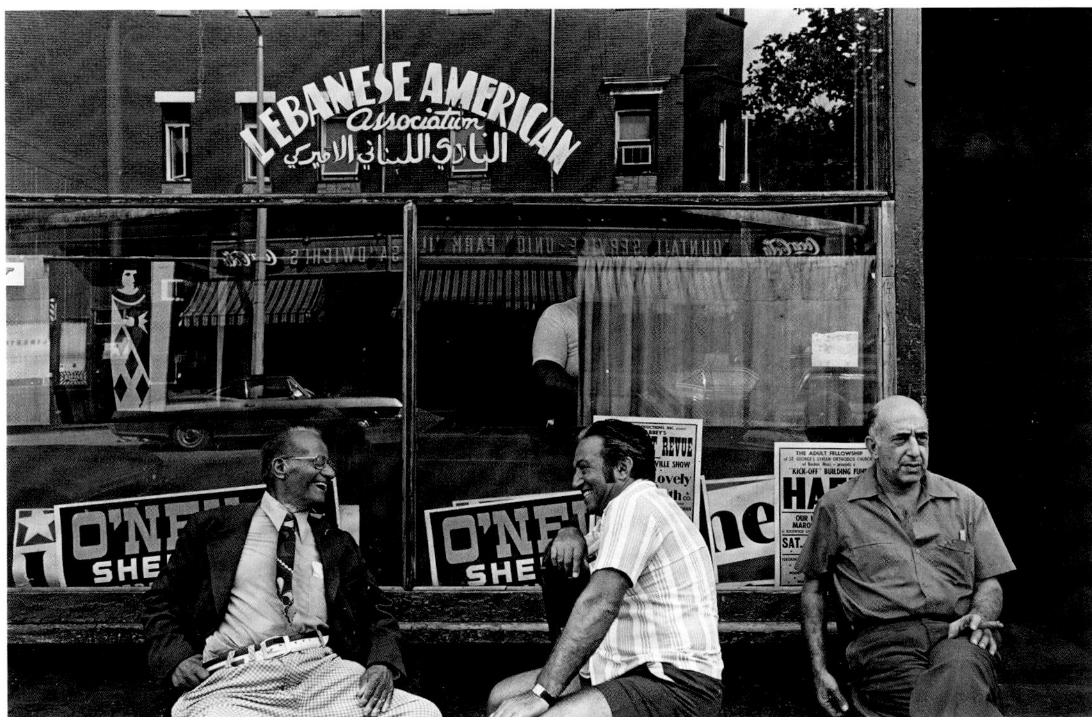

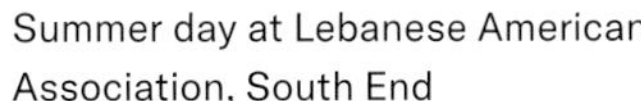
Summer day at Lebanese American Association, South End

Rosanne Solomon

Before highways and housing developments reshaped Boston's neighborhoods, the South End was home to many immigrant communities, including a vibrant Lebanese American population. Rosanne Solomon, a second-generation Lebanese American, grew up just blocks from Shawmut Avenue—a street that once bustled with small shops, groceries, and familiar faces. Though her family moved to Roslindale in the 1950s, following their church and a wider wave of suburban migration, she remembers returning to the South End, specifically the Lebanese American Association, as a teenager.

Shawmut Avenue was a shopping street, and everybody would go down there to get their vegetables and their groceries and their ethnic foods and whatever. And the guys would be sitting outside and you'd kibitz with them, talking with them back and forth. "Hi, how are you, I haven't seen you in a while. Where are the kids? What's this? What's that?" A very laid back social experience. If you wanted to see people or see friends or anything, that's the neighborhood you'd go to. . . . I can remember once distinctly, I was a teenage kid, and I wanted to go home, and I checked my pocket and I didn't have a quarter to get on the train. So I went in and I looked around to see who I knew, and I went to one of the guys I know. I said, "Uncle"—you call everybody uncle. Everybody's your uncle or aunt. You never call anybody by their first name—"Uncle, I need a quarter to go home. Can you give me a quarter?" . . . They would do anything for you. I mean, you knew, as a kid, if you went there, anybody would help you. It's that kind of a feeling—comfort, a homey, cozy, family feeling.

Moran family baptism, South Boston

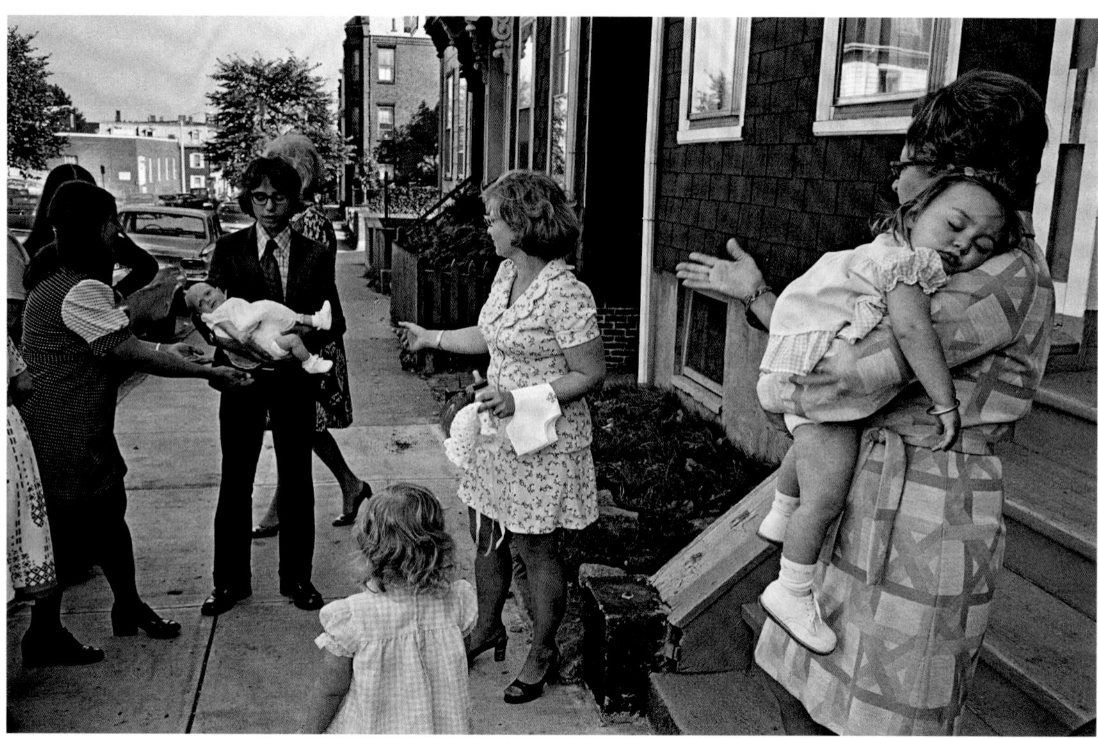

George and Carolyn Moran

In the fall of 1974, four generations of the Moran family gathered in South Boston for the baptism of baby Lila. The photo shows former Boston Public School teacher Carolyn Moran, holding a baby bottle, surrounded by family. Lila is in the arms of her uncle and godfather, Alan Sammartino. At the time, Carolyn and her husband, George Moran (not pictured), also a BPS teacher, were raising their young family in the South Boston home where George had grown up. As the school desegregation crisis unfolded that September, the Morans found themselves at the center of a city in conflict. George and Carolyn reflect on that time—on escorting the photographer Constantine Manos through the neighborhood, the tensions, and the decision to eventually leave.

I accompanied him [Manos] for the entire day because, you have to realize, at that time the press was persona non grata. In fact, they were stoned at times during the busing crisis. So, being a neighborhood person, I stayed with him at all times throughout the whole neighborhood because I was a known quantity and not considered to be a threat. . . . I explained the history of the whole neighborhood to him, about the different breakdowns of the neighborhood, that people from Galway lived on 8th Street, people from Cork, my family, lived on 4th Street. So everything was really subdivided according to where in Europe the families came from. And he was extremely personable. He was inquisitive about everything, about the history, even what was going on socially at the time with the desegregation process.

On an afternoon in December, when I was teaching in the North End, Carolyn and I had planned that afternoon that I would go right home and pick her and the children up and take the children and let them get something to eat, and Carolyn could go Christmas shopping. I came around the corner where our house was on 4th Street, and the street was totally inundated with cars, double and triple parked. . . . And around the corner came this huge mass of humanity, with police on horses, with clubs, coming down the street. And that kind of did it for me. I did not want to have my family living in conditions such as that. . . . And I realized it was a tremendous social upheaval going on, but I didn't want anybody hurt. And that is what made us think seriously about moving. —George Moran

We also both had been Boston Public School teachers . . . so we had a certain allegiance, and that was difficult. . . . I used to take the children on walks in the carriage and go around the block and so forth, and I couldn't do that anymore. There was a fear that the children would be hurt. None of our daughters were, at that point, in school but that would soon be happening, and I think as educators that was a big deal to us, that we wanted them in a school system that we felt would be safe and so forth. . . . But it was not easy. . . . [there was] a feeling that we were betraying people. . . . I don't think that the decision we made was unlike the decision a lot of people made. If we had not had children, it might have been different. —Carolyn Moran

Jim Stewart

Jim Stewart grew up in Jamaica Plain and attended English High School, where his father was the football coach. Jim was a three-sport athlete playing hockey, baseball, and football. Jim entered English High in 1974, the same year Boston implemented court-ordered desegregation through forced busing. English High School had previously been a placement-exam school, and its student body somewhat reflected the diversity of the city. In the 1960s, the Boston School Committee voted to change English to an open-enrollment school and restructured middle schools in the system based on neighborhood. These changes, along with the larger demographic shift in Boston, transformed English into a predominantly Black high school. With the onset of busing, white students from neighborhoods like West Roxbury were reassigned to schools like English. Amid shrinking enrollment and rising tensions, Jim remembers the violence—but also the camaraderie of his football team during that tumultuous first year.

There were periods, especially in the '70s, with the changing of the city, with the busing issues and the desegregation, it changed the complexity of the school, I think. But as teammates, we bonded very much so that we created a brothership that will last a lifetime because of how we felt about each other, you know, [during] *the trying times of the city. And I think we overcame the adversity to keep the tradition going. . . . I mean, '74 to '77, with the busing issues and as a white kid playing with a lot of African American kids, I faced a lot of verbal abuse when we played games in different areas of the city, you know. But it made me a better person, I think. I think the respect that I got from my teammates and, you know, I protected them too.*

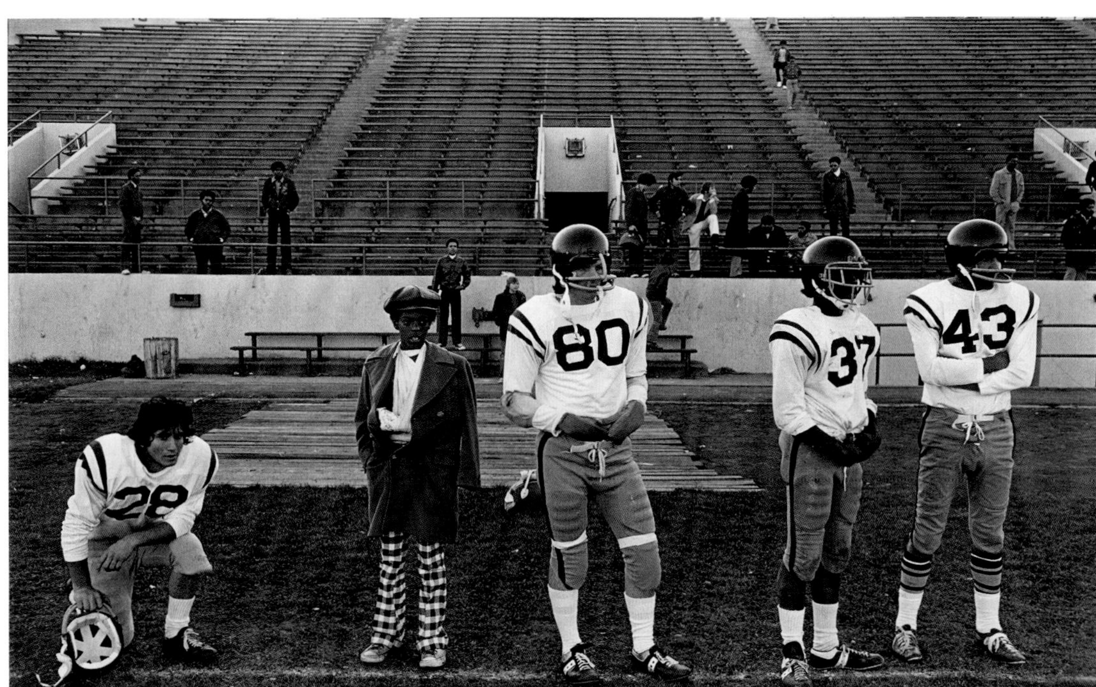

English High School football game, White Stadium

Cedric Turner

Cedric Turner was a high school student from Mattapan attending English High School at the start of Boston's school desegregation order in September 1974. A member of the football team, Turner (not pictured) recalls the racial hostility on and off the field.

About three weeks earlier, before the Southie game, we played East Boston at East Boston. And we was coming in and we were stoned by old ladies, old men, grandmas, grandpas. They stoned us, called us all types of names. And we went in there—we were so traumatized—we went in there, and in fact that was one of the three games that year we lost. Because we was like, these cats are stoning us. We had to duck down and everything, right? So even though East Boston had us beat—they beat us like 38 to nothing, right?—they stoned us on the way out. . . . So then we're supposed to play Southie in Southie. And Peterkin [English High School Headmaster Robert Peterkin] said, Oh, hell no. Because he knew Eastie was bad, but had we gone into Southie, it would have been murderous. I mean they would not have hesitated to have us killed. It was that dead bad. Peterkin said, I'm not gonna send my kids to Southie. . . . Finally he said, Let's have a neutral site. So they decided the neutral site was going to be Roslindale. . . . But that did not stop them from showing up fully armed . . . It was Southie! It was parents and, you know, community people. . . . But then, once our coach saw that, he made a phone call and 15 minutes later, our sideline was totally armed . . . knives, everything. It was like, you know, people was ready. And people in our community wasn't about to sit on back and let us get jacked up like that.

But at the end of the day it was a really hard game. . . . They had a running back by the name of Joyce, hardcore guy. . . . He was the toughest dude I ever played against in my life. We was pounding him. He was just like grunting and moaning and spitting up stuff. Did not come out the game. Matter of fact, he scored the winning touchdown. And then the game was over, and everyone went home. It was kind of like a mutual thing where you got arms, they got arms, everyone's gonna go home. Right?

Twenty-five years later, I'm downtown at 1010 Mass Ave. I'm working for the school department. This kid comes out of 1010 Mass Ave. . . . I said, man, I know you from somewhere . . . He said, yeah, I recognize your face. And I said, what high school you go to? . . . He said, I went to Southie. And I said, And I went to English. And we both just cracked up laughing. . . . And we sat out there and talked for like two hours; we just talked about shit, right? And I'm like, man, what a cool-ass guy. And we came away saying that we was just pawns. We was just pawns. They was just using us for some nefarious game. We was only kids. And, you know, it really did not have to be like that. It really, really didn't.

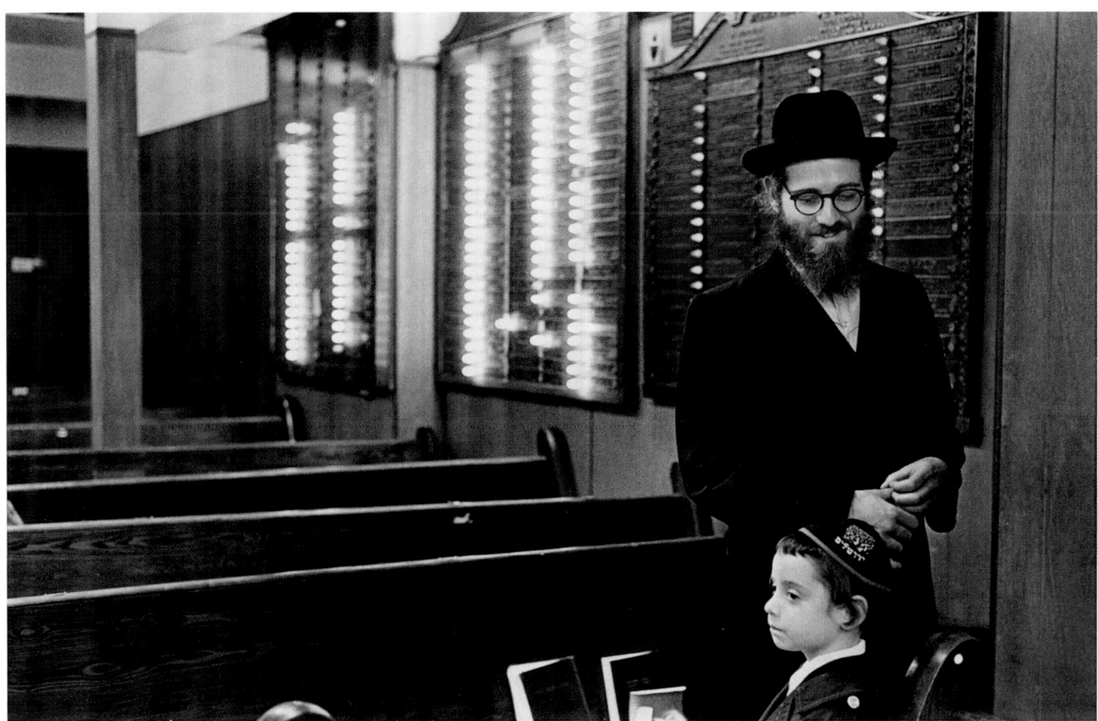

Father and son before service at Boston Chassidic Center, Brookline

Naftali Brawer

Naftali Brawer grew up in Brookline's Jewish community, where Friday nights marked the sacred transition into the Sabbath. Surrounded by the quiet strength of tradition and the watchful gaze of his father, Brawer appears still and contemplative in this photograph, captured just before the start of Shabbat. He reflects on that moment as one frozen in time, rich with meaning and memory.

At the moment I'm reading a lot of Byung-Chul Han, the Korean-German philosopher and social critic. One of the things he writes about is the demise of community as a result of all the noise we project. He says that a real community is comfortable with silence. And for a moment I go, well, he's never been in a Jewish community! But I think what he means by silence is there isn't a need to be performative. So, there's noise—of course there's noise. There's prayer, there's song—at least for Jews, there is lots of loud, animated conversation—but you don't have to outperform anyone else. This is what he means by silence. You collectively hold a narrative together, and you each instinctively know your place within that narrative.

And so, I'm looking at this picture. And I think to myself, what a privilege to take a little kid, who at least in this picture looks very pensive and sensitive, and anchor him deeply within a community, which is what my father is doing.

And I think about Boston today, or more broadly, our country, which is a very fragmented place. And I wish that all four- or five-year-old kids, whatever their parents' worldview, religious identity, ethnic or cultural heritage, find a sense of community. That their parents can raise them in the kind of anchored, thick community where you feel secure and loved, like I was privileged to experience. Where you instinctively know your place in your people's story. Where you feel that you belong in the truest sense. A quiet belonging, where you don't have to apologize or defend yourself or assert yourself. This is what this picture is bringing up for me: the sense of community, the advent of a sacred moment, and this gift that one generation is passing to the next.

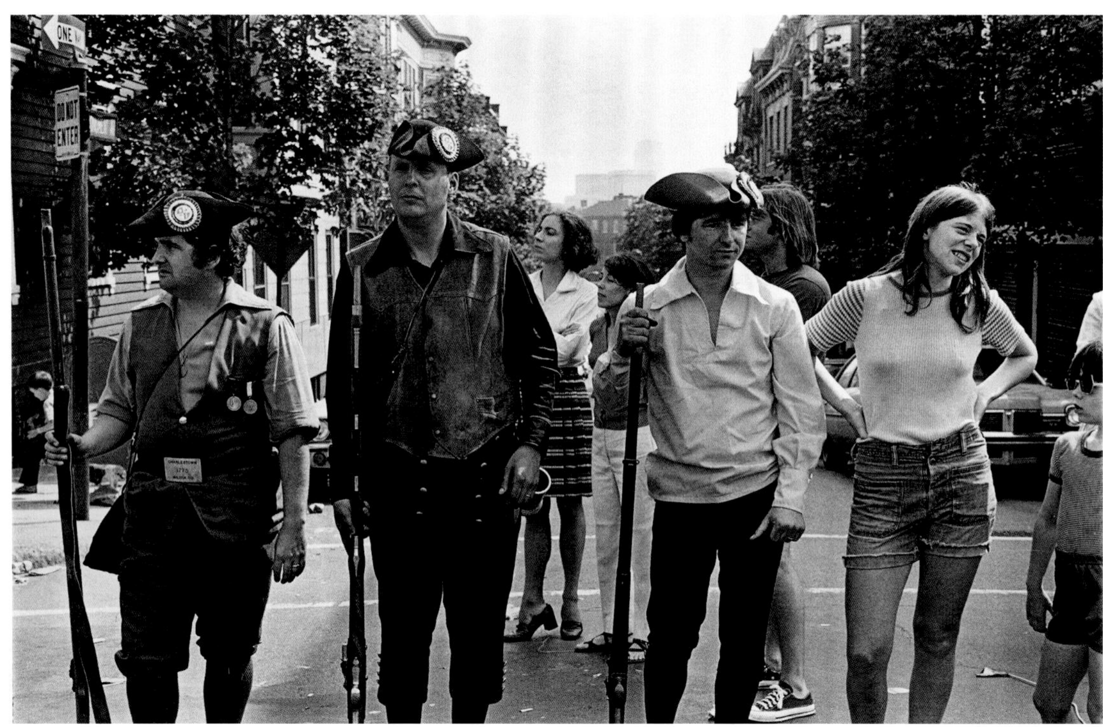

Participants and spectators at Bunker Hill Day, Charlestown

Roger Chesebrough

Roger Chesebrough was born and raised in Charlestown. He joined the neighborhood militia in 1972 and remained an active member. As part of the militia, Roger would march in neighborhood parades and travel throughout the city to participate in other patriotic events and reenactments. He still has his musket today.

[I bought the musket] from Lew Horton's. That's the place that sold guns and stuff, but especially muskets. . . . All of it, the whole uniform, was made. My friends helped me to make it; my sister helped me to make it. . . .

Once in a while, the musket is operational. You put the powder in, and you put the rest down the barrel. But what I did a couple times, I took a little bit of black powder, I put it where it's supposed to go, put the thing down, and pulled the hand thing back, and the fledge went on the spark, and it went boom.

This book is published in conjunction with the exhibition *Where's Boston? Fifty Years Later*, presented at the Boston Athenaeum from June 15 to December 12, 2026.

Funding was provided by the Rosalie Thorne McKenna Foundation

ISBN: 978-1-64657-054-6
Library of Congress Control Number: 2025951009

Published by The Boston Athenaeum
bostonathenaeum.org

Available through:
ARTBOOK | D.A.P.
75 Broad Street, Suite 630
New York, NY 10004
artbook.com

Produced by Marquand Books, Seattle
marquandbooks.com

Edited by Jean Dykstra
Designed by Ryan Polich
Typeset in GT America by Maggie Lee
Proofread by Bruno George
Color management by I/O Color, Seattle
Printed and bound in China by Artron Art Group

Cover: Demonstrator in front of City Hall, Government Center, p. 52
pp. 2–3: Fireman resting after blaze, Symphony Road, pp. 82–83 (detail)

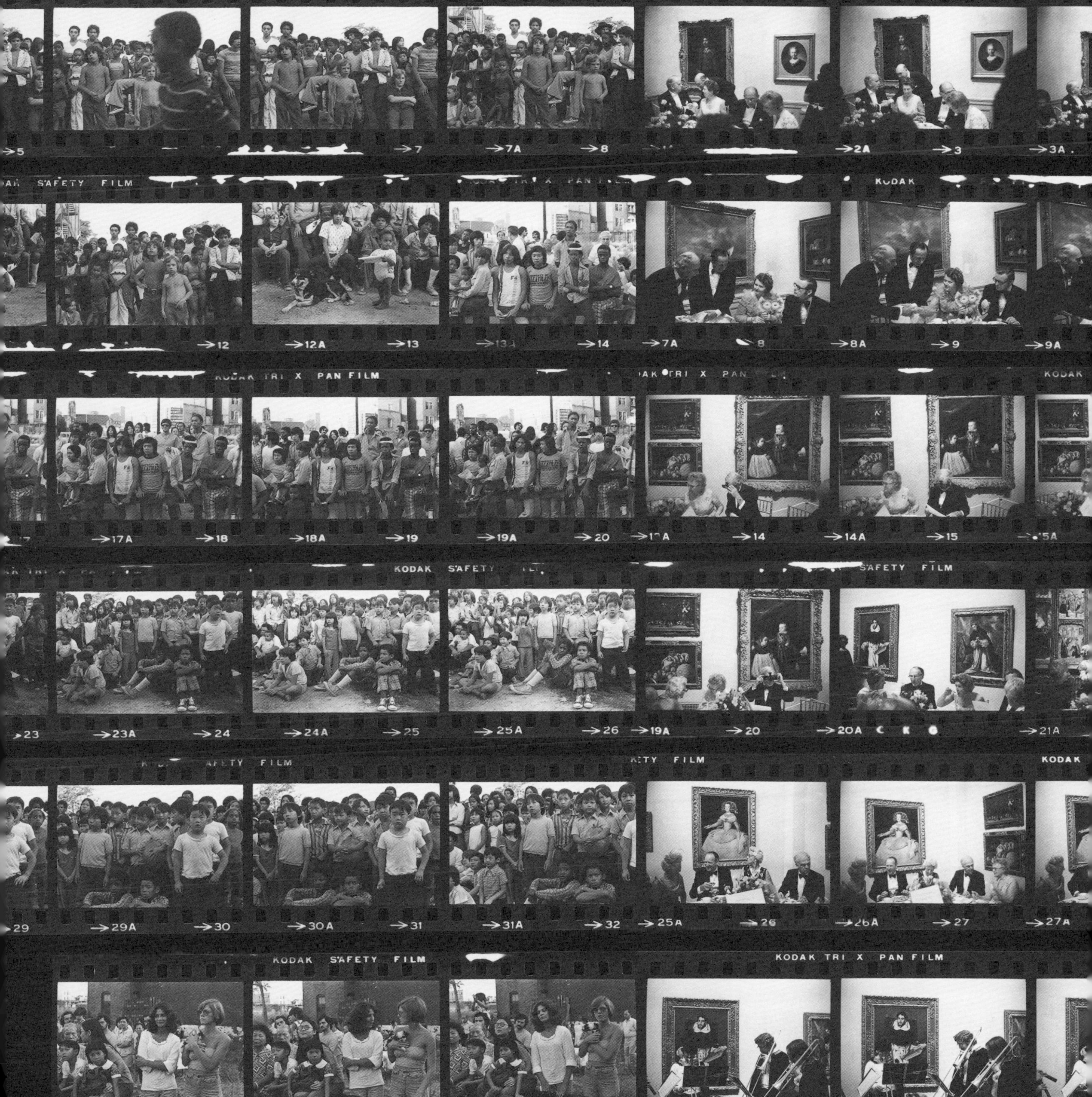

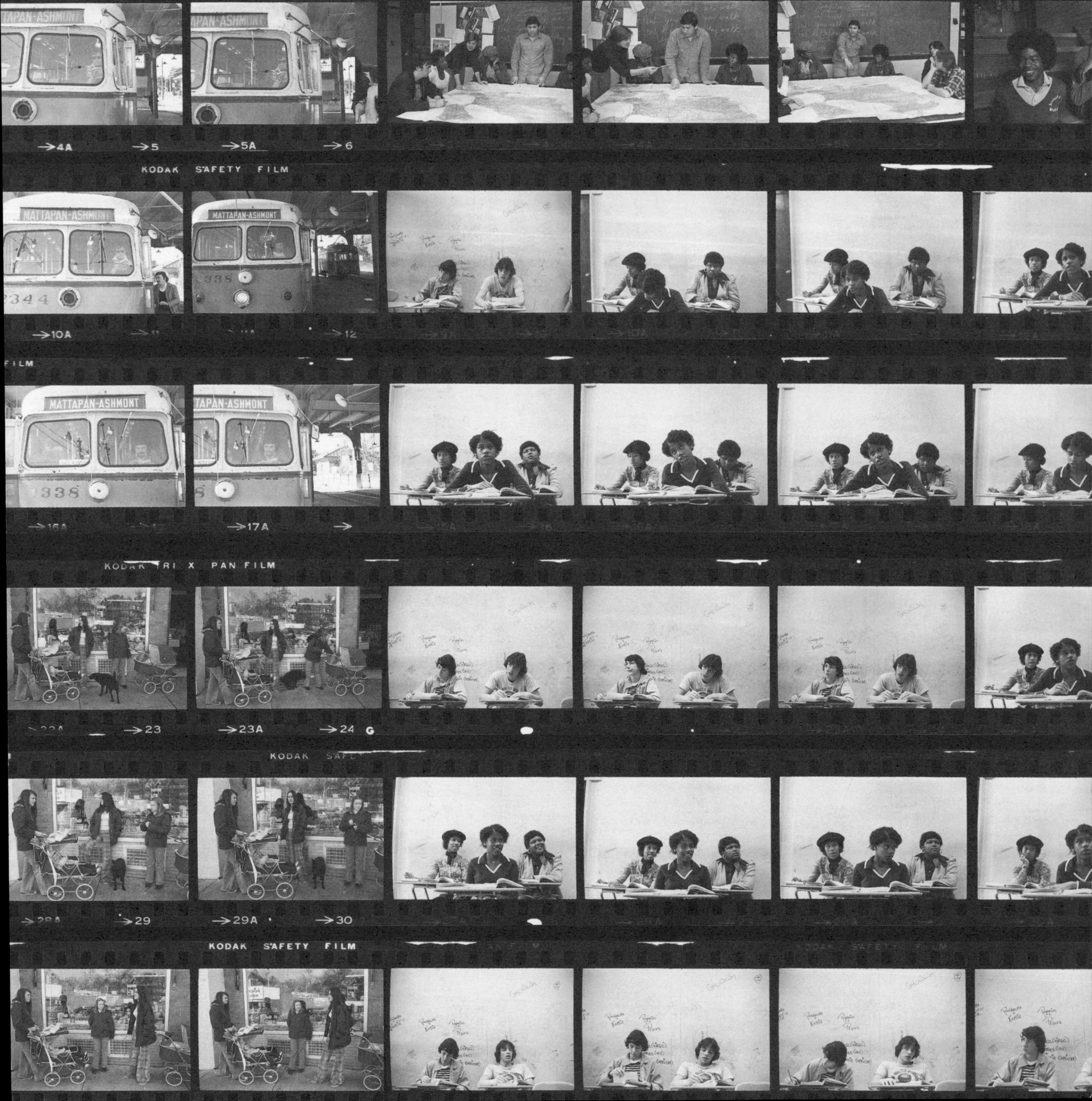

MATTAPAN-ASHMONT
→4A
→5
→5A
→6
KODAK SAFETY FILM
→10A
→12
FILM
→16A
→17A
KODAK TRI X PAN FILM
→23
→23A
→24
KODAK
→29
→29A
→30
KODAK SAFETY FILM